WASHINTON'S
BEST FISHING WATERS™

159 Detailed Maps of 38 of the Best Rivers and Streams

Wilderness
Adventures
Press, Inc.™

Belgrade, Montana

Wilderness Adventures Press is dedicated to making these angling maps as accurate as possible. Please contact us at books@wildadvpress.com to let us know about any information in this book that you feel needs to be corrected. We appreciate your help.

TABLE OF CONTENTS

Washington's Best Fishing Waters, State Map iv
Introduction and Acknowledgments v
Water Conditions and Regulations v
Resources and Legend vi

RIVERS

Bogachiel River 1
Calawah River 6
Chehalis River 9
Columbia River 14
Cowlitz River 26
Elochoman River 29
Elwha River 32
Grande Ronde River 35
Green River 38
Hoh River 41
Hoko River 44
Hood Canal 47
Kalama River 52
Kettle River 55
Klickitat River 59
Lewis River 62
Methow River 66
Okanogan River 70
Pend Oreille River 74
Queets River 77
Quillayute River 81
Rocky Ford Creek 84
Samish River 87
Sanpoil River 90
Satsop River 94
Sauk River 98
Skagit River 101
Skykomish River 107
Snake River 112
Snohomish River 119
Snoqualmie River 122
Sol Duc River 127
Spokane River 131
Stillaguamish River 134
Washougal River 140
Wenatchee River 143
Wynoochee River 147
Yakima River 151

RIVERS AND STREAMS

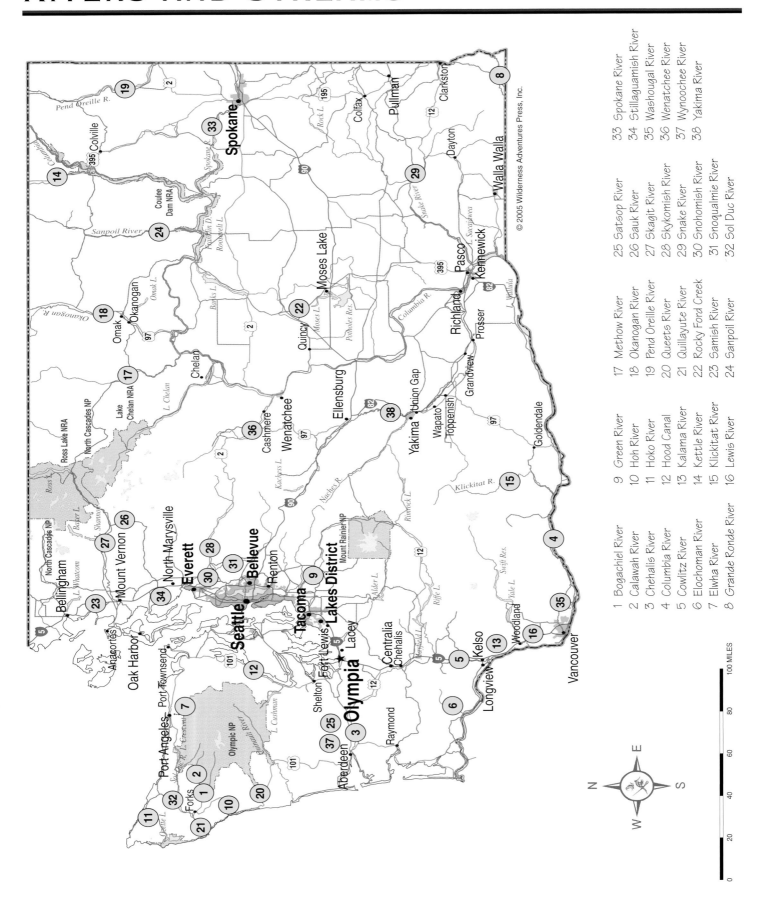

© 2005 Wilderness Adventures Press, Inc.

1 Bogachiel River
2 Calawah River
3 Chehalis River
4 Columbia River
5 Cowlitz River
6 Elochoman River
7 Elwha River
8 Grande Ronde River
9 Green River
10 Hoh River
11 Hoko River
12 Hood Canal
13 Kalama River
14 Kettle River
15 Klickitat River
16 Lewis River
17 Methow River
18 Okanogan River
19 Pend Oreille River
20 Queets River
21 Quillayute River
22 Rocky Ford Creek
23 Samish River
24 Sanpoil River
25 Satsop River
26 Sauk River
27 Skagit River
28 Skykomish River
29 Snake River
30 Snohomish River
31 Snoqualmie River
32 Sol Duc River
33 Spokane River
34 Stillaguamish River
35 Washougal River
36 Wenatchee River
37 Wynoochee River
38 Yakima River

INTRODUCTION AND ACKNOWLEDGMENTS

Washington State has tremendous fishing on its waters: from steelhead and salmon, to trout and many warmwater species. *Washington's Best Fishing Waters* is the third book in our great map book series. Chris Camuto of Gray's Sporting Journal says of our first book, *Colorado's Best Fishing Waters*, " This book has by far the clearest road and river maps I've ever seen in a guidebook, all in a decent scale so that you can get on good water off state highways and local roads with a minimum of fuss and second guessing."

This comprehensive map book contains 162 full-page maps and covers 38 rivers. Our maps are based on the U.S. Geological Survey maps and include a wealth of useful angling information, along with an overview of the fishing opportunities and the fish found in each water. Access points are clearly indicated, along with boat ramps, campgrounds, and roads and trails. We also show public access in the national forests and state lands. The information our book provides enables you to get to many overlooked areas and waters that result in a better overall angling experience. Each water has an overview map showing the entire river. Then we break the river down into more detailed maps, each showing a smaller section of the river that gives you a more comprehensive view than you will find in other map books.

The waters are listed in alphabetical order for easy reference without the need to consult an index. For the best and latest information on fishing regulations and water conditions, contact your fly-fishing shops and outdoor stores near the water you plan to fish. It is always a good idea to contact Washington State fish and game commission for information on fishing regulations.

We want to extend our special thanks to Peter Corbett, Brett Wedeking, and Dan Lemaich with Creekside Angling in Issaquah, Washington for their help in critiquing the maps. If there are any mistakes in the maps it is our fault not theirs.

WATER CONDITIONS AND REGULATIONS

With so many of Washington's rivers being coastal streams, affected by tides and frequent rain, the water conditions and the quality of the fishing can change frequently. For example, you may have enjoyed a fabulous day of fishing for steelhead along a particular sandbar, and marked the area for future angling days, only to return in a month or sometimes even a day and find the area completely different. The changes in the river characteristics merely become part of the challenge, and add to the overall experience. If you have fished it once you definitely have not fished it a thousand times. Each time you visit your favorite Washington stream you will have a new and exciting experience that will keep you coming back.

Along with the frequent changes in river characteristics, there are many changes in regulations throughout the season. Closures and openings of fisheries are not uncommon at any time during the season, as well as other special regulations. Because of the frequent changes we recommend that you call the Fish and Game Department (360-902-2200) ahead of time, to ask about the specific regulations for the stream that you plan to visit, and more specifically the area of that stream. Another great resource for regulations is the Fish and Game website (http://wdfw.wa.gov) where you can download the current season's game fish regulations, as well as the most current changes to the regulations.

WASHINGTON RESOURCES

Washington Department of Fish & Wildlife

WDFW Main Office:

360-902-2200

Natural Resources Building
1111 Washington St. SE
Olympia, WA
98501

Mailing Address:

600 Capitol Way N.
Olympia, WA
98501-1091

On the World Wide Web at:
http://wdfw.wa.gov/

Statewide Resources

Department of Parks and Recreation
360-902-8844
http://www.parks.wa.gov

National Forests of Washington
503-808-2971

National Parks of Washington State
510-817-1300

National Wildlife Refuges of Washington State
503-231-6828

The Washington Outfitters and Guides Association
509-997-1080

LEGEND

——	Interstate	▬	State - Public Land	♣	Picnic Area
═══	Primary Highway	▬	Indian Reservation	✈	Airport
——	Road or Street	▬	National Forest	〜	Rapids
....	Trails	🛥	Boat Launch	▬	Dam
5	Interstate Route	▲	Campsite	⊢——⊣	Railroad
3	State Route	⊕	Ferry		
395	U.S. Route	☺	Marina / Moorage		

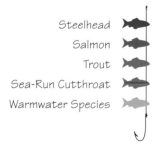

Steelhead
Salmon
Trout
Sea-Run Cutthroat
Warmwater Species

Easily flip through the pages to locate the species you wish to target. Our new fish indicators tell you with the flip of a page what kind of fish are primarily targeted in that particular stream. A blue fish indicates steelhead, a red fish a salmon. A green fish is for trout, and the green with red stripe is for the sea-run cutthroat trout that penetrate Washington's waters. Finally the orange fish indicator is for warm water species. These fish indicators are not suggesting quality of fishing, or that there are not other species in the stream. They are simply a guide to help you find the type of fish you would like to hook up with. Read more on the stream maps themselves to learn about the quality of fishing and access provided.

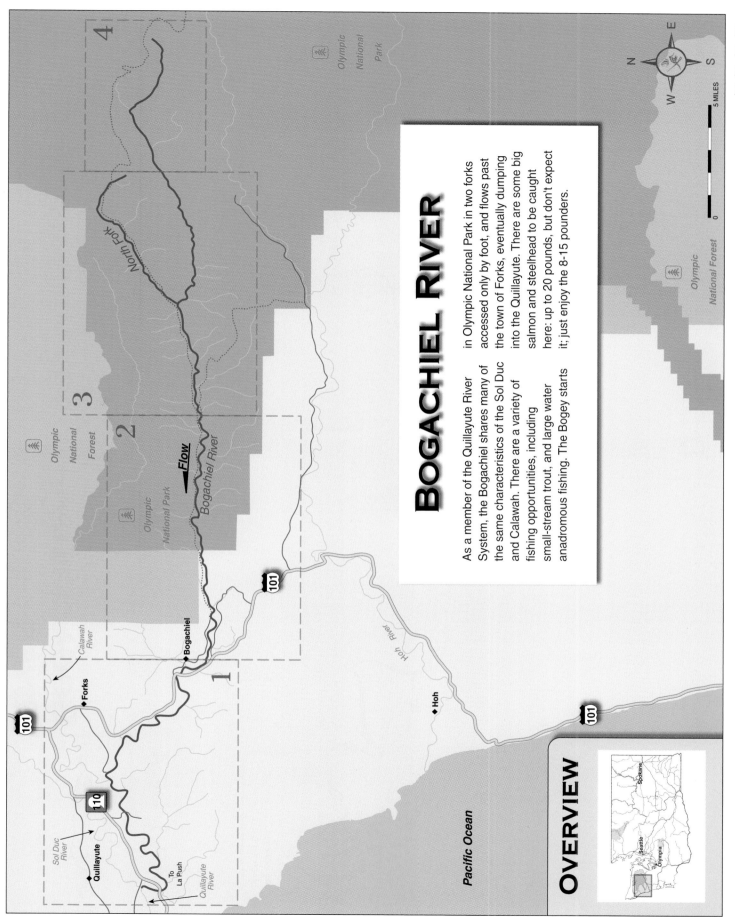

BOGACHIEL RIVER

As a member of the Quillayute River System, the Bogachiel shares many of the same characteristics of the Sol Duc and Calawah. There are a variety of fishing opportunities, including small-stream trout, and large water anadromous fishing. The Bogey starts in Olympic National Park in two forks accessed only by foot, and flows past the town of Forks, eventually dumping into the Quillayute. There are some big salmon and steelhead to be caught here: up to 20 pounds, but don't expect it; just enjoy the 8-15 pounders.

OVERVIEW

Pacific Ocean

5 MILES

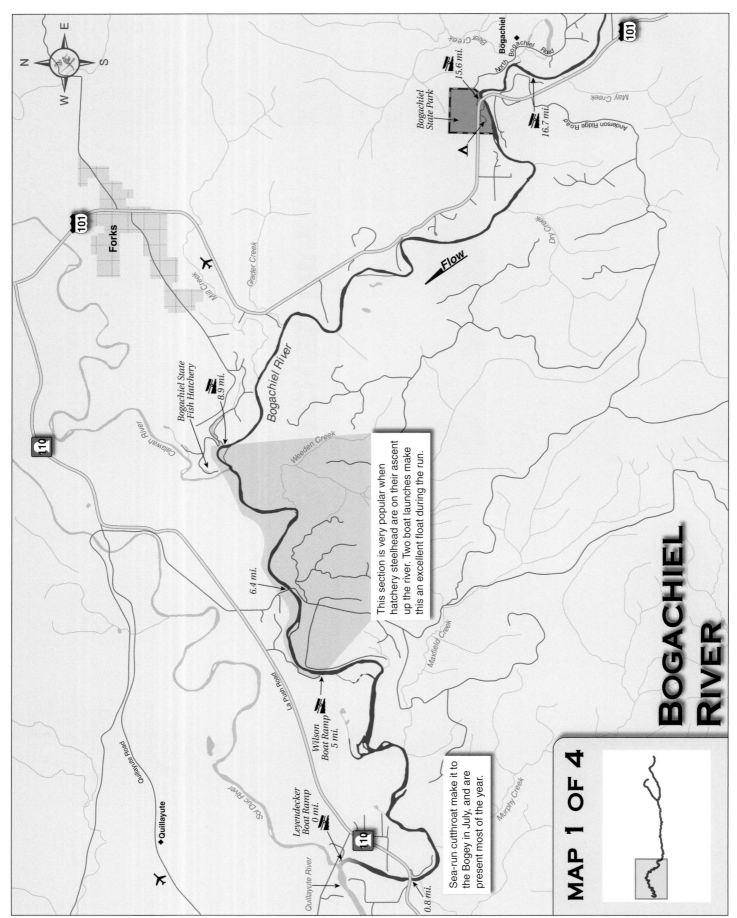

Forks

101

Bogachiel State Fish Hatchery

Calawah River

Mill Creek

Grader Creek

Bogachiel River

8.9 mi.

Weeden Creek

6.4 mi.

This section is very popular when hatchery steelhead are on their ascent up the river. Two boat launches make this an excellent float during the run.

La Push Road

Wilson Boat Ramp 5 mi.

110

Leyendecker Boat Ramp 0 mi.

Quillayute Road

Quillayute River

Sol Duc River

♦ Quillayute

0.8 mi.

Sea-run cutthroat make it to the Bogey in July, and are present most of the year.

110

Flow

Bear Creek

15.6 mi.

Bogachiel

North Bogachiel Road

101

Anderson Ridge Road

16.7 mi.

May Creek

Bogachiel State Park

Dry Creek

△

Maxfield Creek

Murphy Creek

BOGACHIEL RIVER

MAP 1 OF 4

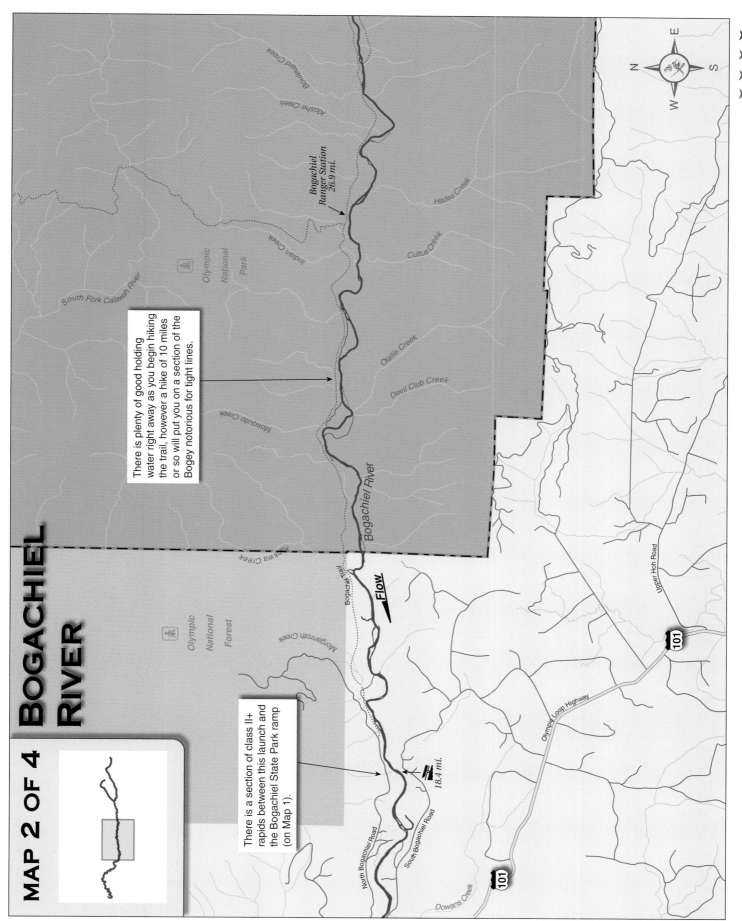

MAP 2 OF 4

BOGACHIEL RIVER

There is plenty of good holding water right away as you begin hiking the trail, however a hike of 10 miles or so will put you on a section of the Bogey notorious for tight lines.

There is a section of class II+ rapids between this launch and the Bogachiel State Park ramp (on Map 1).

Bogachiel Ranger Station 26.9 mi.

Bogachiel River

FLOW

18.4 mi.

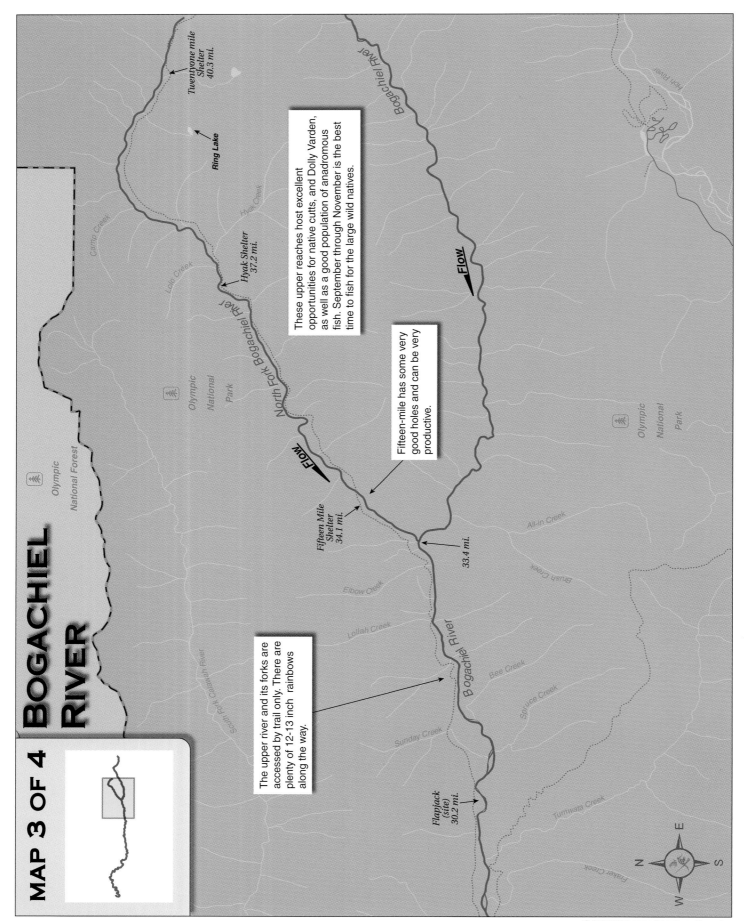

MAP 3 OF 4

BOGACHIEL RIVER

Olympic National Forest

Twentyone mile Shelter 40.3 mi.

Ring Lake

Hyak Creek

Hyak Shelter 37.2 mi.

Camp Creek

Lola Creek

North Fork Bogachiel River

Olympic National Park

South Fork Calawah River

These upper reaches host excellent opportunities for native cutts, and Dolly Varden, as well as a good population of anadromous fish. September through November is the best time to fish for the large wild natives.

Fifteen-mile has some very good holes and can be very productive.

Flow

Flow

Fifteen Mile Shelter 34.1 mi.

33.4 mi.

Elbow Creek

Lollah Creek

All-In Creek

Bush Creek

Bogachiel River

Bee Creek

Spruce Creek

The upper river and its forks are accessed by trail only. There are plenty of 12-13 inch rainbows along the way.

Sunday Creek

Flapjack (site) 30.2 mi.

Olympic National Park

Bogachiel River

Hoh River

Turnwata Creek

Fraser Creek

N E S W

© 2005 Wilderness Adventures Press, Inc.

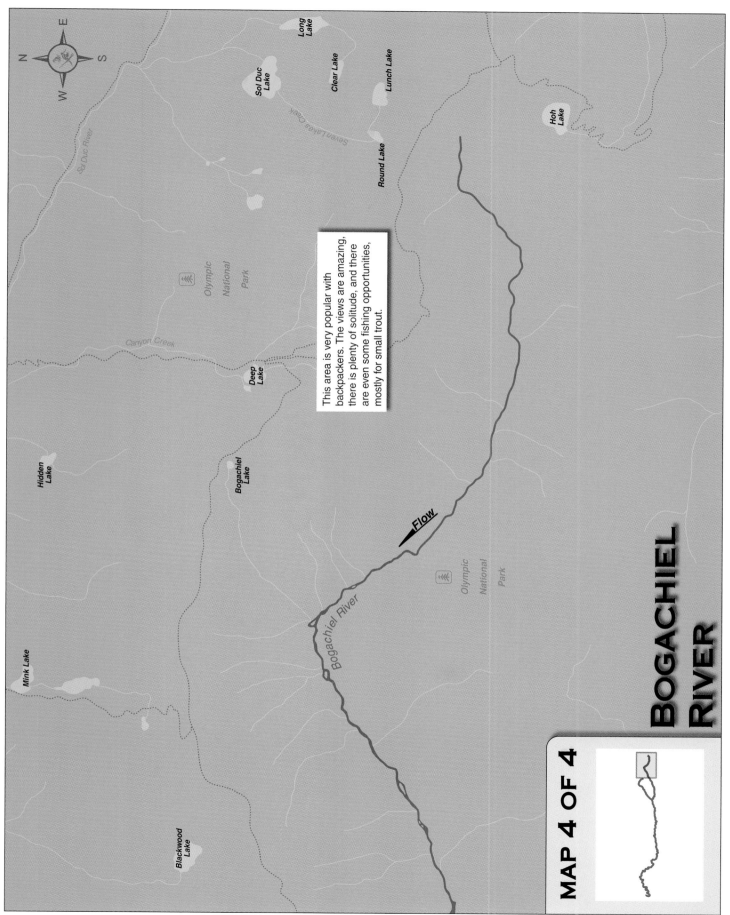

This area is very popular with backpackers. The views are amazing, there is plenty of solitude, and there are even some fishing opportunities, mostly for small trout.

Long Lake

Sol Duc Lake

Clear Lake

Lunch Lake

Hoh Lake

Round Lake

Seven Lakes Creek

Sol Duc River

Olympic National Park

Canyon Creek

Deep Lake

Hidden Lake

Bogachiel Lake

Flow

Mink Lake

Bogachiel River

Olympic National Park

Blackwood Lake

MAP 4 OF 4

BOGACHIEL RIVER

© 2005 Wilderness Adventures Press, Inc.

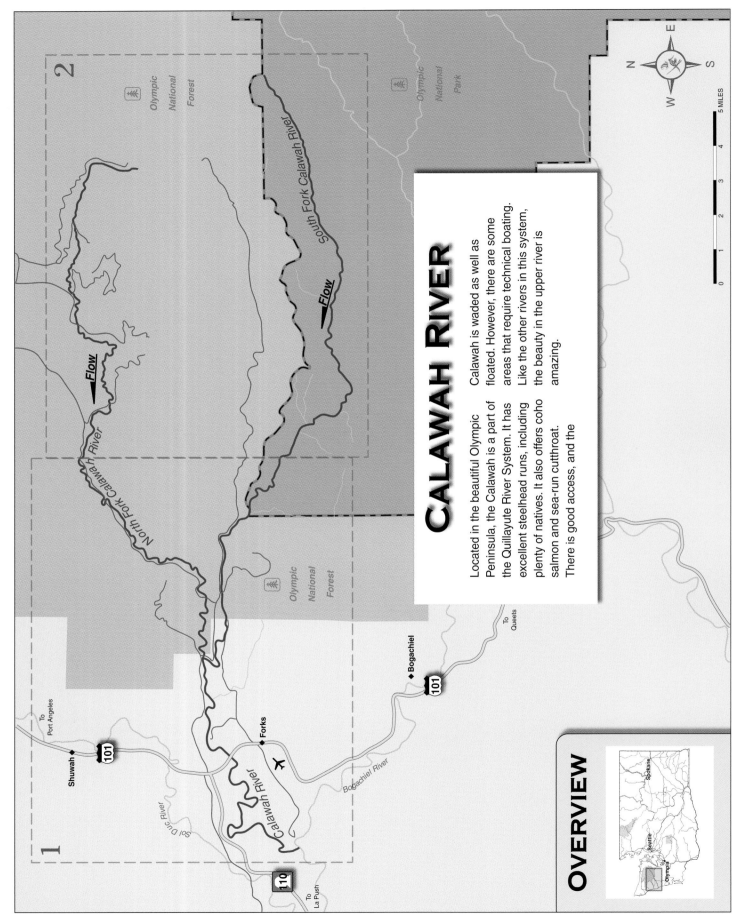

CALAWAH RIVER

Located in the beautiful Olympic Peninsula, the Calawah is a part of the Quillayute River System. It has excellent steelhead runs, including plenty of natives. It also offers coho salmon and sea-run cutthroat. There is good access, and the Calawah is waded as well as floated. However, there are some areas that require technical boating. Like the other rivers in this system, the beauty in the upper river is amazing.

OVERVIEW

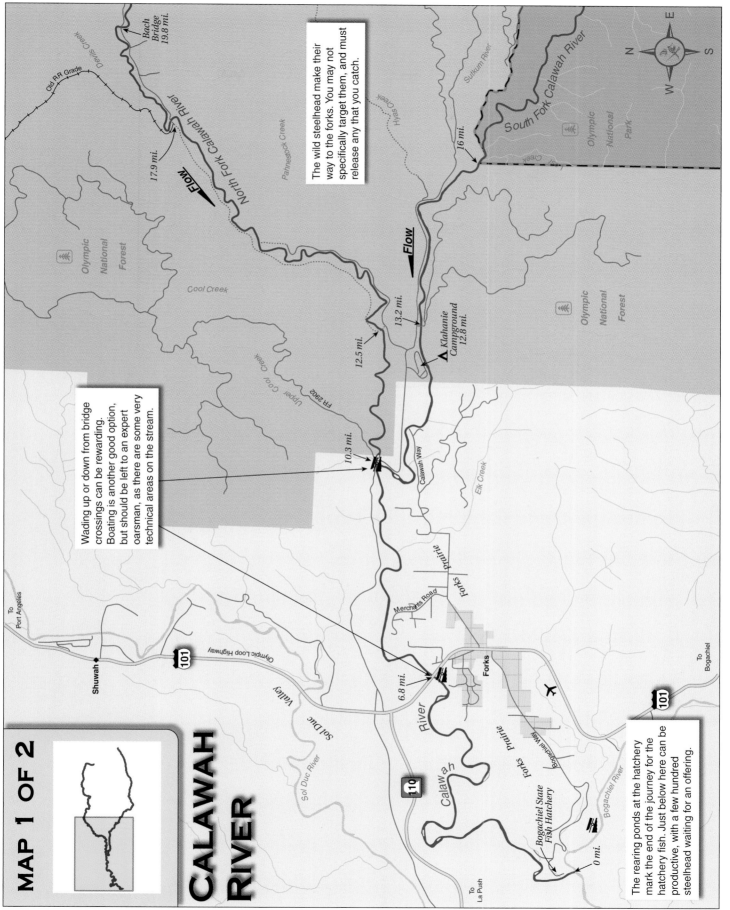

MAP 1 OF 2

CALAWAH RIVER

Bach Bridge 19.8 mi.

Old RR Grade

Davis Creek

North Fork Calawah River

FLOW

17.9 mi.

The wild steelhead make their way to the forks. You may not specifically target them, and must release any that you catch.

Palmestook Creek

Suikum River

South Fork Calawah River

Olympic National Park

Hyas Creek

16 mi.

Flow

Cool Creek

Olympic National Forest

13.2 mi.

12.5 mi.

Klahanie Campground 12.8 mi.

Olympic National Forest

Upper Cool Creek

FR 2902

10.3 mi.

Wading up or down from bridge crossings can be rewarding. Boating is another good option, but should be left to an expert oarsman, as there are some very technical areas on the stream.

Calawah Way

Elk Creek

To Port Angeles

Shuwah

101

Olympic Loop Highway

Forks Prairie

Merchants Road

6.8 mi.

Sol Duc Valley

Sol Duc River

10

River

Forks

Calawah

Forks Prairie

Bogachiel Way

Bogachiel River

To La Push

Bogachiel State Fish Hatchery

0 mi.

101

To Bogachiel

The rearing ponds at the hatchery mark the end of the journey for the hatchery fish. Just below here can be productive, with a few hundred steelhead waiting for an offering.

© 2005 Wilderness Adventures Press, Inc.

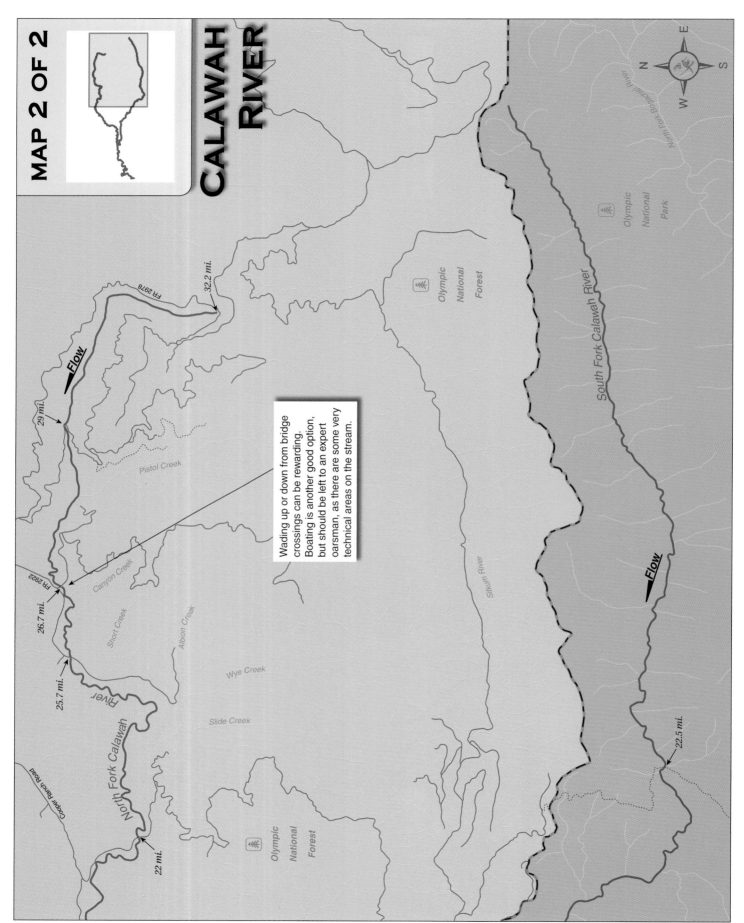

MAP 2 OF 2

CALAWAH RIVER

Wading up or down from bridge crossings can be rewarding. Boating is another good option, but should be left to an expert oarsman, as there are some very technical areas on the stream.

FR 2978

32.2 mi.

Flow

29 mi.

Pistol Creek

Canyon Creek

FR 2922

26.7 mi.

Short Creek

Albion Creek

25.7 mi.

River

Wye Creek

Slide Creek

North Fork Calawah

Cooper Ranch Road

22 mi.

Olympic National Forest

Sitkum River

South Fork Calawah River

Olympic National Forest

Olympic National Park

North Fork Bogachiel River

Flow

22.5 mi.

N E W S

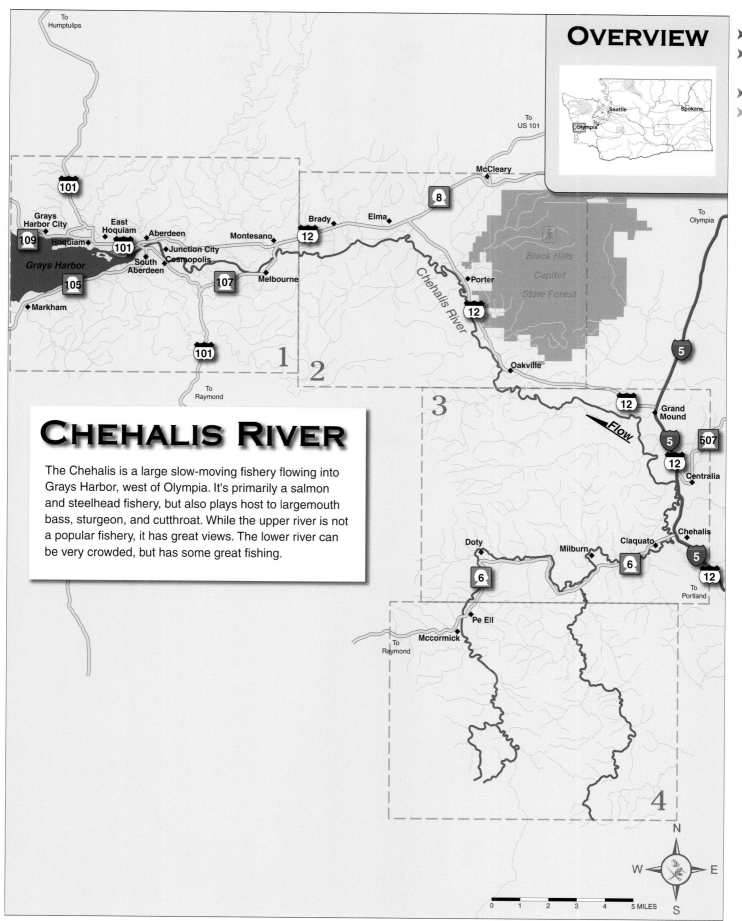

OVERVIEW

CHEHALIS RIVER

The Chehalis is a large slow-moving fishery flowing into Grays Harbor, west of Olympia. It's primarily a salmon and steelhead fishery, but also plays host to largemouth bass, sturgeon, and cutthroat. While the upper river is not a popular fishery, it has great views. The lower river can be very crowded, but has some great fishing.

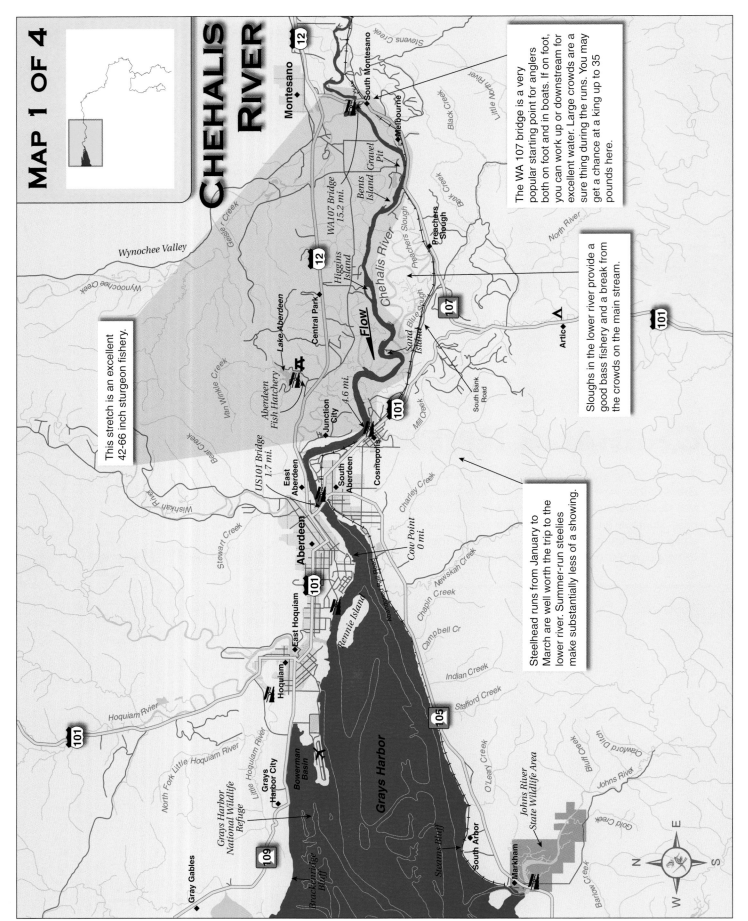

MAP 1 OF 4

CHEHALIS RIVER

The WA 107 bridge is a very popular starting point for anglers both on foot and in boats. If on foot, you can work up or downstream for excellent water. Large crowds are a sure thing during the runs. You may get a chance at a king up to 35 pounds here.

Sloughs in the lower river provide a good bass fishery and a break from the crowds on the main stream.

This stretch is an excellent 42-66 inch sturgeon fishery.

Steelhead runs from January to March are well worth the trip to the lower river. Summer-run steelies make substantially less of a showing.

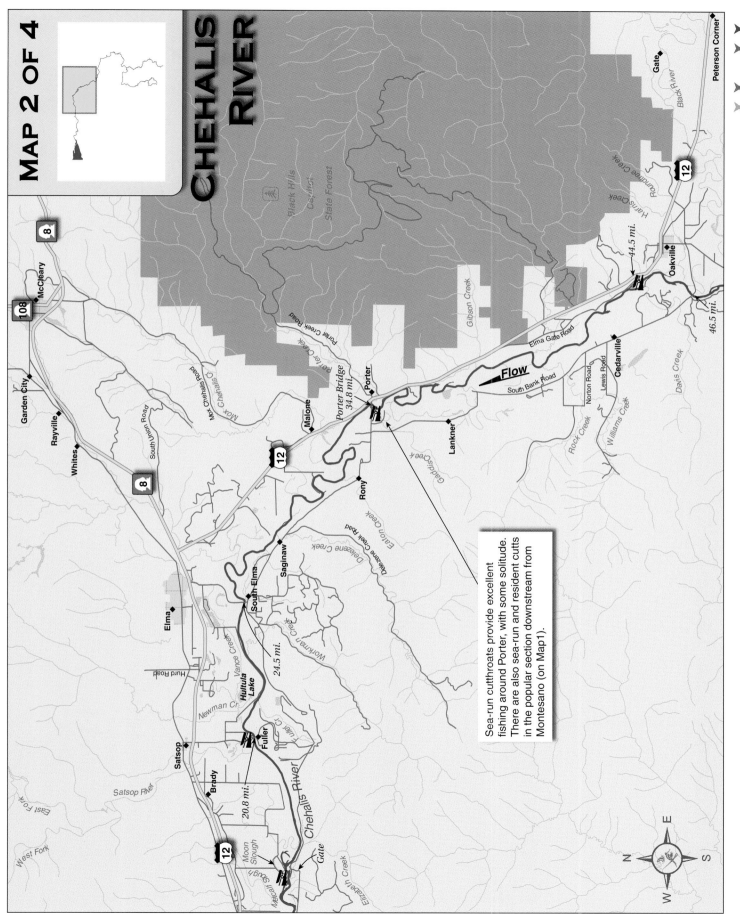

MAP 2 OF 4

CHEHALIS RIVER

Sea-run cutthroats provide excellent fishing around Porter, with some solitude. There are also sea-run and resident cutts in the popular section downstream from Montesano (on Map1).

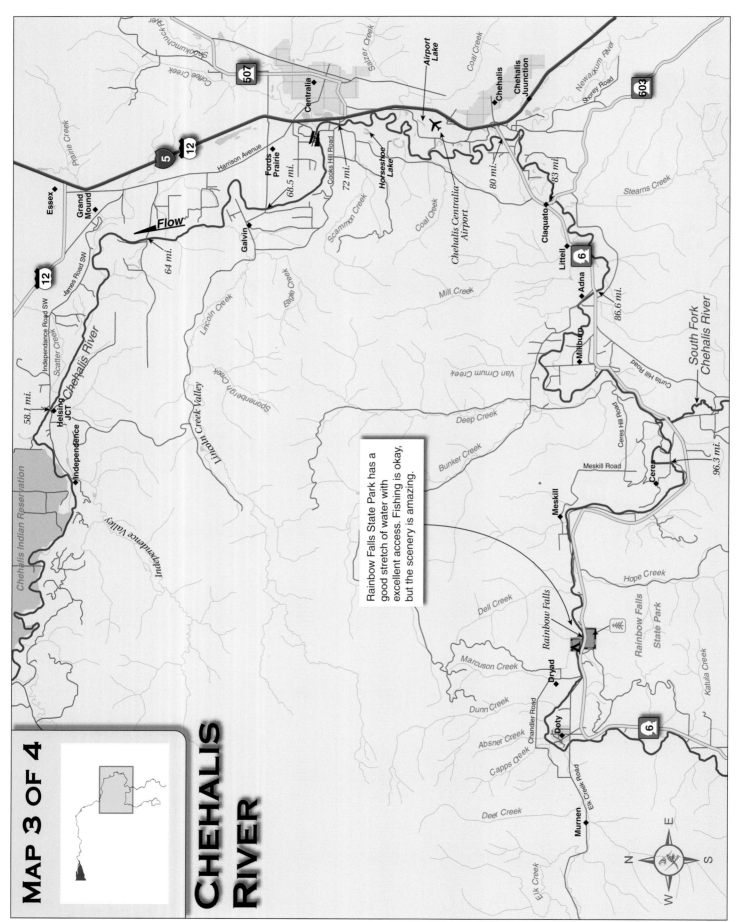

Rainbow Falls State Park has a good stretch of water with excellent access. Fishing is okay, but the scenery is amazing.

MAP 3 OF 4

CHEHALIS RIVER

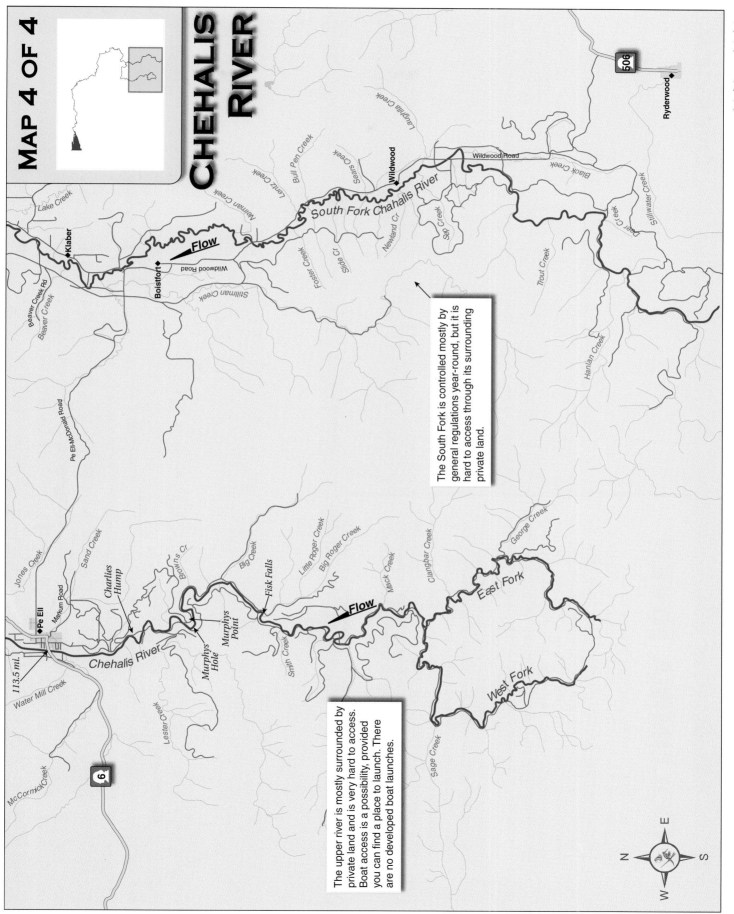

MAP 4 OF 4

CHEHALIS RIVER

Ryderwood

506

Laughlle Creek

Black Creek

Deer Creek

Stillwater Creek

Wildwood

Wildwood Road

South Fork Chehalis River

Bull Pen Creek

Lentz Creek

Sears Creek

Newland Cr

Sel Creek

Trout Creek

Hanlan Creek

Nelman Creek

Lake Creek

Klaber

Flow

Boistfort

Wildwood Road

Foster Creek

Slide Cr

Stillman Creek

Beaver Creek Rd

Beaver Creek

Pe Ell-McDonald Road

The South Fork is controlled mostly by general regulations year-round, but it is hard to access through its surrounding private land.

Jones Creek

Sand Creek

Charlies Hump

Markum Road

Pe Ell

113.5 mi.

Water Mill Creek

Chehalis River

Murphys Hole

Murphys Point

Fisk Falls

Browns Cr

Big Creek

Smith Creek

Little Roger Creek

Big Roger Creek

Mack Creek

Clangbar Creek

George Creek

East Fork

West Fork

Sage Creek

Lester Creek

McCormick Creek

6

The upper river is mostly surrounded by private land and is very hard to access. Boat access is a possibility, provided you can find a place to launch. There are no developed boat launches.

N
E
S
W

© 2005 Wilderness Adventures Press, Inc.

OVERVIEW

COLUMBIA RIVER

The Grand Coulee Dam releases water from the huge impoundment, Franklin D. Roosevelt Lake, to form the Columbia in northeastern Washington. The river flows mostly south until it reaches Oregon. Then Washington and Oregon's largest river forms the border between the two states as it flows west until it reaches the Pacific Ocean. As a single fishery the Columbia would be overwhelming to any angler, as every little section of this great river could have an entire book written about it. The Columbia is mostly made up of a series of dams and lakes, so as a warm water fishery it ranks very well. Nearly every warm water species can be found somewhere between Roosevelt Lake and the Pacific Ocean. The Columbia's tributaries are among the very best salmon and steelhead producers in the state, and the Columbia is the highway for all of them to get to their destinations. The access is very good for nearly the entire journey of the river, especially for those launching a boat. You could easily spend a month on the Columbia and never cast to the same water twice.

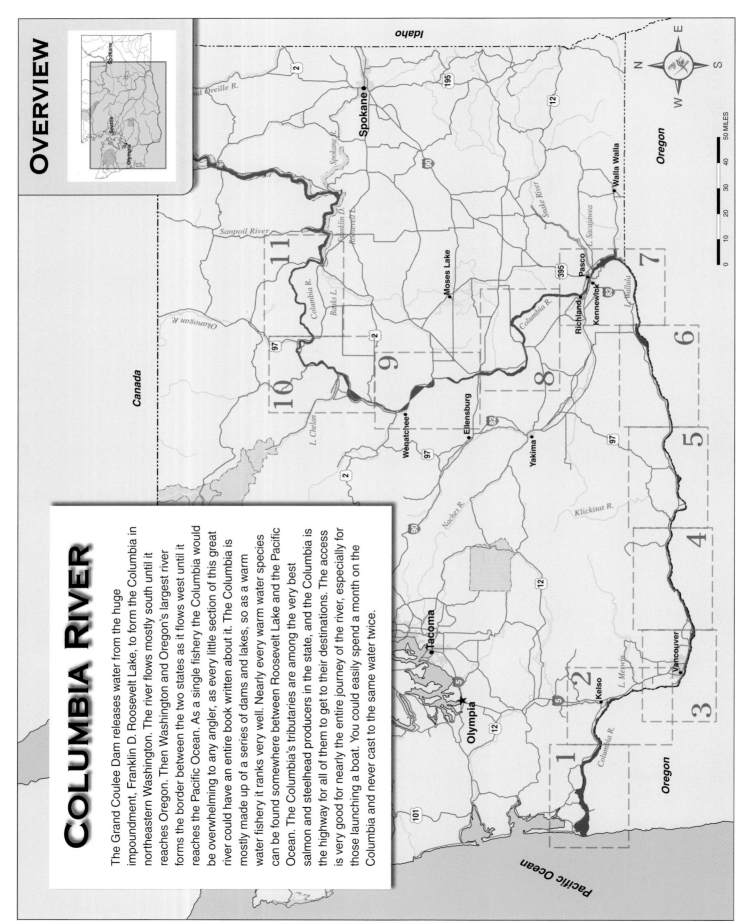

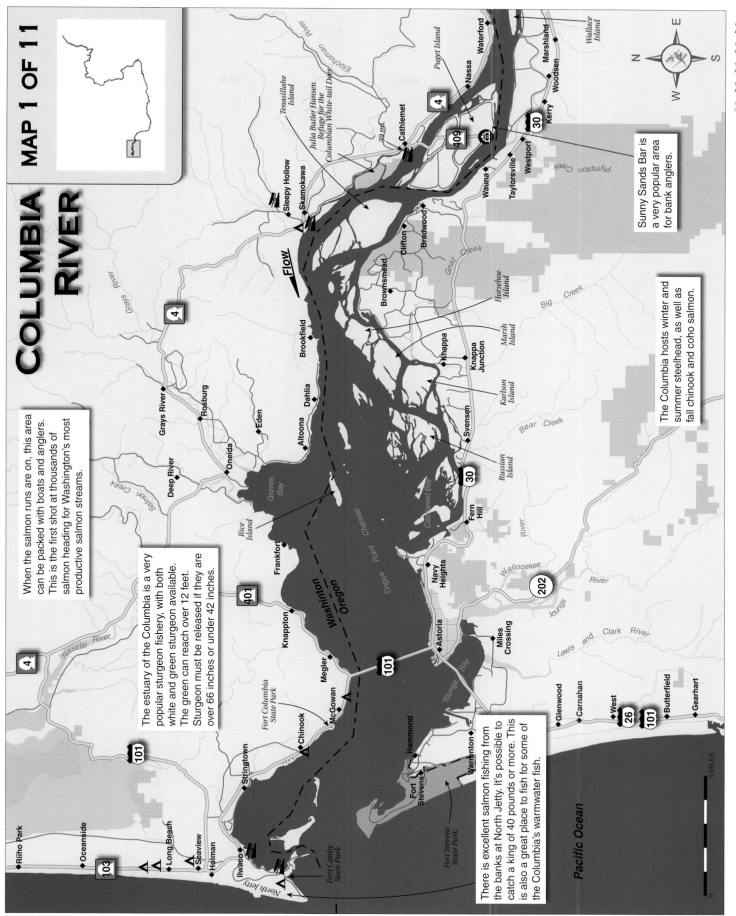

COLUMBIA RIVER

MAP 1 OF 11

FLOW

Washinton
Oregon

When the salmon runs are on, this area can be packed with boats and anglers. This is the first shot at thousands of salmon heading for Washington's most productive salmon streams.

The estuary of the Columbia is a very popular sturgeon fishery, with both white and green sturgeon available. The green can reach over 12 feet. Sturgeon must be released if they are over 66 inches or under 42 inches.

There is excellent salmon fishing from the banks at North Jetty. It's possible to catch a king of 40 pounds or more. This is also a great place to fish for some of the Columbia's warmwater fish.

Sunny Sands Bar is a very popular area for bank anglers.

The Columbia hosts winter and summer steelhead, as well as fall chinook and coho salmon.

Elochoman River
Grays River
Naselle River
Deep River
Salmon Creek
Plympton Creek
Gnat Creek
Big Creek
Bear Creek
Walllooskee River
Youngs River
Lewis and Clark River

Riiho Park
Oceanside
Long Beach
Seaview
Holman
Ilwaco
North Jetty
Fort Canby State Park
Stringtown
Chinook
McGowan
Fort Columbia State Park
Megler
Knappton
Frankfort
Grays River
Rosburg
Oneida
Eden
Deep River
Dahlia
Altoona
Brookfield
Sleepy Hollow
Skamokawa
Tenasillahe Island
Julia Butler Hansen Refuge for the Columbian White-tail Deer
39 mi.
Cathlemet
Puget Island
Waterford
Nassa
Marshland
Wallace Island
Woodsen
Kerry
Westport
Taylorsville
Wauna
Clifton
Bradwood
Brownsmead
Horsehoe Island
Knappa
Knappa Junction
Marsh Island
Karlson Island
Svensen
Russian Island
Fern Hill
Navy Heights
Astoria
Miles Crossing
Warrenton
Hammond
Fort Stevens
Fort Stevens State Park
Rice Island
Graves Bay
Cathlamet Bay
Tongue Point Channel
Youngs Bay
Glenwood
Carnahan
West
Butterfield
Gearhart

Pacific Ocean

5 MILES

N
E
W
S

© 2005 Wilderness Adventures Press, Inc.

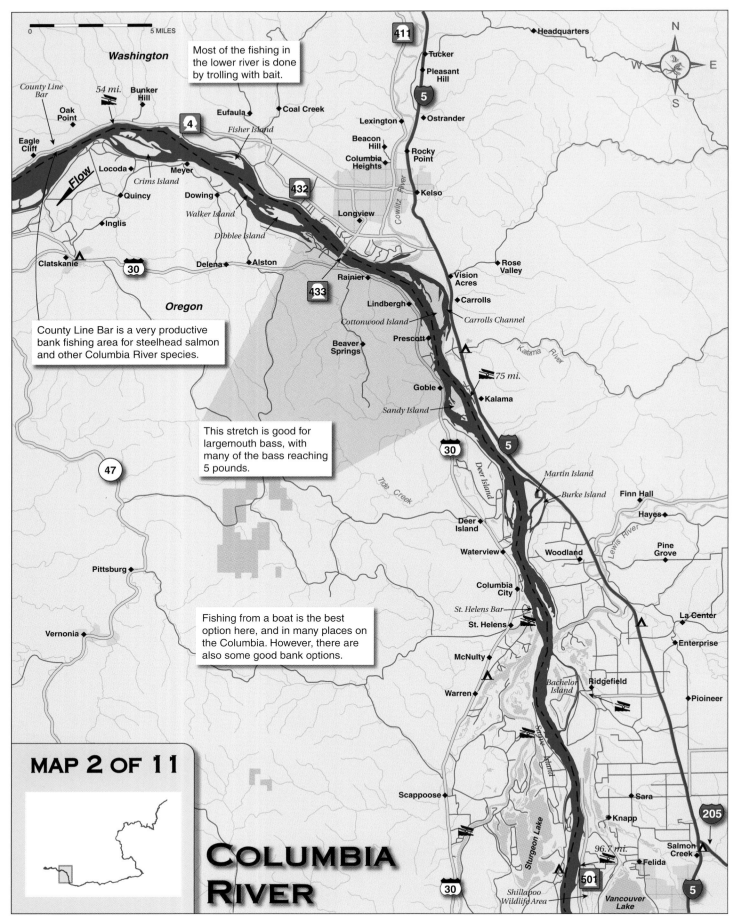

Most of the fishing in the lower river is done by trolling with bait.

County Line Bar is a very productive bank fishing area for steelhead salmon and other Columbia River species.

This stretch is good for largemouth bass, with many of the bass reaching 5 pounds.

Fishing from a boat is the best option here, and in many places on the Columbia. However, there are also some good bank options.

MAP 2 OF 11

COLUMBIA RIVER

© 2005 Wilderness Adventures Press, Inc.

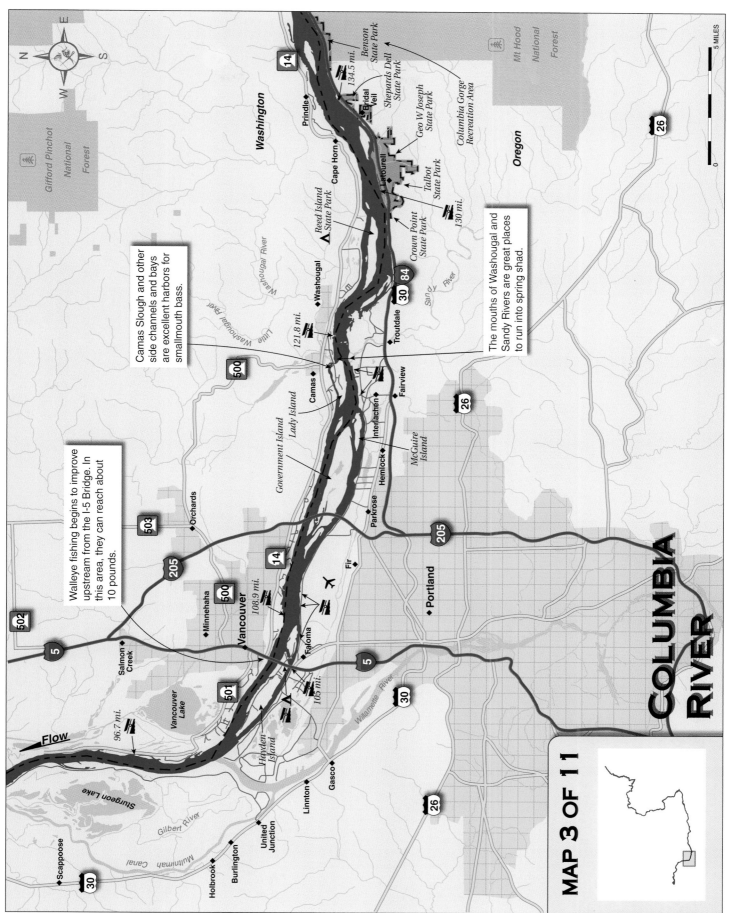

Walleye fishing begins to improve upstream from the I-5 Bridge. In this area, they can reach about 10 pounds.

Camas Slough and other side channels and bays are excellent harbors for smallmouth bass.

The mouths of Washougal and Sandy Rivers are great places to run into spring shad.

Washington

Oregon

Gifford Pinchot National Forest

Mt Hood National Forest

Benson State Park

Shepards Dell State Park

134.5 mi.

Bridal Veil

Prindle

Geo W Joseph State Park

Columbia Gorge Recreation Area

Cape Horn

Latourell

Talbot State Park

Crown Point State Park

130 mi.

Reed Island State Park

Washougal River

Washougal

Sandy River

84

30

Troutdale

Little Washougal River

121.8 mi.

500

Camas

Lady Island

Fairview

Government Island

Interlachen

McGuire Island

Hemlock

Parkrose

Orchards

503

205

26

Fir

14

Portland

205

Minnehaha

500

Vancouver

108.9 mi.

502

5

501

Salmon Creek

Paloma

105 mi.

Willamette River

30

5

Flow

96.7 mi.

Vancouver Lake

Hayden Island

30

26

Sturgeon Lake

Gasco

Gilbert River

Linnton

Multnomah Canal

United Junction

Burlington

Holbrook

Scappoose

30

MAP 3 OF 11

COLUMBIA RIVER

5 MILES

26

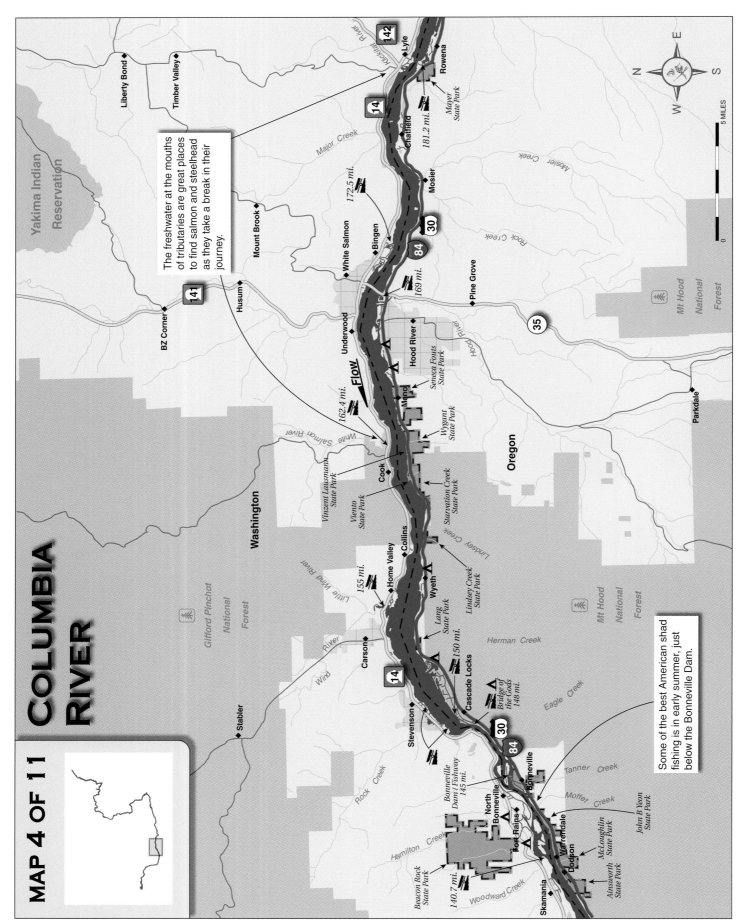

MAP 4 OF 11

COLUMBIA RIVER

The freshwater at the mouths of tributaries are great places to find salmon and steelhead as they take a break in their journey.

Some of the best American shad fishing is in early summer, just below the Bonneville Dam.

Yakima Indian Reservation

Liberty Bond

Timber Valley

BZ Corner
141

Husum

Mount Brook

Stabler

Washington

Gifford Pinchot National Forest

Wind River

Little Wind River

Carson

Stevenson

Home Valley
155 mi.

Collins

Wyeth
150 mi.

Lang State Park

Cook
162.4 mi.

White Salmon River

FLOW

Underwood
169 mi.

White Salmon

Bingen

Major Creek

Klickitat River

Lyle
142
14

Chatfield
181.2 mi.

Rowena

Mayer State Park

Mosier
172.5 mi.

30

84

Pine Grove

Rock Creek

Mosier Creek

Mt Hood National Forest

35

Hood River

Seneca Fouts State Park

Menol

Wygant State Park

Vinzent Lausmann State Park

Viento State Park

Starvation Creek State Park

Lindsey Creek

Lindsey Creek State Park

Oregon

Herman Creek

Eagle Creek

Mt Hood National Forest

Parkdale

Hood River

Cascade Locks

Bridge of the Gods
148 mi.

30

84

14

Bonneville Dam / Fishway
145 mi.

North Bonneville

Port Rains
140.7 mi.

Beacon Rock State Park

Bonneville

Tanner Creek

Moffet Creek

John B Yeon State Park

McLoughlin State Park

Warrendale

Dodson

Ainsworth State Park

Skamania

Woodward Creek

Hamilton Creek

Rock Creek

5 MILES

N E S W

© 2005 Wilderness Adventures Press, Inc.

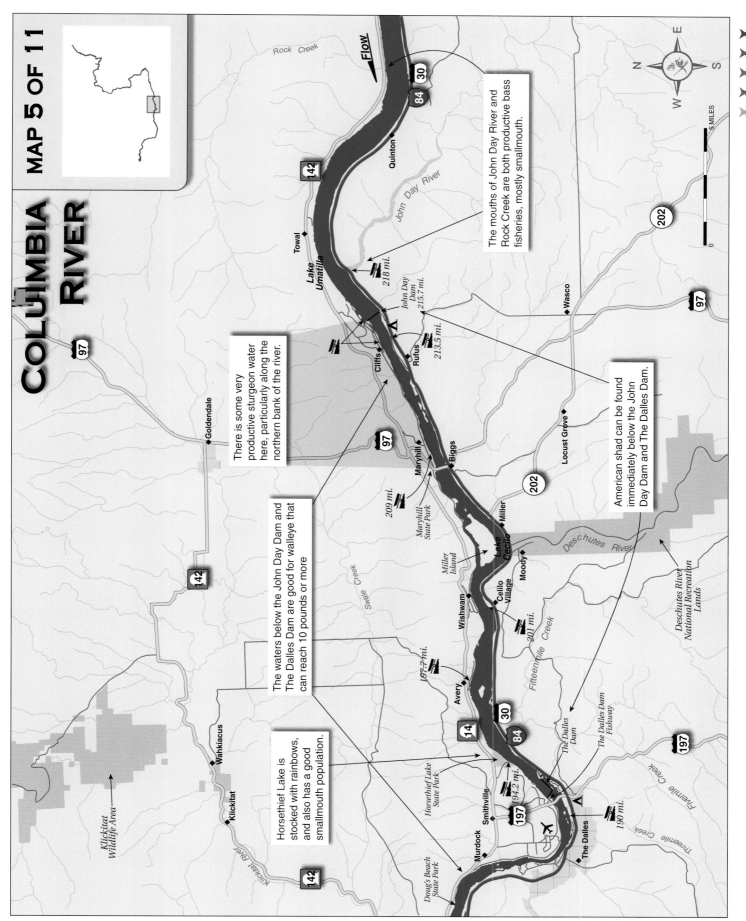

COLUMBIA RIVER

MAP 5 OF 11

Flow

The mouths of John Day River and Rock Creek are both productive bass fisheries, mostly smallmouth.

There is some very productive sturgeon water here, particularly along the northern bank of the river.

The waters below the John Day Dam and The Dalles Dam are good for walleye that can reach 10 pounds or more

American shad can be found immediately below the John Day Dam and The Dalles Dam.

Horsethief Lake is stocked with rainbows, and also has a good smallmouth population.

Rock Creek

Quinton

John Day River

Towal

Lake Umatilla

218 mi.

John Day Dam 215.7 mi.

Wasco

Rufus

213.5 mi.

Cliffs

Goldendale

Biggs

Maryhill

209 mi.

Maryhill State Park

97

Locust Grove

202

Miller

Lake Celilo

Moody

Deschutes River

Miller Island

Swale Creek

Wishram

Celilo Village

201 mi.

Fifteenmile Creek

Deschutes River National Recreation Lands

Wahkiacus

Klickitat

Klickitat Wildlife Area

Klickitat River

Avery

197.7 mi.

14

30

84

The Dalles Dam

The Dalles Dam Fishway

197

Horsethief Lake State Park

Smithville

194.2 mi.

197

Murdock

Doug's Beach State Park

190 mi.

The Dalles

Fivemile Creek

Threemile Creek

N E S W

5 MILES

0

© 2005 Wilderness Adventures Press, Inc.

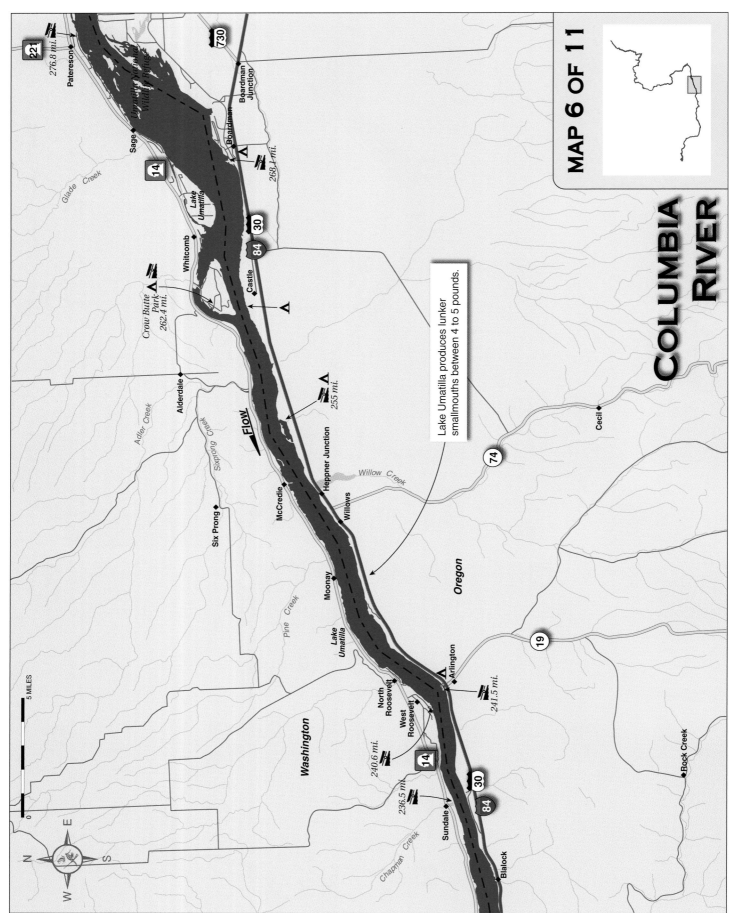

MAP 6 OF 11

COLUMBIA RIVER

Lake Umatilla produces lunker smallmouths between 4 to 5 pounds.

Flow

Washington

Oregon

Lake Umatilla

Lake Umatilla

276.8 mi.

268.1 mi.

262.4 mi.

255 mi.

241.5 mi.

240.6 mi.

236.5 mi.

Patereson

Sage

Whitcomb

Castle

Crow Butte Park

Alderdale

Six Prong

McCredie

Heppner Junction

Willows

Moonay

North Roosevelt

West Roosevelt

Arlington

Sundale

Blalock

Boardman

Boardman Junction

Cecil

Rock Creek

Umatilla National Wildlife Refuge

Glade Creek

Adler Creek

Sixprong Creek

Pine Creek

Willow Creek

Chapman Creek

5 MILES

N E S W

© 2005 Wilderness Adventures Press, Inc.

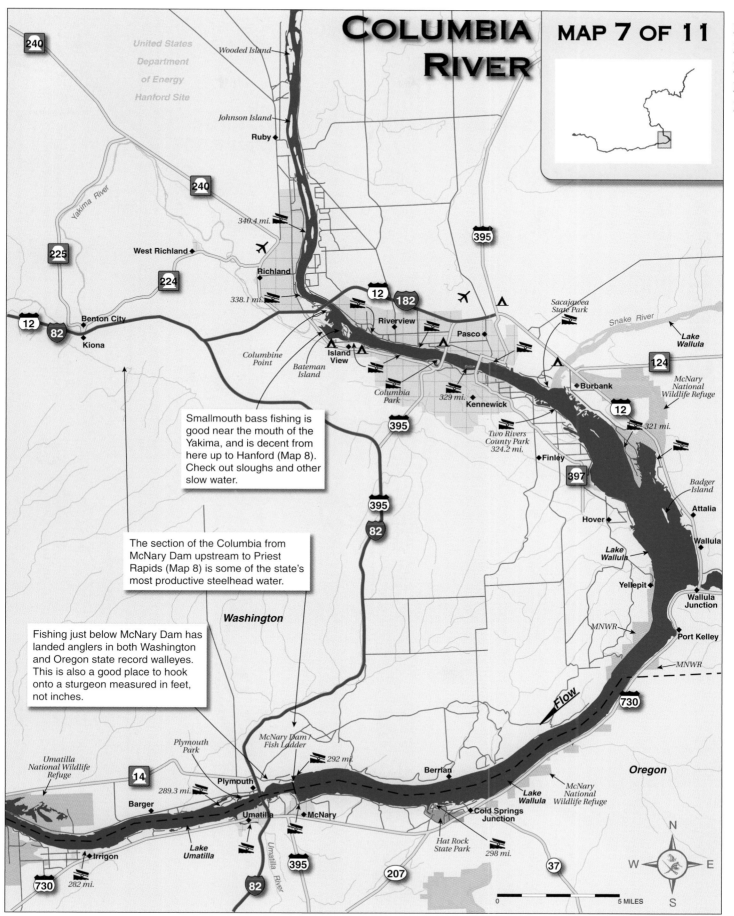

COLUMBIA RIVER

MAP **7** OF **11**

United States
Department
of Energy
Hanford Site

Wooded Island

Johnson Island

Ruby

340.4 mi.

West Richland

Richland

338.1 mi.

Benton City

Kiona

Columbine Point

Bateman Island

Island View

Columbia Park

Riverview

Pasco

Sacajawea State Park

Snake River

Lake Wallula

McNary National Wildlife Refuge

Burbank

329 mi.

Kennewick

Two Rivers County Park
324.2 mi.

Finley

321 mi.

Badger Island

Attalia

Hover

Wallula

Lake Wallula

Yellepit

Wallula Junction

MNWR

Port Kelley

MNWR

Smallmouth bass fishing is good near the mouth of the Yakima, and is decent from here up to Hanford (Map 8). Check out sloughs and other slow water.

The section of the Columbia from McNary Dam upstream to Priest Rapids (Map 8) is some of the state's most productive steelhead water.

Fishing just below McNary Dam has landed anglers in both Washington and Oregon state record walleyes. This is also a good place to hook onto a sturgeon measured in feet, not inches.

Washington

Flow

730

McNary Dam Fish Ladder

Plymouth Park

292 mi.

Berrian

Oregon

Umatilla National Wildlife Refuge

Plymouth

289.3 mi.

Barger

Umatilla

McNary

Lake Umatilla

Cold Springs Junction

Lake Wallula

McNary National Wildlife Refuge

Hat Rock State Park

298 mi.

Irrigon

730

282 mi.

N

W   E

S

0   5 MILES

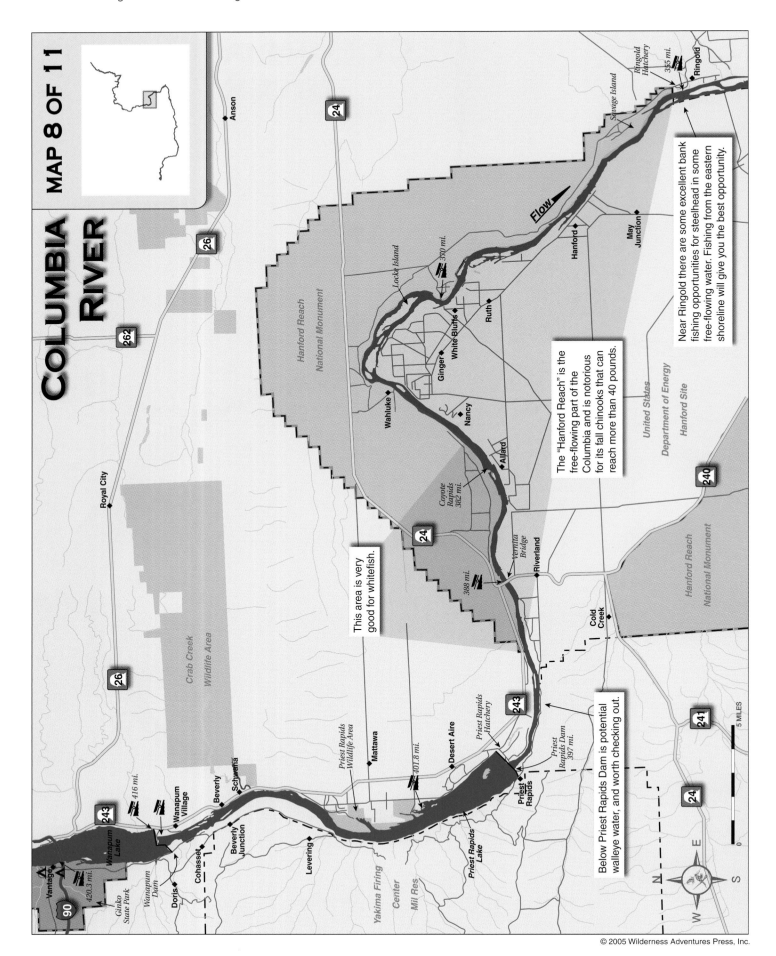

MAP 8 OF 11

COLUMBIA RIVER

The "Hanford Reach" is the free-flowing part of the Columbia and is notorious for its fall chinooks that can reach more than 40 pounds.

Near Ringold there are some excellent bank fishing opportunities for steelhead in some free-flowing water. Fishing from the eastern shoreline will give you the best opportunity.

This area is very good for whitefish.

Below Priest Rapids Dam is potential walleye water, and worth checking out.

Flow

Ringold Hatchery
355 mi.
Ringold

Savage Island

May Junction

Hanford

United States
Department of Energy
Hanford Site

Locke Island
370 mi.

Ginger
White Bluffs
Ruth

Wahluke
Nancy

Allard

Coyote Rapids
382 mi.

Vernita Bridge
Riverland

388 mi.

Cold Creek

Hanford Reach
National Monument

Hanford Reach
National Monument

Anson

24

26

262

Royal City

26

243

Crab Creek
Wildlife Area

Priest Rapids
Wildlife Area

Mattawa

401.8 mi.

Desert Aire

Priest Rapids
Hatchery

Priest Rapids Dam
397 mi.

Priest Rapids

Priest Rapids
Lake

Schwana

Beverly

Beverly
Junction

Levering

Cohasset

Doris

Wanapum
Village

Wanapum
Dam

416 mi.

243

Wanapum
Lake

Ginko State Park

Vantage
420.3 mi.

90

Yakima Firing Center Mil Res.

240

241

241

24

5 MILES

0

N
W   E
S

© 2005 Wilderness Adventures Press, Inc.

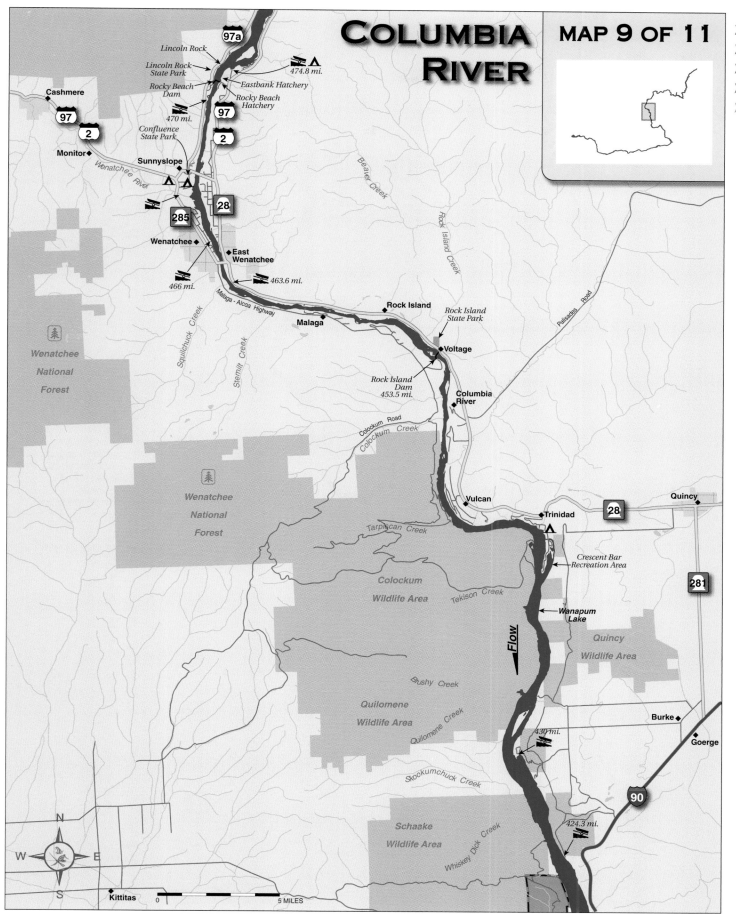

MAP 9 OF 11

COLUMBIA RIVER

Lincoln Rock

Lincoln Rock State Park

Rocky Beach Dam

Eastbank Hatchery

Rocky Beach Hatchery

474.8 mi.

470 mi.

Confluence State Park

Sunnyslope

Cashmere

Monitor

Wenatchee River

Wenatchee

East Wenatchee

466 mi.

463.6 mi.

Malaga - Alcoa Highway

Squilchuck Creek

Stemilt Creek

Malaga

Rock Island

Rock Island State Park

Voltage

Rock Island Dam 453.5 mi.

Columbia River

Palisades Road

Beaver Creek

Rock Island Creek

Wenatchee National Forest

Wenatchee National Forest

Colockum Road

Colockum Creek

Vulcan

Trinidad

Tarpiscan Creek

Colockum Wildlife Area

Tekison Creek

Crescent Bar Recreation Area

Wanapum Lake

Quincy

Quincy Wildlife Area

Burke

Goerge

Flow

Bushy Creek

Quilomene Wildlife Area

Quilomene Creek

Skookumchuck Creek

430 mi.

Schaake Wildlife Area

Whiskey Dick Creek

424.3 mi.

Kittitas

N
W   E
S

0   5 MILES

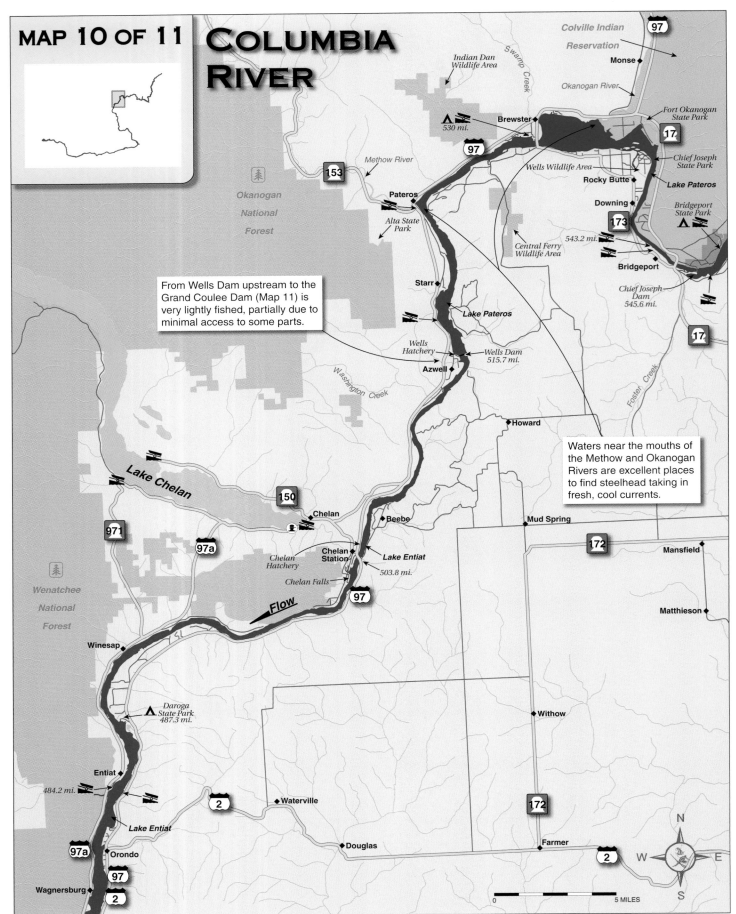

MAP 10 OF 11

COLUMBIA RIVER

From Wells Dam upstream to the Grand Coulee Dam (Map 11) is very lightly fished, partially due to minimal access to some parts.

Waters near the mouths of the Methow and Okanogan Rivers are excellent places to find steelhead taking in fresh, cool currents.

Colville Indian Reservation

Monse

Indian Dan Wildlife Area

Fort Okanogan State Park

Okanogan River

Brewster

530 mi.

Wells Wildlife Area

Chief Joseph State Park

Rocky Butte

Lake Pateros

Downing

Bridgeport State Park

Methow River

Pateros

Central Ferry Wildlife Area

543.2 mi.

Bridgeport

Okanogan National Forest

Alta State Park

Starr

Lake Pateros

Chief Joseph Dam 545.6 mi.

Wells Hatchery

Wells Dam 515.7 mi.

Azwell

Washington Creek

Howard

Foster Creek

Lake Chelan

150

Chelan

Beebe

Mud Spring

Mansfield

Chelan Hatchery

Chelan Station

Lake Entiat

172

971

97a

Chelan Falls

503.8 mi.

Matthieson

Wenatchee National Forest

Flow

Winesap

Withow

Daroga State Park 487.3 mi.

Entiat

484.2 mi.

2

Waterville

172

Lake Entiat

Douglas

Farmer

97a

Orondo

2

Wagnersburg

2

N W E S

0   5 MILES

© 2005 Wilderness Adventures Press, Inc.

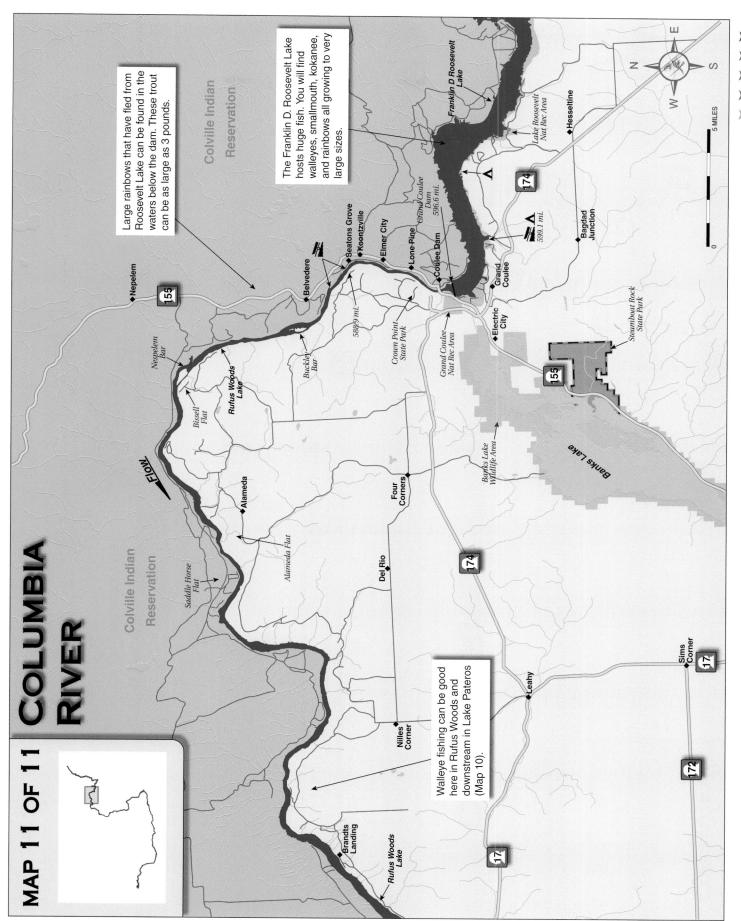

MAP 11 OF 11 | COLUMBIA RIVER

COLUMBIA RIVER

Large rainbows that have fled from Roosevelt Lake can be found in the waters below the dam. These trout can be as large as 3 pounds.

The Franklin D. Roosevelt Lake hosts huge fish. You will find walleyes, smallmouth, kokanee, and rainbows all growing to very large sizes.

Walleye fishing can be good here in Rufus Woods and downstream in Lake Pateros (Map 10).

Colville Indian Reservation

Colville Indian Reservation

Nepelem

Belvedere

Seatons Grove
Koontzville
Elmer City
Lone Pine

Grand Coulee Dam
596.6 mi.

Coulee Dam

Grand Coulee

Franklin D Roosevelt Lake

Lake Roosevelt Nat Rec Area

Hesseltine

Bagdad Junction

599.1 mi.

Electric City

Grand Coulee Nat Rec Area

Steamboat Rock State Park

Banks Lake

Nespelem Bar

Buckley Bar

588.9 mi.

Crown Point State Park

Bissell Flat

Rufus Woods Lake

Alameda

Four Corners

Del Rio

Barks Lake Wildlife Area

FLOW

Saddle Horse Flat

Alameda Flat

Nilles Corner

Leahy

Sims Corner

Brandts Landing

Rufus Woods Lake

5 MILES

N E S W

© 2005 Wilderness Adventures Press, Inc.

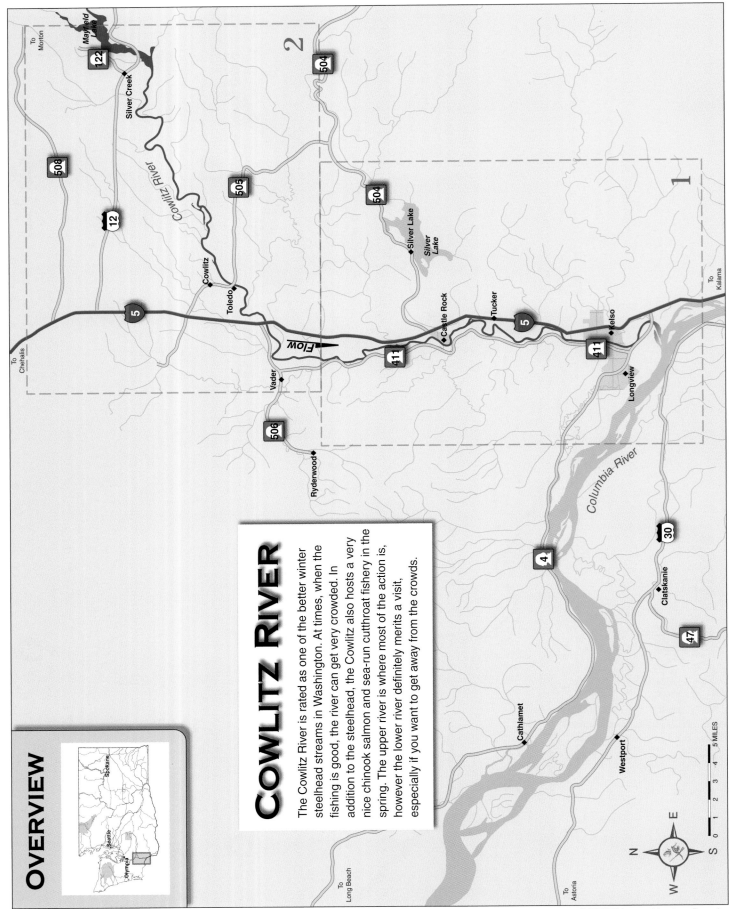

OVERVIEW

COWLITZ RIVER

The Cowlitz River is rated as one of the better winter steelhead streams in Washington. At times, when the fishing is good, the river can get very crowded. In addition to the steelhead, the Cowlitz also hosts a very nice chinook salmon and sea-run cutthroat fishery in the spring. The upper river is where most of the action is, however the lower river definitely merits a visit, especially if you want to get away from the crowds.

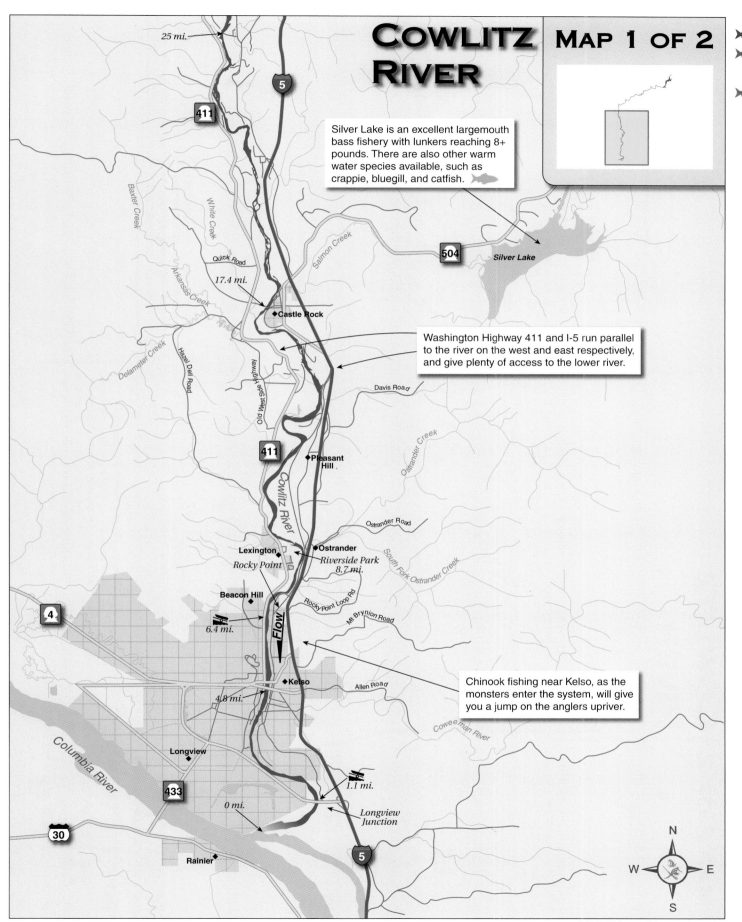

COWLITZ RIVER

MAP 1 OF 2

25 mi.

411

5

Silver Lake is an excellent largemouth bass fishery with lunkers reaching 8+ pounds. There are also other warm water species available, such as crappie, bluegill, and catfish.

504

Silver Lake

Baxter Creek

White Creek

Quick Road

17.4 mi.

Salmon Creek

Arkansas Creek

◆Castle Rock

Washington Highway 411 and I-5 run parallel to the river on the west and east respectively, and give plenty of access to the lower river.

Delameter Creek

Hazel Dell Road

Old West Side Highway

Davis Road

Ostrander Creek

411

◆Pleasant Hill

Cowlitz River

Ostrander Road

Lexington ◇

◆Ostrander

Riverside Park 8.7 mi.

Rocky Point

South Fork Ostrander Creek

Beacon Hill ◆

Rocky Point Loop Rd

Flow

6.4 mi.

Mt Brynion Road

4

Chinook fishing near Kelso, as the monsters enter the system, will give you a jump on the anglers upriver.

◆Kelso

Allen Road

4.8 mi.

Coweeman River

Longview ◆

433

1.1 mi.

0 mi.

Longview Junction

30

5

Rainier ◆

N
W E
S

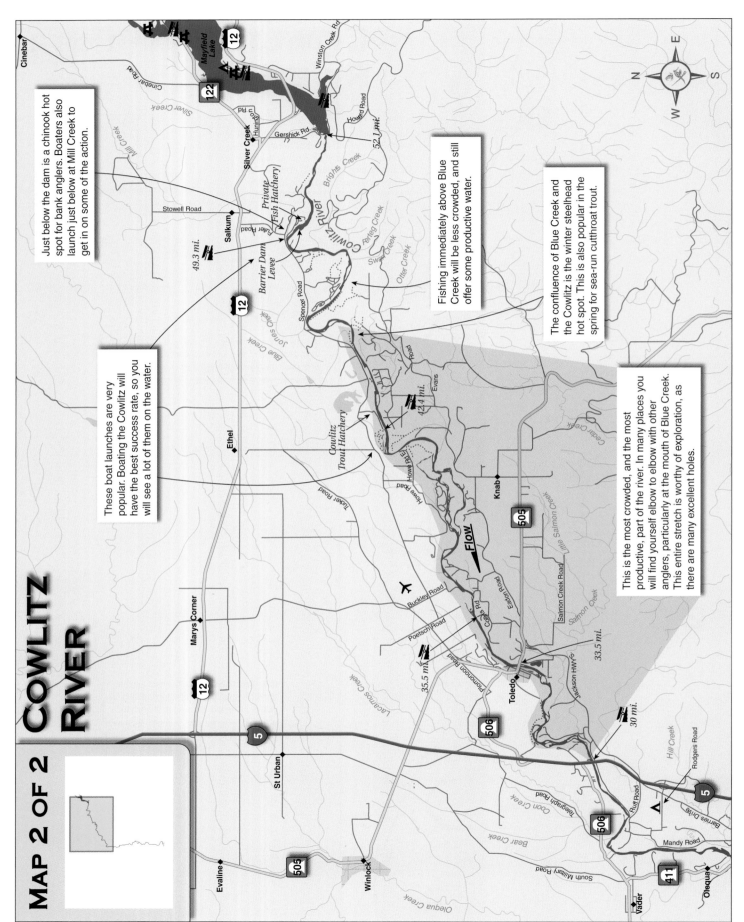

MAP 2 OF 2

COWLITZ RIVER

Just below the dam is a chinook hot spot for bank anglers. Boaters also launch just below at Mill Creek to get in on some of the action.

These boat launches are very popular. Boating the Cowlitz will have the best success rate, so you will see a lot of them on the water.

Fishing immediately above Blue Creek will be less crowded, and still offer some productive water.

The confluence of Blue Creek and the Cowlitz is the winter steelhead hot spot. This is also popular in the spring for sea-run cutthroat trout.

This is the most crowded, and the most productive, part of the river. In many places you will find yourself elbow to elbow with other anglers, particularly at the mouth of Blue Creek. This entire stretch is worthy of exploration, as there are many excellent holes.

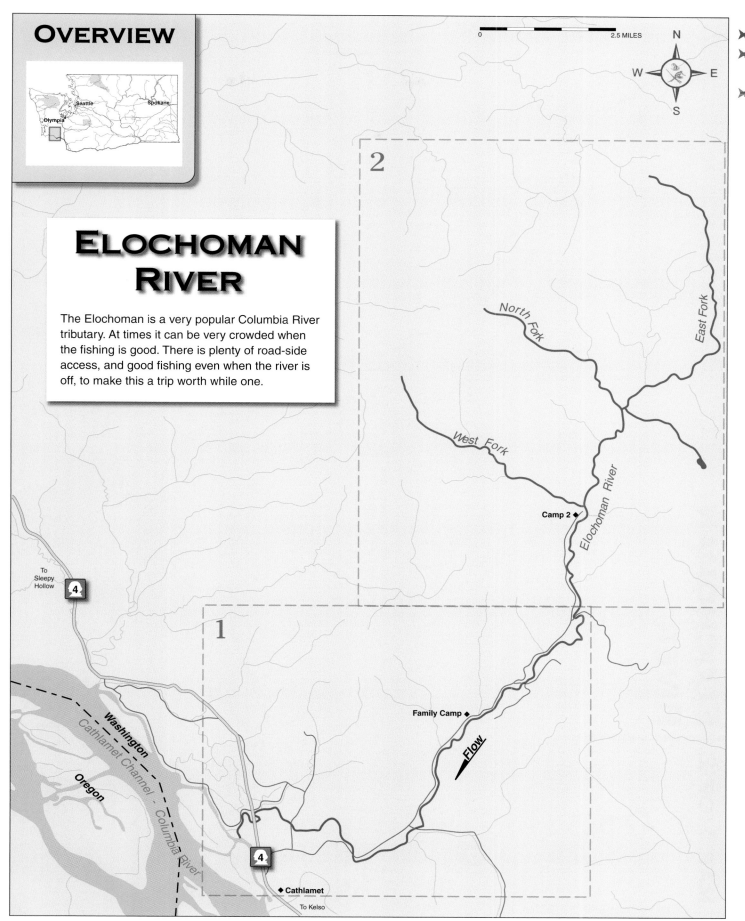

OVERVIEW

ELOCHOMAN RIVER

The Elochoman is a very popular Columbia River tributary. At times it can be very crowded when the fishing is good. There is plenty of road-side access, and good fishing even when the river is off, to make this a trip worth while one.

0   2.5 MILES

N
W · E
S

Seattle
Spokane
Olympia

2

North Fork

East Fork

West Fork

Elochoman River

Camp 2 ◆

To Sleepy Hollow

4

1

Washington
Oregon

Cathlamet Channel · Columbia River

Family Camp ◆

Flow

4

◆ Cathlamet

To Kelso

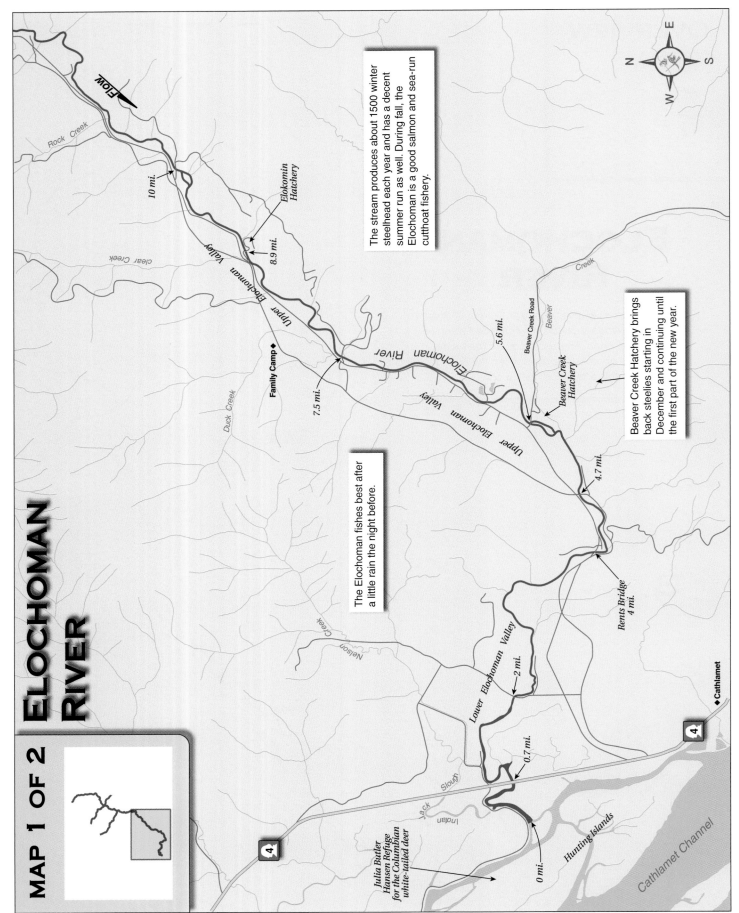

MAP 1 OF 2

ELOCHOMAN RIVER

The stream produces about 1500 winter steelhead each year and has a decent summer run as well. During fall, the Elochoman is a good salmon and sea-run cutthoat fishery.

Beaver Creek Hatchery brings back steelies starting in December and continuing until the first part of the new year.

The Elochoman fishes best after a little rain the night before.

Julia Butler Hansen Refuge for the Columbian white-tailed deer

Flow

Rock Creek

10 mi.

Clear Creek

Elokomin Hatchery

8.9 mi.

Upper Elochoman Valley

Duck Creek

Family Camp ◆

7.5 mi.

Elochoman River

Upper Elochoman Valley

5.6 mi.

Beaver Creek Road

Beaver Creek

Beaver Creek Hatchery

4.7 mi.

Rents Bridge 4 mi.

Nelson Creek

Lower Elochoman Valley

2 mi.

0.7 mi.

Jack Slough

Indian

0 mi.

Hunting Islands

◆ Cathlamet

Cathlamet Channel

4

4

© 2005 Wilderness Adventures Press, Inc.

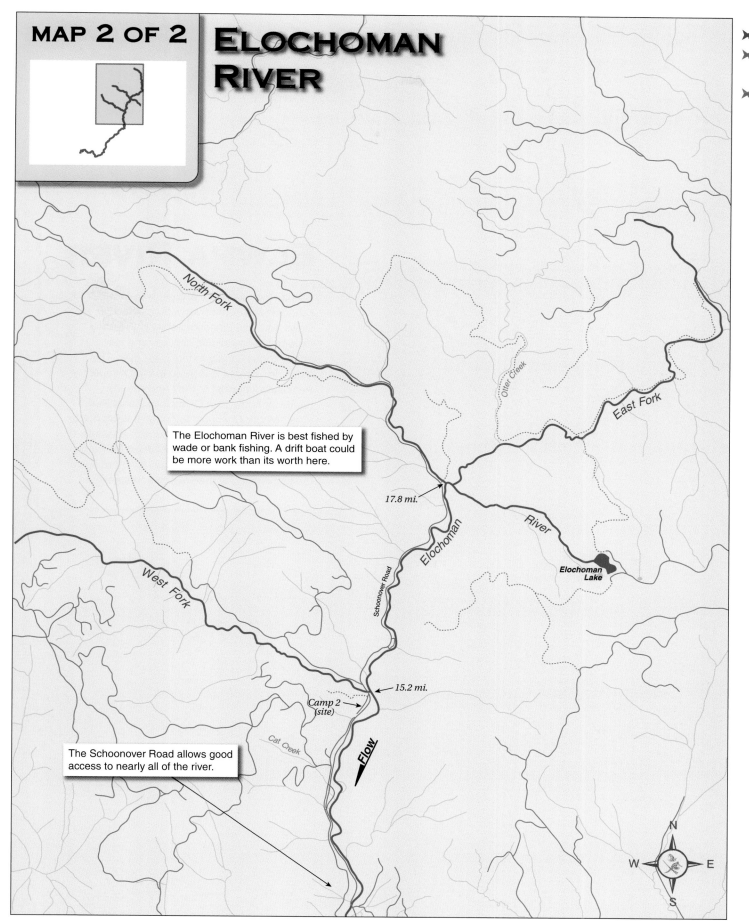

MAP 2 OF 2

ELOCHOMAN RIVER

North Fork

Otter Creek

East Fork

The Elochoman River is best fished by wade or bank fishing. A drift boat could be more work than its worth here.

17.8 mi.

Elochoman

River

Elochoman
Lake

West Fork

Schoonover Road

15.2 mi.

Camp 2
(site)

Cat Creek

Flow

The Schoonover Road allows good access to nearly all of the river.

N
W E
S

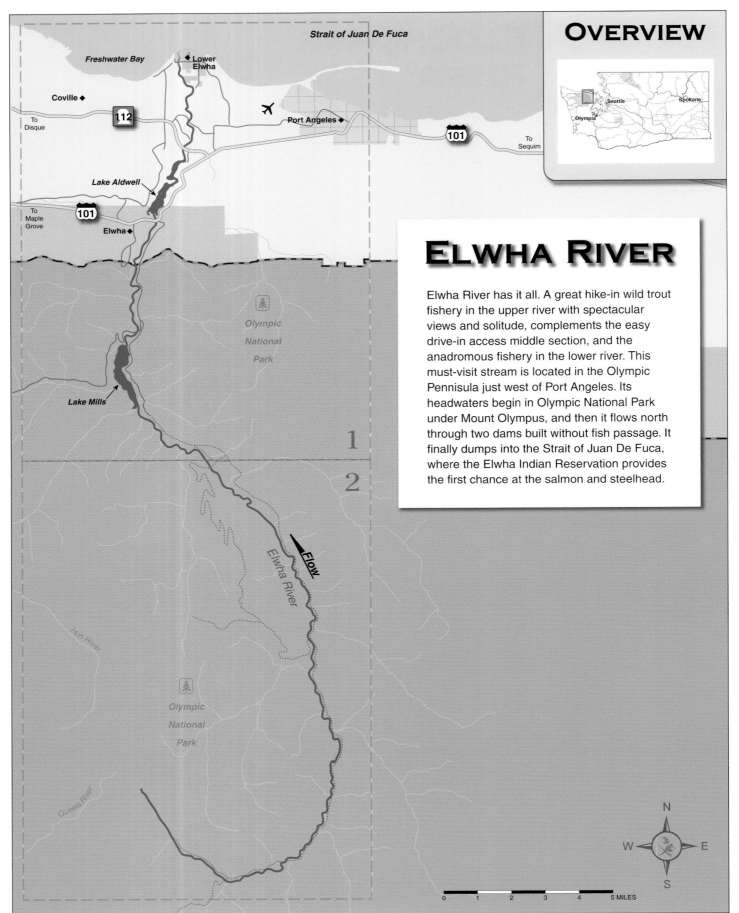

OVERVIEW

ELWHA RIVER

Elwha River has it all. A great hike-in wild trout fishery in the upper river with spectacular views and solitude, complements the easy drive-in access middle section, and the anadromous fishery in the lower river. This must-visit stream is located in the Olympic Pennisula just west of Port Angeles. Its headwaters begin in Olympic National Park under Mount Olympus, and then it flows north through two dams built without fish passage. It finally dumps into the Strait of Juan De Fuca, where the Elwha Indian Reservation provides the first chance at the salmon and steelhead.

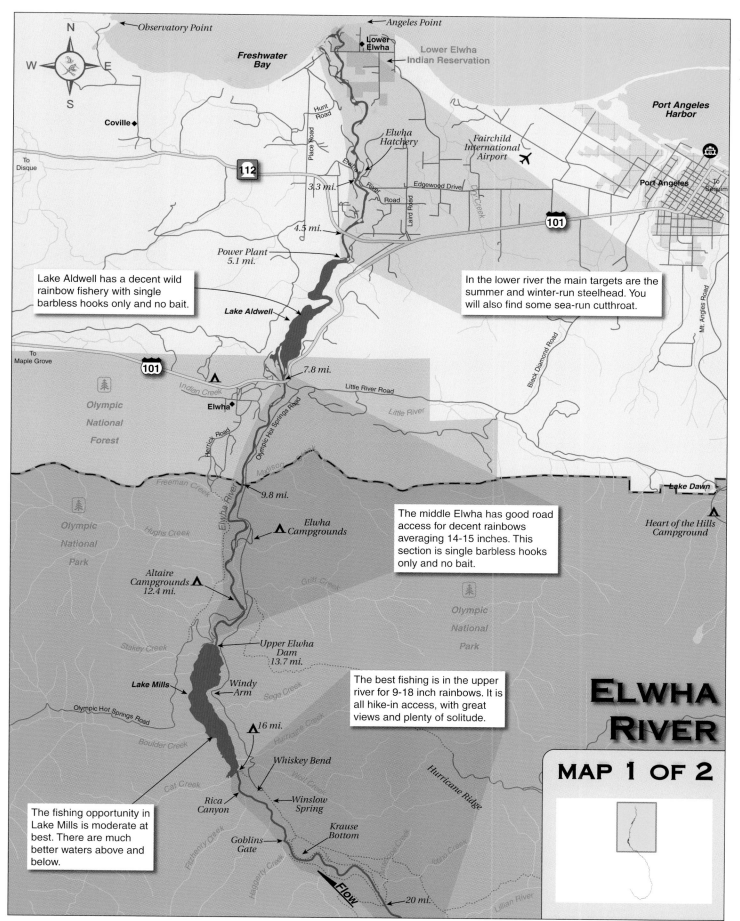

N

W E

S

Observatory Point

Angeles Point

Lower Elwha

Lower Elwha
Indian Reservation

Freshwater
Bay

Port Angeles
Harbor

Coville

Hunt
Road

Elwha
Hatchery

Fairchild
International
Airport

Place Road

To
Disque

112

3.3 mi.

Elwha

River
Road

Edgewood Drive

Laird Road

Dry Creek

101

Port Angeles

To
Sequim

Mt. Angeles Road

4.5 mi.

Power Plant
5.1 mi.

Lake Aldwell has a decent wild
rainbow fishery with single
barbless hooks only and no bait.

Lake Aldwell

In the lower river the main targets are the
summer and winter-run steelhead. You
will also find some sea-run cutthroat.

To
Maple Grove

101

Indian Creek

7.8 mi.

Little River Road

Little River

Black Diamond Road

Olympic

National

Forest

Elwha

Herrick Road

Olympic Hot Springs Road

Madison

Freeman Creek

Elwha River

9.8 mi.

Lake Dawn

Olympic

National

Park

Hughs Creek

Elwha
Campgrounds

The middle Elwha has good road
access for decent rainbows
averaging 14-15 inches. This
section is single barbless hooks
only and no bait.

Heart of the Hills
Campground

Altaire
Campgrounds
12.4 mi.

Griff Creek

Stakey Creek

Upper Elwha
Dam
13.7 mi.

Olympic

National

Park

Lake Mills

Windy
Arm

Sege Creek

Olympic Hot Springs Road

16 mi.

Hurricane Creek

The best fishing is in the upper
river for 9-18 inch rainbows. It is
all hike-in access, with great
views and plenty of solitude.

ELWHA

Boulder Creek

Cat Creek

Whiskey Bend

Wolf Creek

Hurricane Ridge

RIVER

MAP 1 OF 2

Rica
Canyon

Winslow
Spring

Krause
Bottom

The fishing opportunity in
Lake Mills is moderate at
best. There are much
better waters above and
below.

Fitzhenry Creek

Goblins
Gate

Haggerty Creek

Flow

Idaho Creek

20 mi.

Lillian River

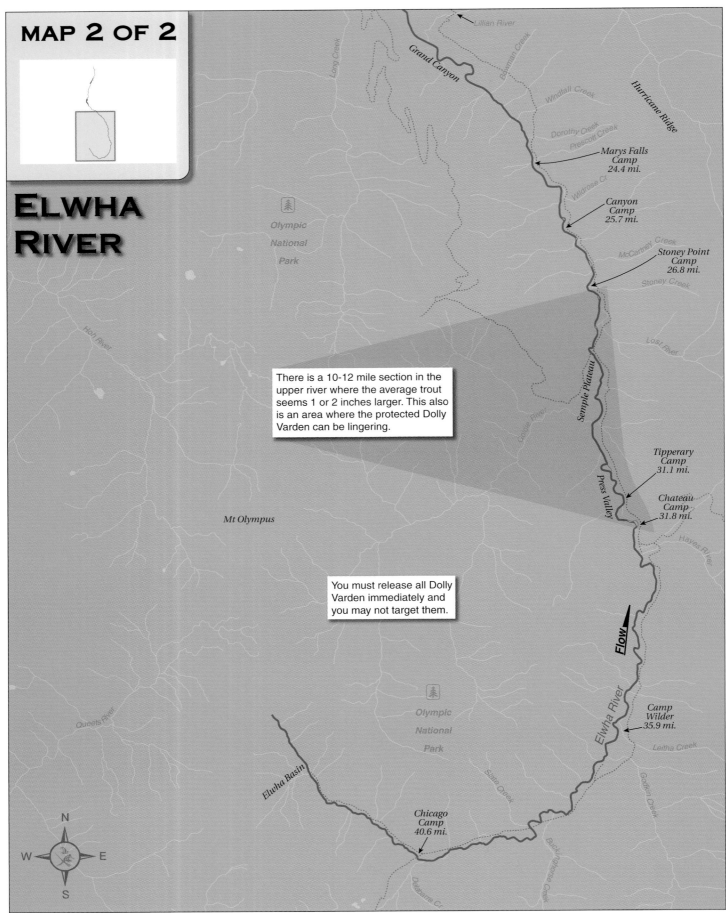

MAP 2 OF 2

ELWHA RIVER

Lillian River

Grand Canyon

Bowman Creek

Windfall Creek

Hurricane Ridge

Long Creek

Dorothy Creek

Prescott Creek

Marys Falls
Camp
24.4 mi.

Wildrose Cr

Canyon
Camp
25.7 mi.

Olympic
National
Park

McCartney Creek

Stoney Point
Camp
26.8 mi.

Stoney Creek

Hoh River

Lost River

Semple Plateau

There is a 10-12 mile section in the
upper river where the average trout
seems 1 or 2 inches larger. This also
is an area where the protected Dolly
Varden can be lingering.

Goose River

Tipperary
Camp
31.1 mi.

Press Valley

Chateau
Camp
31.8 mi.

Mt Olympus

Hayes River

You must release all Dolly
Varden immediately and
you may not target them.

Flow

Olympic
National
Park

Queets River

Elwha River

Camp
Wilder
35.9 mi.

Leitha Creek

Godkin Creek

Elwha Basin

State Creek

Chicago
Camp
40.6 mi.

Buckinghorse Creek

N
W   E
S

Delabarre Cr

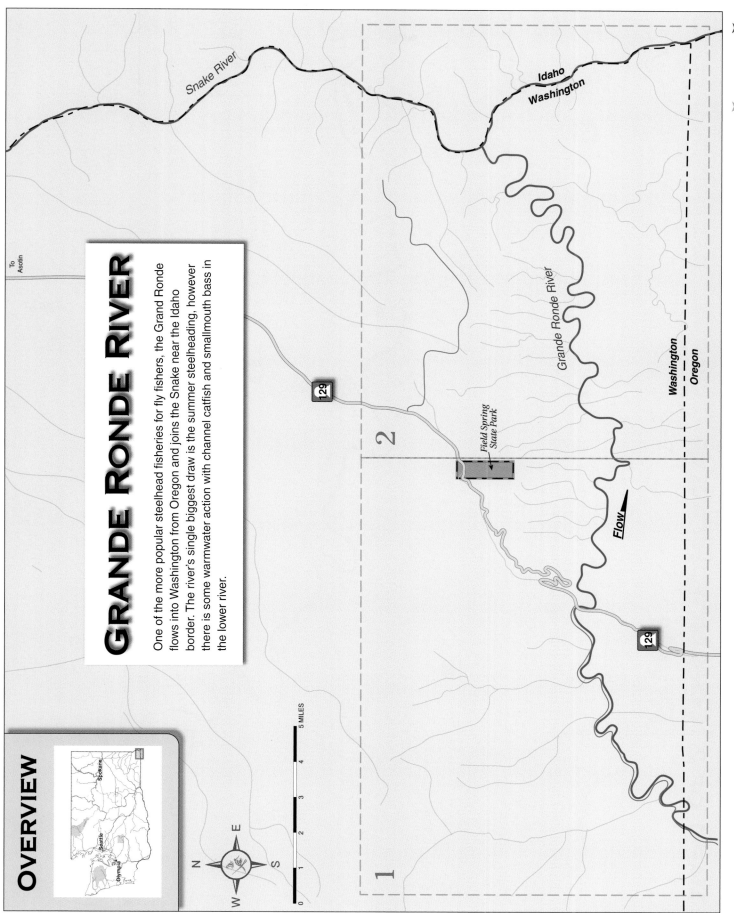

GRANDE RONDE RIVER

One of the more popular steelhead fisheries for fly fishers, the Grand Ronde flows into Washington from Oregon and joins the Snake near the Idaho border. The river's single biggest draw is the summer steelheading, however there is some warmwater action with channel catfish and smallmouth bass in the lower river.

Snake River

Idaho
Washington

Grande Ronde River

Field Spring State Park

Washington
Oregon

Flow

129

129

To Asotin

2

1

OVERVIEW

Spokane

Seattle

Olympia

N
E
S
W

0 1 2 3 4 5 MILES

MAP 1 OF 2

GRANDE RONDE RIVER

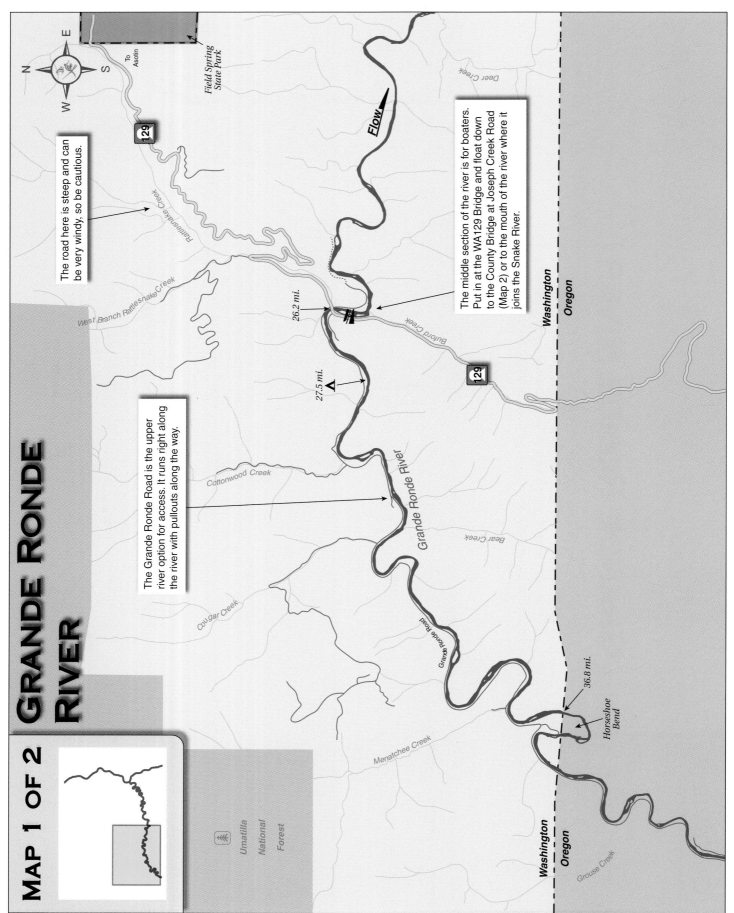

The road here is steep and can be very windy, so be cautious.

The Grande Ronde Road is the upper river option for access. It runs right along the river with pullouts along the way.

The middle section of the river is for boaters. Put in at the WA129 Bridge and float down to the County Bridge at Joseph Creek Road (Map 2) or to the mouth of the river where it joins the Snake River.

Field Spring State Park

To Asotin

129

Rattlesnake Creek

West Branch Rattlesnake Creek

Flow

Deer Creek

Buford Creek

129

26.2 mi.

27.5 mi.

Cottonwood Creek

Cougar Creek

Grande Ronde River

Bear Creek

Grande Ronde Road

Menatchee Creek

36.8 mi.

Horseshoe Bend

Grouse Creek

Washington
Oregon

Umatilla National Forest

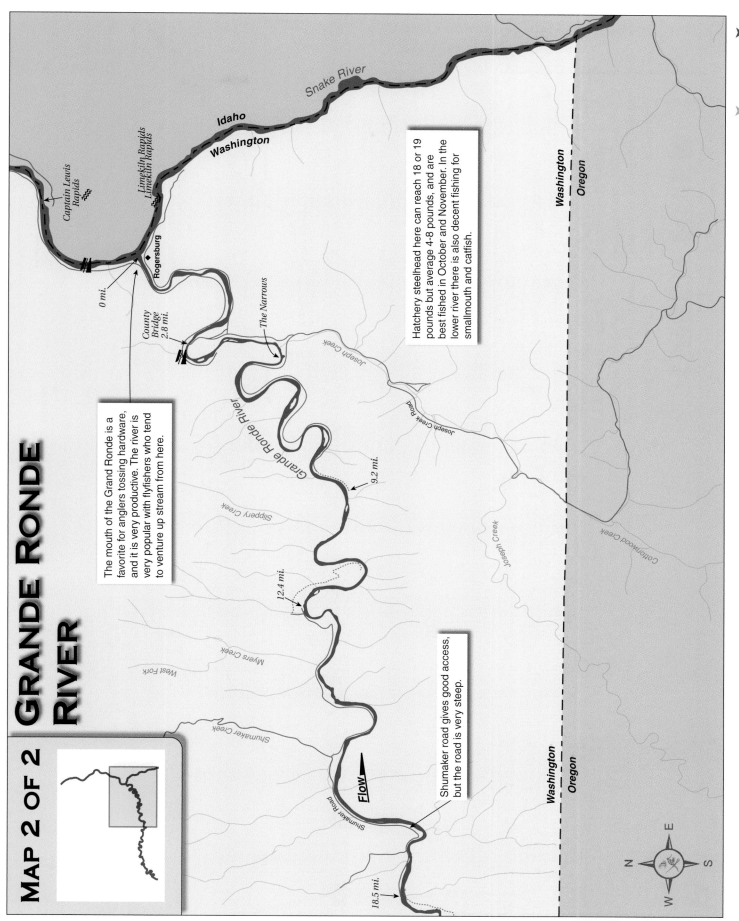

MAP 2 OF 2 GRANDE RONDE RIVER

The mouth of the Grand Ronde is a favorite for anglers tossing hardware, and it is very productive. The river is very popular with flyfishers who tend to venture up stream from here.

Hatchery steelhead here can reach 18 or 19 pounds but average 4-8 pounds, and are best fished in October and November. In the lower river there is also decent fishing for smallmouth and catfish.

Shumaker road gives good access, but the road is very steep.

Captain Lewis Rapids

Limekiln Rapids
Limekiln Rapids

Snake River

Idaho

Washington

Rogersburg

0 mi.

County Bridge 2.8 mi.

The Narrows

Joseph Creek

Grande Ronde River

Slippery Creek

9.2 mi.

12.4 mi.

Myers Creek

West Fork

Shumaker Creek

Joseph Creek

Cottonwood Creek

Joseph Creek Road

Washington
Oregon

Washington
Oregon

Flow

Shumaker Road

18.5 mi.

N
E
S
W

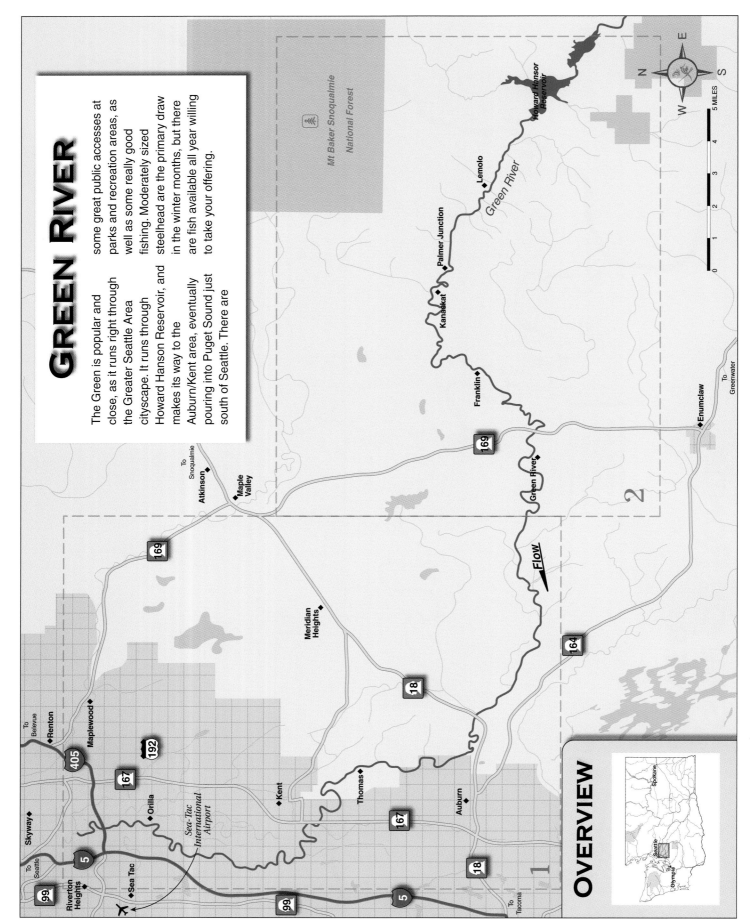

GREEN RIVER

The Green is popular and close, as it runs right through the Greater Seattle Area cityscape. It runs through Howard Hanson Reservoir, and makes its way to the Auburn/Kent area, eventually pouring into Puget Sound just south of Seattle. There are some great public accesses at parks and recreation areas, as well as some really good fishing. Moderately sized steelhead are the primary draw in the winter months, but there are fish available all year willing to take your offering.

OVERVIEW

© 2005 Wilderness Adventures Press, Inc.

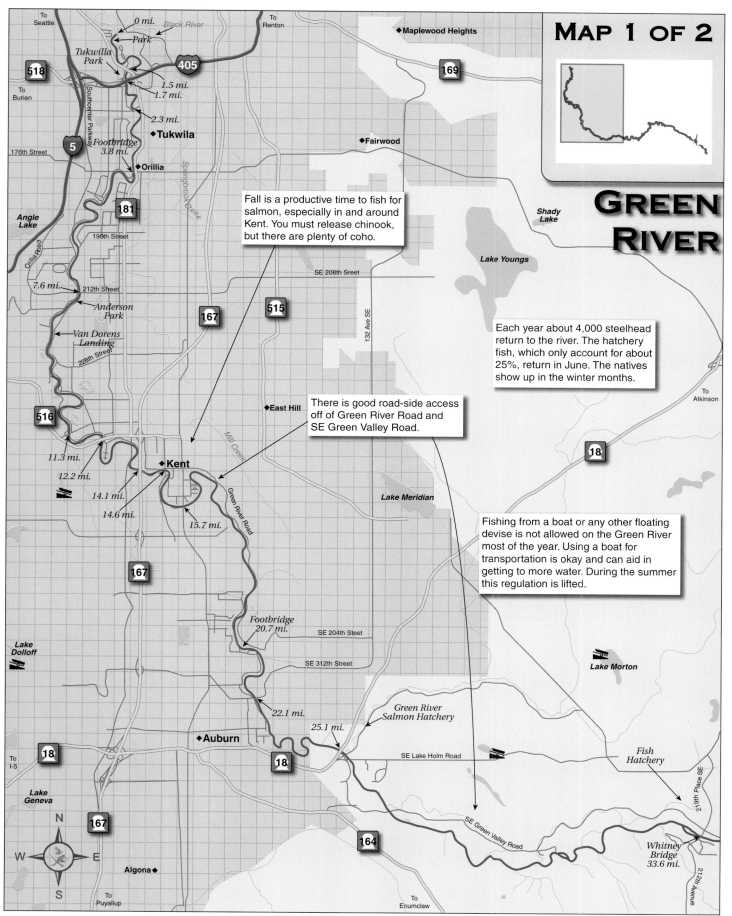

MAP 1 OF 2

GREEN RIVER

To Seattle

0 mi.
Park
Black River

Tukwilla Park

518

1.5 mi.
1.7 mi.

405

To Renton

To Burien

Maplewood Heights

169

Southcenter Parkway

2.3 mi.

Tukwila

5

176th Street

Footbridge
3.8 mi.

Orillia

181

Fairwood

Angle Lake

190th Street

Springbrook Creek

Shady Lake

Fall is a productive time to fish for salmon, especially in and around Kent. You must release chinook, but there are plenty of coho.

Lake Youngs

Orillia Road

7.6 mi.

212th Street

Anderson Park

Van Dorens Landing

228th Street

167

515

SE 208th Street

132 Ave SE

Each year about 4,000 steelhead return to the river. The hatchery fish, which only account for about 25%, return in June. The natives show up in the winter months.

516

East Hill

There is good road-side access off of Green River Road and SE Green Valley Road.

Mill Creek

To Atkinson

18

11.3 mi.

12.2 mi.

Kent

14.1 mi.

14.6 mi.

15.7 mi.

Green River Road

Lake Meridian

Fishing from a boat or any other floating devise is not allowed on the Green River most of the year. Using a boat for transportation is okay and can aid in getting to more water. During the summer this regulation is lifted.

167

Footbridge
20.7 mi.

SE 204th Steet

SE 312th Street

Lake Dolloff

Lake Morton

22.1 mi.

25.1 mi.

Green River Salmon Hatchery

Auburn

18

18

To I-5

SE Lake Holm Road

Fish Hatchery

219th Place SE

Lake Geneva

N

167

164

SE Green Valley Road

Whitney Bridge
33.6 mi.

212th Avenue

W   E

Algona

S

To Puyallup

To Enumclaw

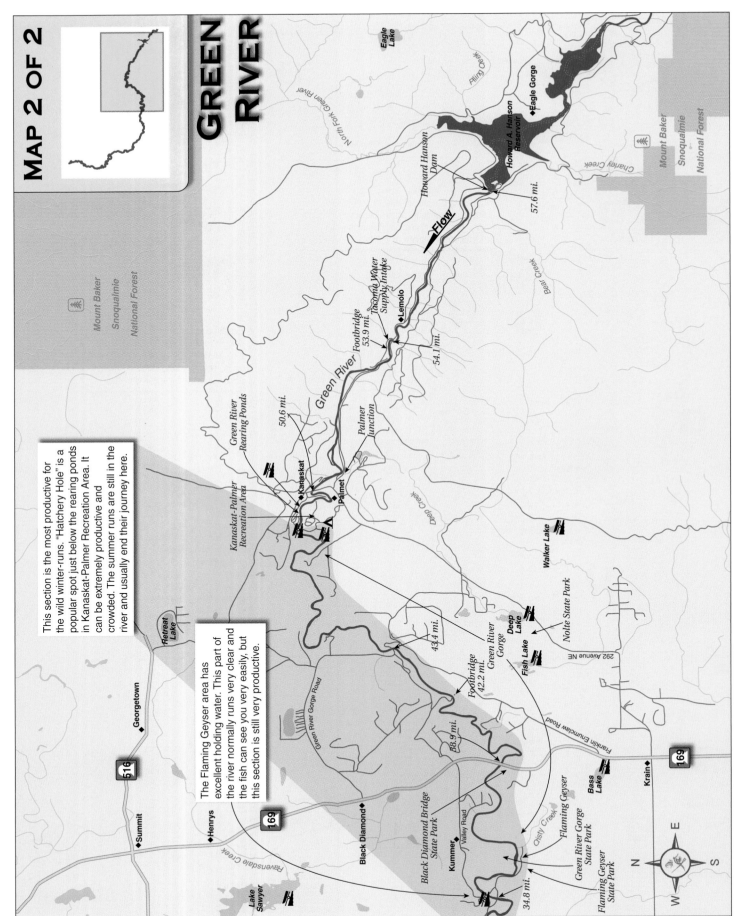

MAP 2 OF 2

GREEN RIVER

This section is the most productive for the wild winter-runs. "Hatchery Hole" is a popular spot just below the rearing ponds in Kanaskat-Palmer Recreation Area. It can be extremely productive and crowded. The summer runs are still in the river and usually end their journey here.

The Flaming Geyser area has excellent holding water. This part of the river normally runs very clear and the fish can see you very easily, but this section is still very productive.

© 2005 Wilderness Adventures Press, Inc.

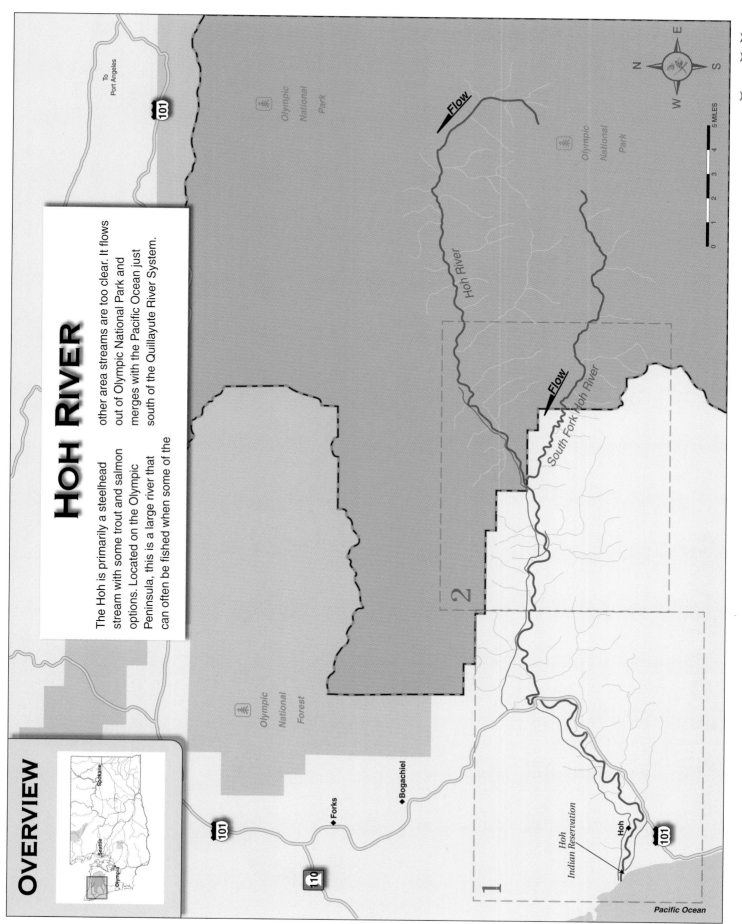

HOH RIVER

The Hoh is primarily a steelhead stream with some trout and salmon options. Located on the Olympic Peninsula, this is a large river that can often be fished when some of the other area streams are too clear. It flows out of Olympic National Park and merges with the Pacific Ocean just south of the Quillayute River System.

OVERVIEW

Flow

Flow

Hoh River

South Fork Hoh River

Olympic National Park

Olympic National Park

Olympic National Forest

To Port Angeles

101

101

110

101

Forks

Bogachiel

Hoh

Hoh Indian Reservation

Pacific Ocean

5 MILES
0 1 2 3 4

N E S W

Spokane
Seattle
Olympia

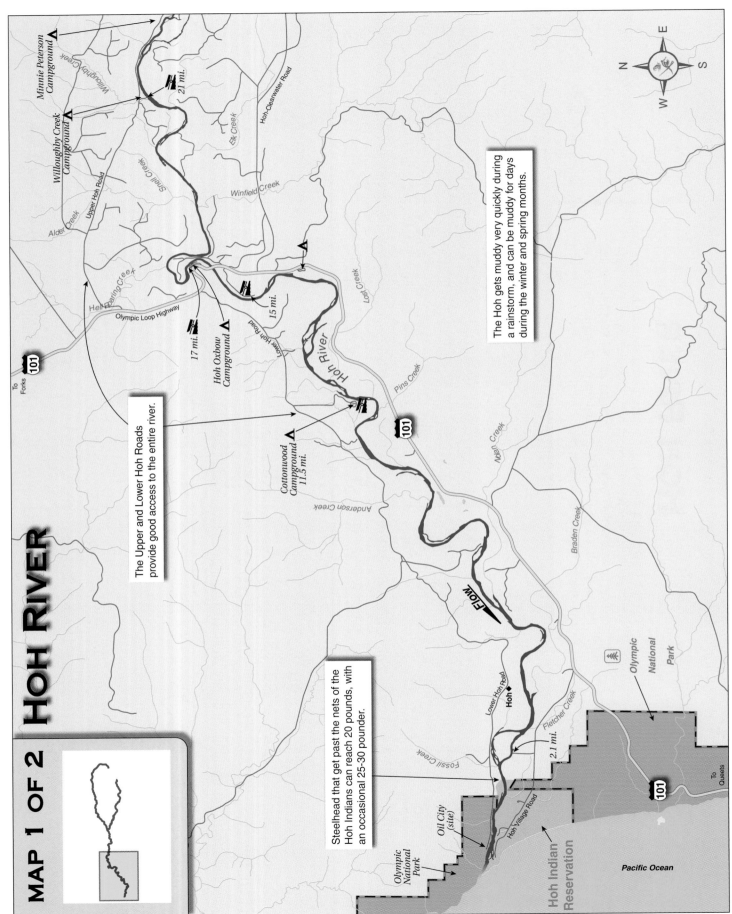

MAP 1 OF 2   HOH RIVER

The Upper and Lower Hoh Roads provide good access to the entire river.

The Hoh gets muddy very quickly during a rainstorm, and can be muddy for days during the winter and spring months.

Steelhead that get past the nets of the Hoh Indians can reach 20 pounds, with an occasional 25-30 pounder.

Minnie Peterson Campground

Willoughby Creek Campground

Willoughby Creek

21 mi.

Hoh-Clearwater Road

Elk Creek

Shell Creek

Winfield Creek

Upper Hoh Road

Alder Creek

Bar ing Creek

Hell

Olympic Loop Highway

17 mi.

15 mi.

Hoh Oxbow Campground

Lower Hoh Road

Lost Creek

Hoh River

To Forks

101

Cottonwood Campground 11.5 mi.

Anderson Creek

Pins Creek

101

Nolan Creek

Braden Creek

FLOW

Lower Hoh Road

Hoh

Fletcher Creek

2.1 mi.

Fossil Creek

Olympic National Park

Oil City (site)

Hoh Village Road

101

To Queets

Olympic National Park

Hoh Indian Reservation

Pacific Ocean

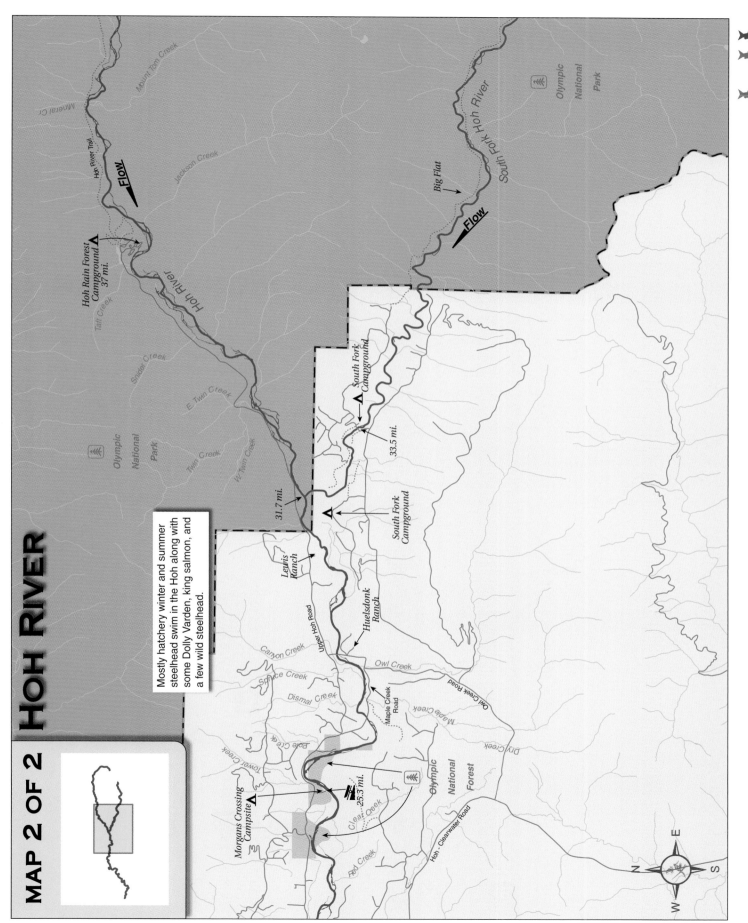

MAP 2 OF 2

HOH RIVER

Mostly hatchery winter and summer steelhead swim in the Hoh along with some Dolly Varden, king salmon, and a few wild steelhead.

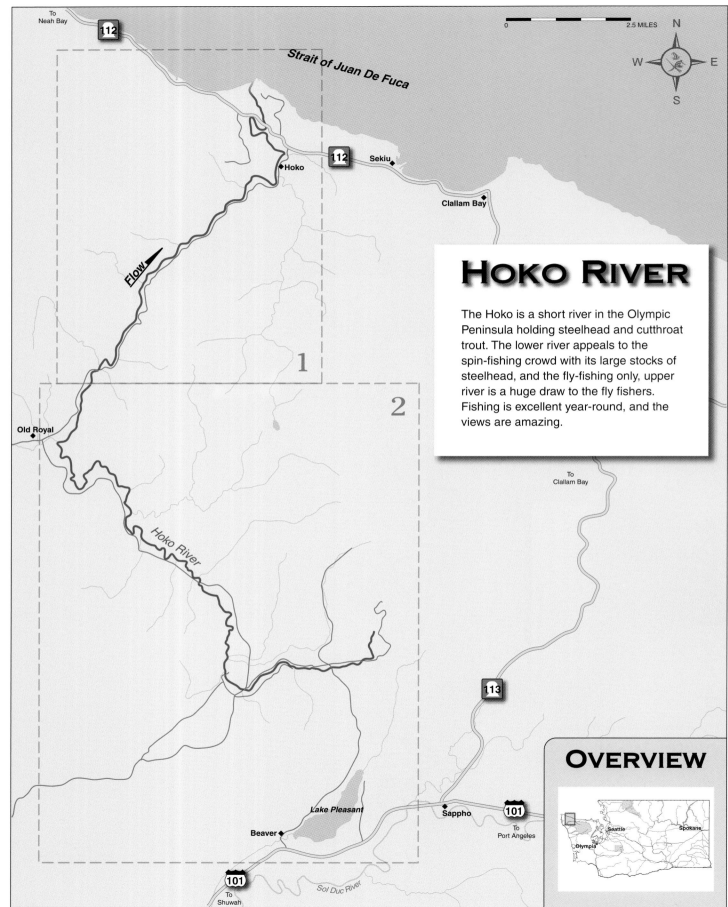

HOKO RIVER

The Hoko is a short river in the Olympic Peninsula holding steelhead and cutthroat trout. The lower river appeals to the spin-fishing crowd with its large stocks of steelhead, and the fly-fishing only, upper river is a huge draw to the fly fishers. Fishing is excellent year-round, and the views are amazing.

OVERVIEW

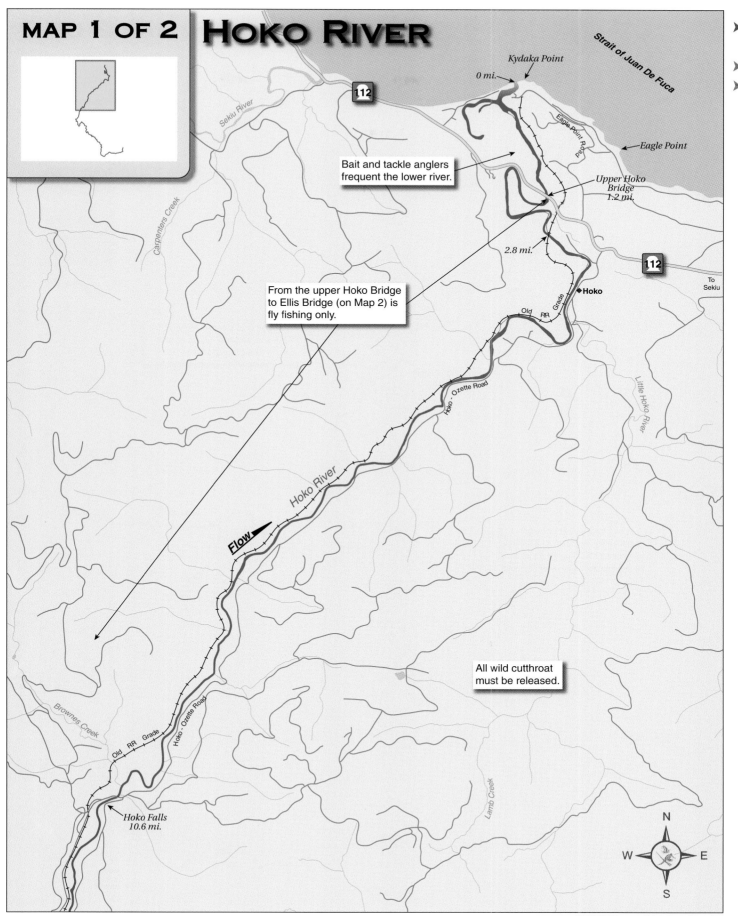

MAP 1 OF 2 | **HOKO RIVER**

Strait of Juan De Fuca

Kydaka Point

0 mi.

12

Eagle Point

Eagle Point Road

Bait and tackle anglers
frequent the lower river.

Upper Hoko
Bridge
1.2 mi.

2.8 mi.

112

Hoko

To
Sekiu

From the upper Hoko Bridge
to Ellis Bridge (on Map 2) is
fly fishing only.

Old RR Grade

Sekiu River

Carpenters Creek

Little Hoko River

Hoko - Ozette Road

Hoko River

Flow

All wild cutthroat
must be released.

Lamb Creek

Brownes Creek

Old RR Grade

Hoko - Ozette Road

Hoko Falls
10.6 mi.

N
W   E
S

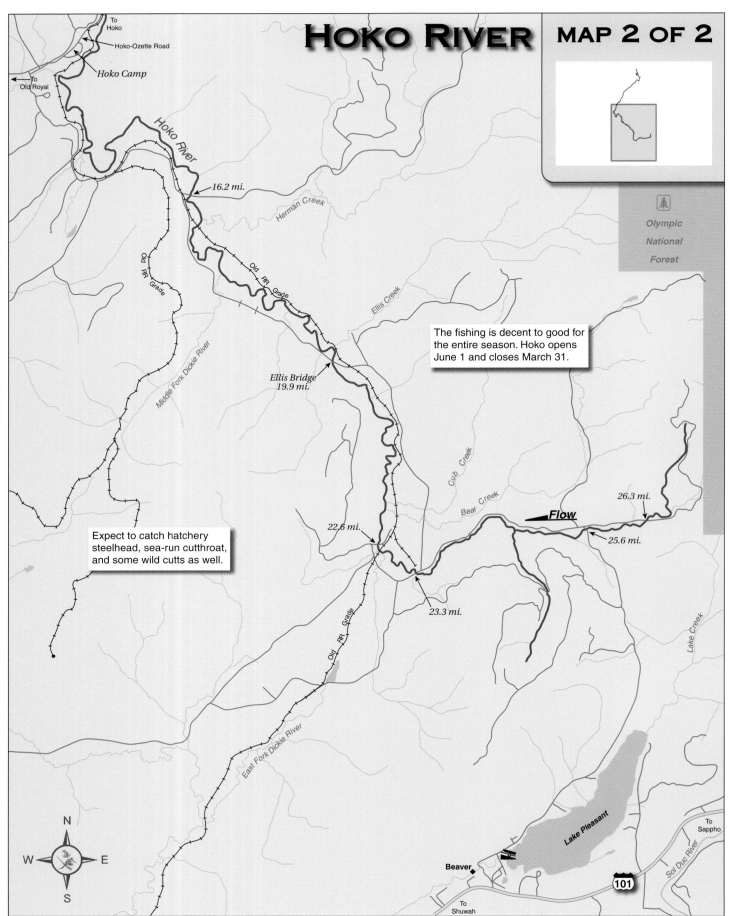

HOKO RIVER MAP 2 OF 2

To Hoko

Hoko-Ozette Road

Hoko Camp

To Old Royal

Hoko River

16.2 mi.

Herman Creek

Old RR Grade

Old RR Grade

Olympic National Forest

Ellis Creek

The fishing is decent to good for the entire season. Hoko opens June 1 and closes March 31.

Middle Fork Dickie River

Ellis Bridge 19.9 mi.

Cub Creek

26.3 mi.

Bear Creek

Flow

25.6 mi.

22.6 mi.

Expect to catch hatchery steelhead, sea-run cutthroat, and some wild cutts as well.

23.3 mi.

Old RR Grade

Lake Creek

East Fork Dickie River

N
W E
S

Lake Pleasant

To Sappho

Beaver

101

Sol Duc River

To Shuwah

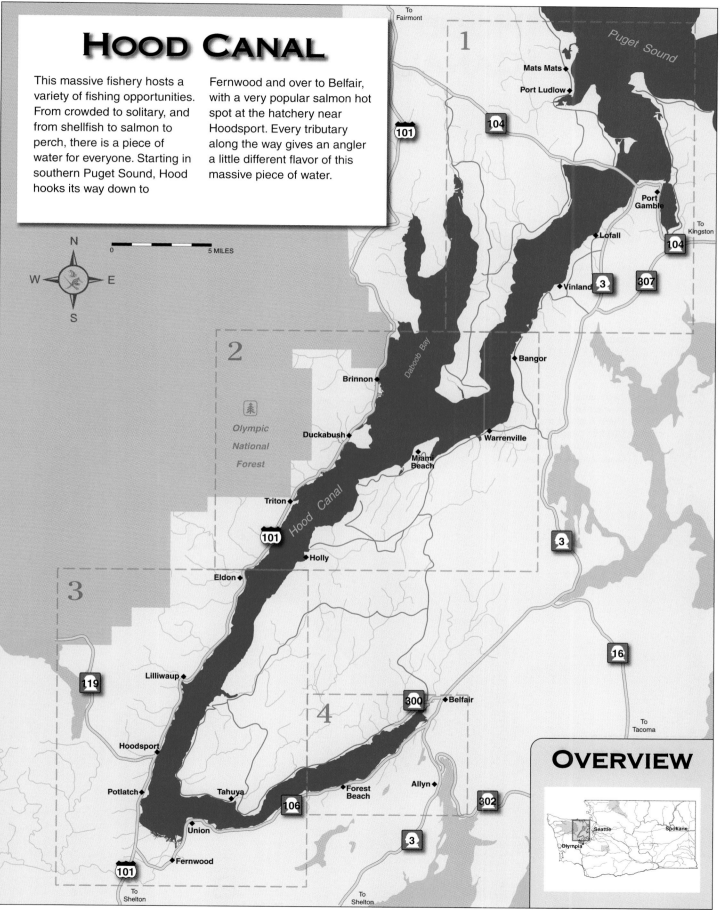

HOOD CANAL

This massive fishery hosts a variety of fishing opportunities. From crowded to solitary, and from shellfish to salmon to perch, there is a piece of water for everyone. Starting in southern Puget Sound, Hood hooks its way down to Fernwood and over to Belfair, with a very popular salmon hot spot at the hatchery near Hoodsport. Every tributary along the way gives an angler a little different flavor of this massive piece of water.

0   5 MILES

N
W   E
S

1

Puget Sound

To Fairmont

Mats Mats
Port Ludlow

104

101

Port Gamble

Lofall

To Kingston

104

Vinland   3   307

Dabob Bay

Bangor

2

Olympic

National

Forest

Brinnon

Duckabush

Warrenville

Miami Beach

Triton

Hood Canal

101

Holly

Eldon

3

3

16

119

Lilliwaup

4

300   Belfair

To Tacoma

Hoodsport

Potlatch   Tahuya   106   Forest Beach   Allyn   302

3

Union

Fernwood

101

To Shelton

To Shelton

OVERVIEW

Seattle   Spokane

Olympia

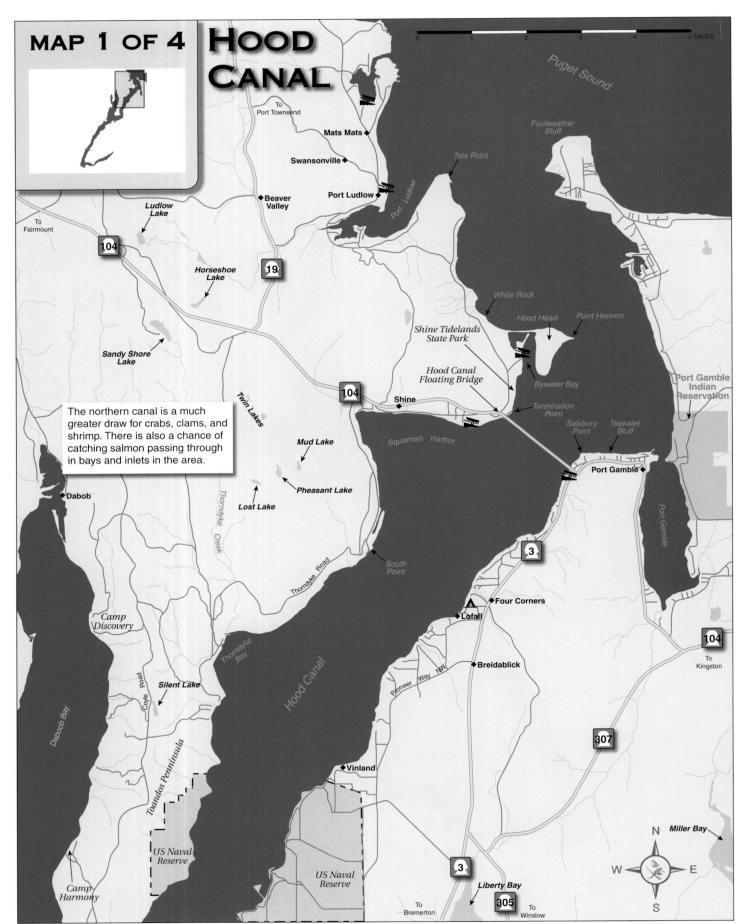

MAP 1 OF 4 HOOD CANAL

Puget Sound

To Port Townsend

Mats Mats

Swansonville

Beaver Valley

Port Ludlow

Port Ludlow

Tala Point

Foulweather Bluff

Ludlow Lake

To Fairmount

104

19

Horseshoe Lake

White Rock

Hood Head

Point Hannon

Shine Tidelands State Park

Hood Canal Floating Bridge

Bywater Bay

Port Gamble Indian Reservation

Sandy Shore Lake

104

Shine

Termination Point

Salsbury Point

Teekalet Bluff

The northern canal is a much greater draw for crabs, clams, and shrimp. There is also a chance of catching salmon passing through in bays and inlets in the area.

Twin Lakes

Mud Lake

Squamish Harbor

Port Gamble

Dabob

Pheasant Lake

Lost Lake

Thorndyke Creek

South Point

3

Port Gamble

Thorndyke Road

Four Corners

Lofall

104

To Kingston

Camp Discovery

Thorndyke Bay

Silent Lake

Breidablick

Coyle Road

Pioneer Way NW

Daboob Bay

Toandos Penninsula

Hood Canal

307

Vinland

US Naval Reserve

US Naval Reserve

3

Miller Bay

N
W   E
S

Camp Harmony

Liberty Bay

305

To Bremerton

To Winslow

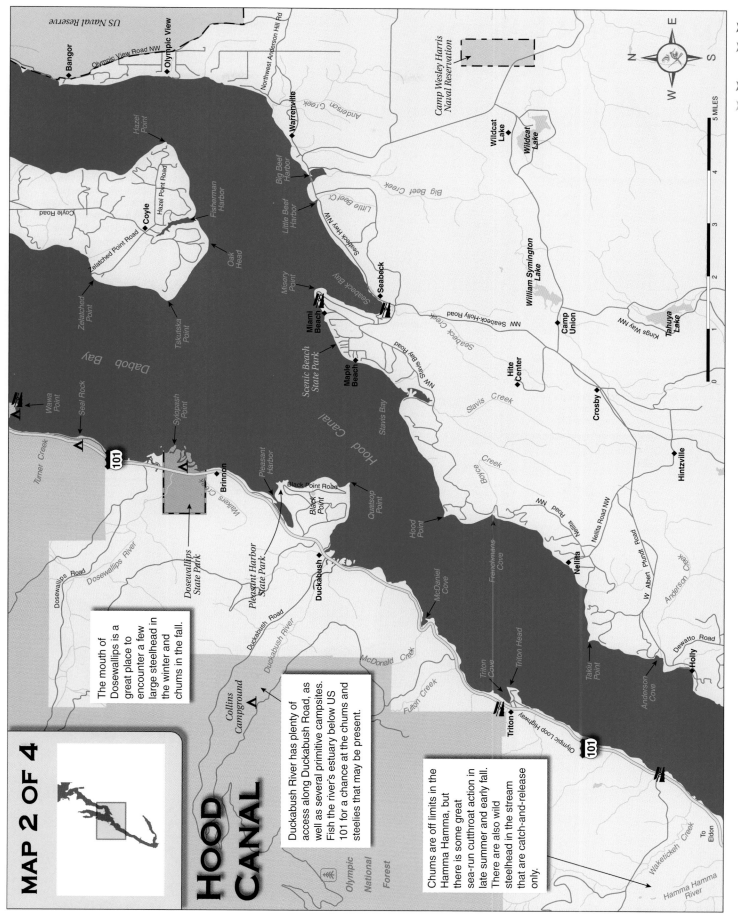

MAP 2 OF 4

HOOD CANAL

The mouth of the Dosewallips is a great place to encounter a few large steelhead in the winter and chums in the fall.

Duckabush River has plenty of access along Duckabush Road, as well as several primitive campsites. Fish the river's estuary below US 101 for a chance at the chums and steelies that may be present.

Chums are off limits in the Hamma Hamma, but there is some great sea-run cutthroat action in late summer and early fall. There are also wild steelhead in the stream that are catch-and-release only.

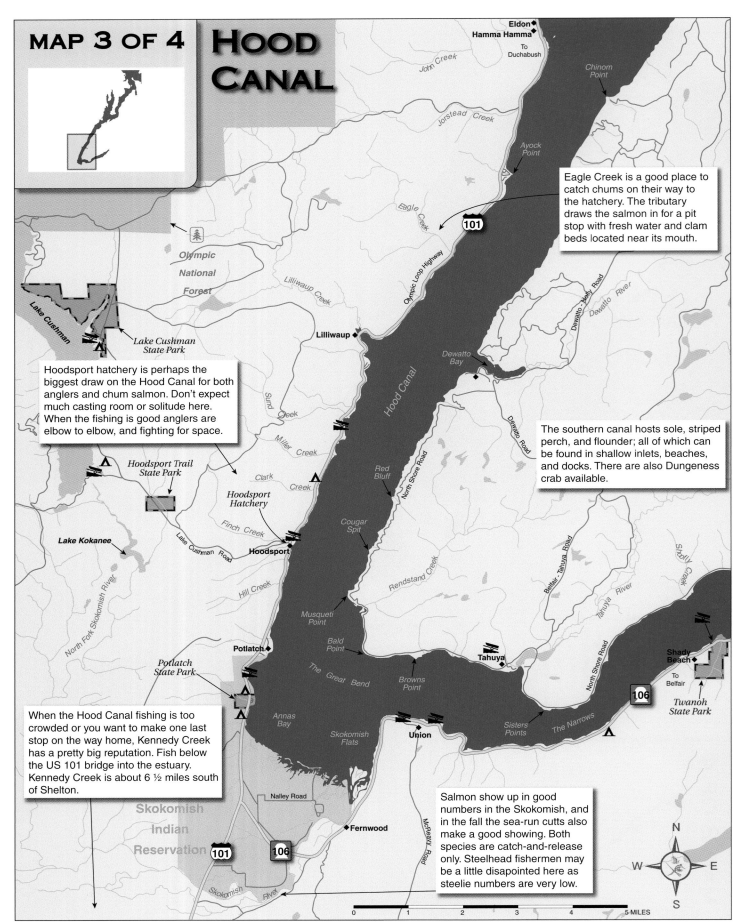

MAP 3 OF 4

HOOD CANAL

Eagle Creek is a good place to catch chums on their way to the hatchery. The tributary draws the salmon in for a pit stop with fresh water and clam beds located near its mouth.

Hoodsport hatchery is perhaps the biggest draw on the Hood Canal for both anglers and chum salmon. Don't expect much casting room or solitude here. When the fishing is good anglers are elbow to elbow, and fighting for space.

The southern canal hosts sole, striped perch, and flounder; all of which can be found in shallow inlets, beaches, and docks. There are also Dungeness crab available.

When the Hood Canal fishing is too crowded or you want to make one last stop on the way home, Kennedy Creek has a pretty big reputation. Fish below the US 101 bridge into the estuary. Kennedy Creek is about 6 ½ miles south of Shelton.

Salmon show up in good numbers in the Skokomish, and in the fall the sea-run cutts also make a good showing. Both species are catch-and-release only. Steelhead fishermen may be a little disapointed here as steelie numbers are very low.

0   1   2   3   4   5 MILES

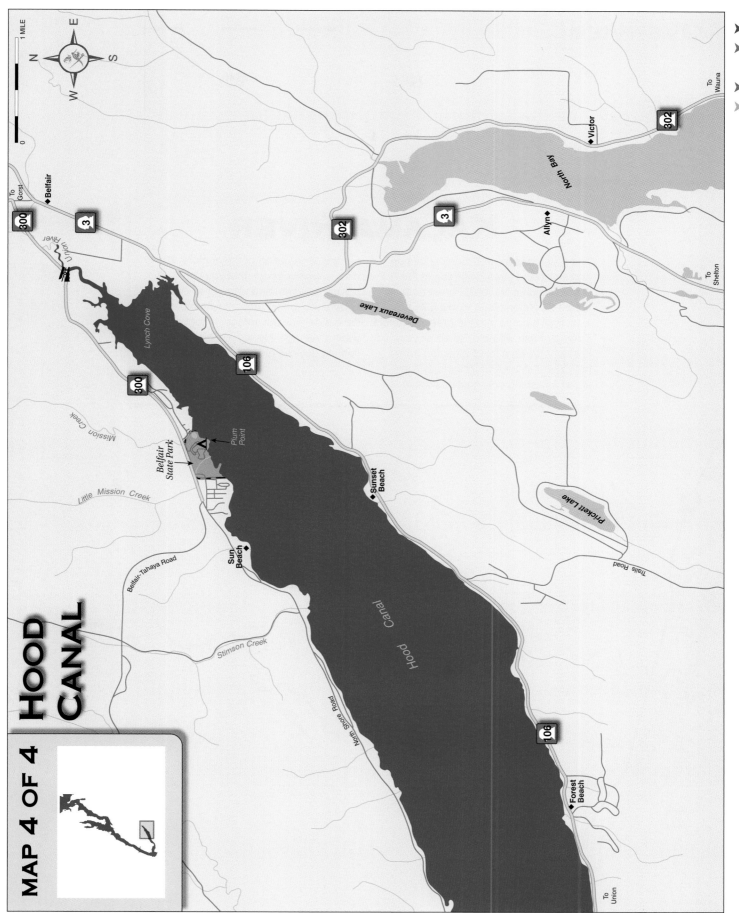

MAP 4 OF 4

HOOD
CANAL

1 MILE

N E
W S

To Gorst

◆ Belfair

Union River

To Wauna

302

◆ Victor

North Bay

3

302

3

◆ Allyn

To Shelton

300

3

Lynch Cove

Devereaux Lake

106

Mission Creek

300

Belfair State Park

Plum Point

Little Mission Creek

Prickett Lake

Sunset Beach

Trails Road

Belfair-Tahaya Road

Sun Beach

Stimson Creek

Hood Canal

North Shore Road

Hood

106

Forest Beach

To Union

OVERVIEW

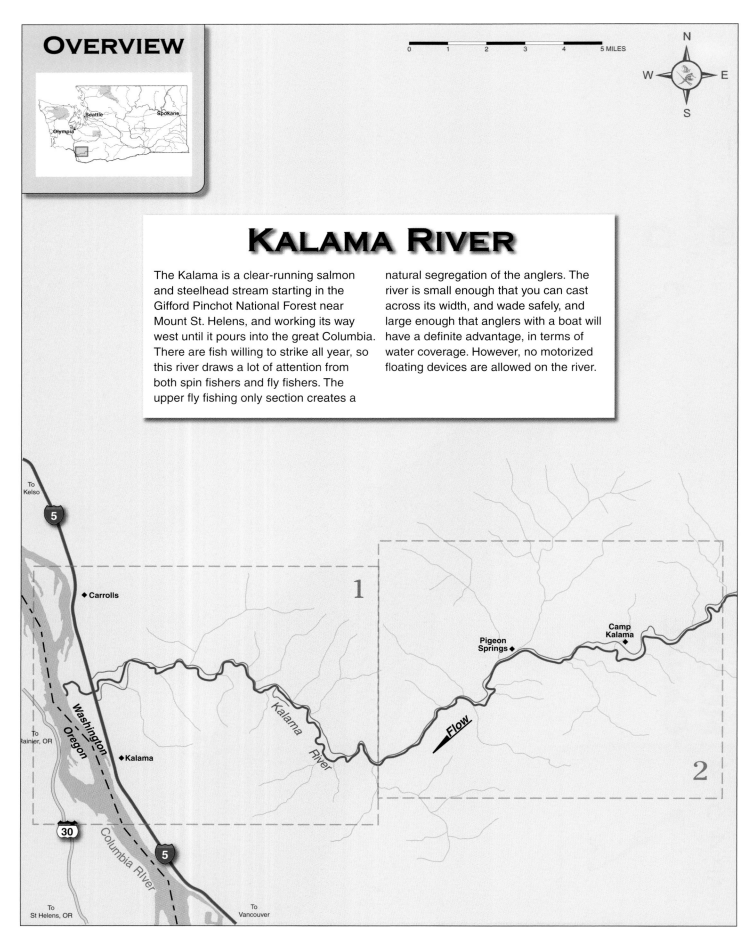

0 1 2 3 4 5 MILES

N
W E
S

KALAMA RIVER

The Kalama is a clear-running salmon and steelhead stream starting in the Gifford Pinchot National Forest near Mount St. Helens, and working its way west until it pours into the great Columbia. There are fish willing to strike all year, so this river draws a lot of attention from both spin fishers and fly fishers. The upper fly fishing only section creates a natural segregation of the anglers. The river is small enough that you can cast across its width, and wade safely, and large enough that anglers with a boat will have a definite advantage, in terms of water coverage. However, no motorized floating devices are allowed on the river.

To Kelso

5

◆ Carrolls

1

Camp Kalama ◆

Pigeon Springs ◆

To Rainier, OR

Washington Oregon

◆ Kalama

Kalama River

Flow

2

To St Helens, OR

30

Columbia River

5

To Vancouver

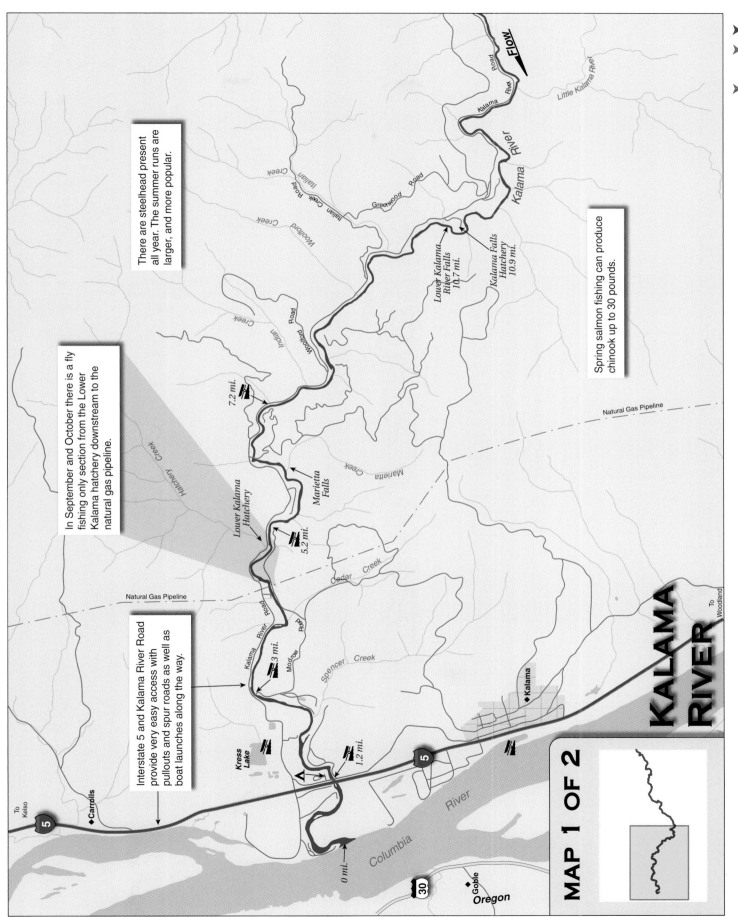

There are steelhead present all year. The summer runs are larger, and more popular.

In September and October there is a fly fishing only section from the Lower Kalama hatchery downstream to the natural gas pipeline.

Interstate 5 and Kalama River Road provide very easy access with pullouts and spur roads as well as boat launches along the way.

Spring salmon fishing can produce chinook up to 30 pounds.

FLOW

Little Kalama River

Kalama River

Road

Kalama River

Greenwood Road

Italian Creek Road

Italian Creek

Woolford Creek

Lower Kalama River Falls
10.7 mi.

Kalama Falls Hatchery
10.9 mi.

Natural Gas Pipeline

Indian Creek

Woolford Road

7.2 mi.

Hatchery Creek

Lower Kalama Hatchery

Marietta Falls

Marietta Creek

5.2 mi.

Cedar Creek

Natural Gas Pipeline

Kalama River Road

Modrow Road

3 mi.

Spencer Creek

Kress Lake

1.2 mi.

5

Kalama

To Woodland

KALAMA RIVER

MAP 1 OF 2

To Kelso

Carrolls

5

0 mi.

Columbia River

30

Goble

Oregon

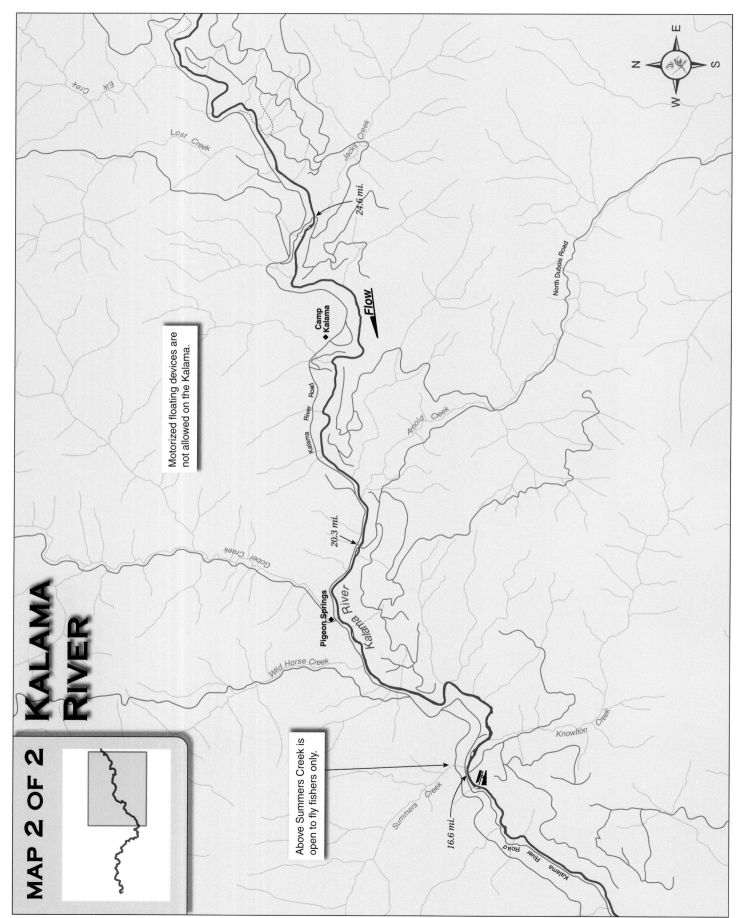

MAP 2 OF 2

KALAMA RIVER

Motorized floating devices are not allowed on the Kalama.

Above Summers Creek is open to fly fishers only.

Camp Kalama

Pigeon Springs

Flow

24.6 mi.

20.3 mi.

16.6 mi.

Elk Creek

Lost Creek

Jacks Creek

North Dubois Road

Kalama River Road

Arnold Creek

Gobar Creek

Kalama River

Wild Horse Creek

Summers Creek

Knowlton Creek

Kalama River Road

© 2005 Wilderness Adventures Press, Inc.

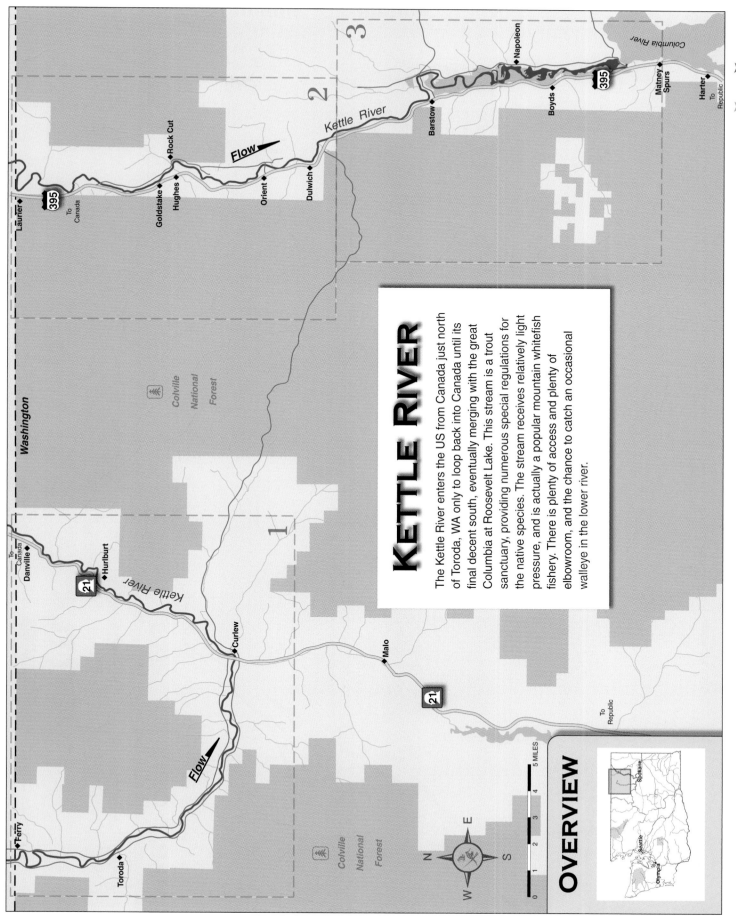

KETTLE RIVER

The Kettle River enters the US from Canada just north of Toroda, WA only to loop back into Canada until its final decent south, eventually merging with the great Columbia at Roosevelt Lake. This stream is a trout sanctuary, providing numerous special regulations for the native species. The stream receives relatively light pressure, and is actually a popular mountain whitefish fishery. There is plenty of access and plenty of elbowroom, and the chance to catch an occasional walleye in the lower river.

OVERVIEW

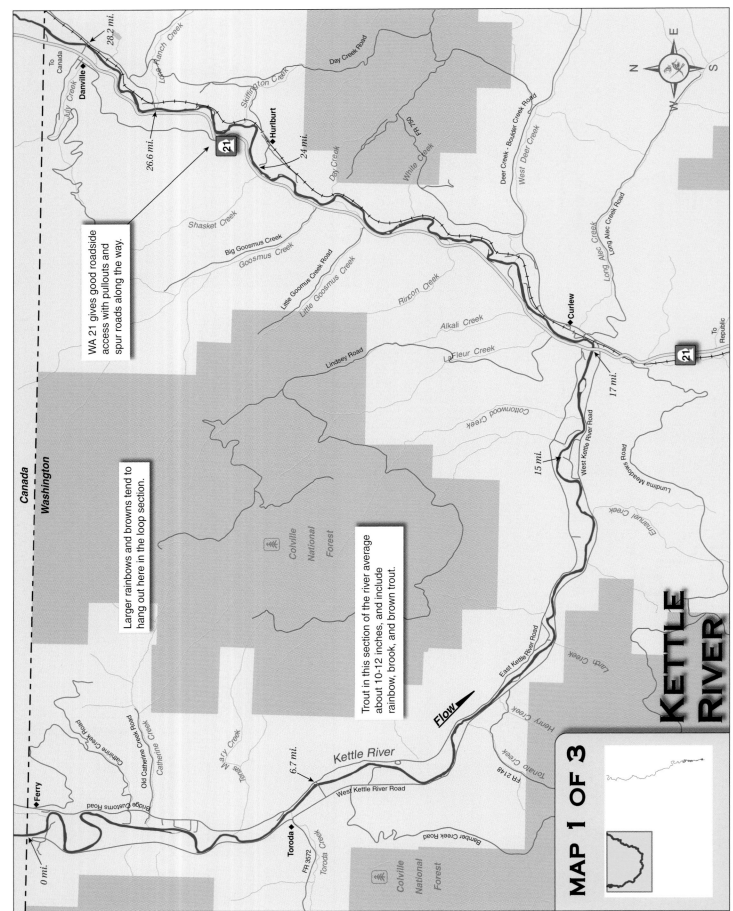

WA 21 gives good roadside access with pullouts and spur roads along the way.

Larger rainbows and browns tend to hang out here in the loop section.

Trout in this section of the river average about 10-12 inches, and include rainbow, brook, and brown trout.

Canada

Washington

Colville National Forest

Flow

Kettle River

Colville National Forest

KETTLE RIVER

MAP 1 OF 3

© 2005 Wilderness Adventures Press, Inc.

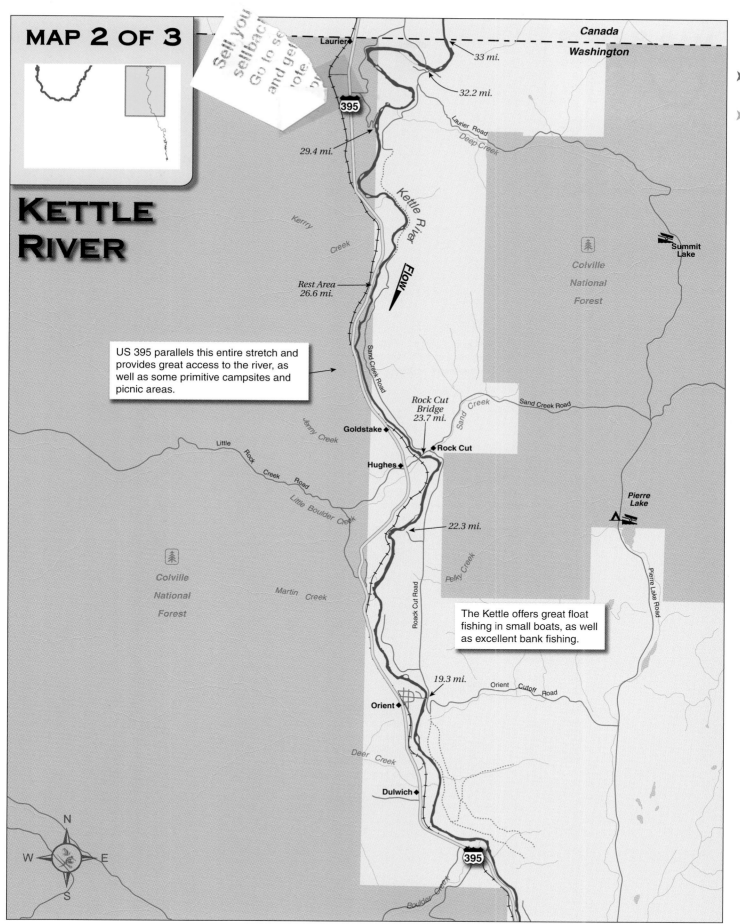

MAP 2 OF 3

KETTLE RIVER

US 395 parallels this entire stretch and provides great access to the river, as well as some primitive campsites and picnic areas.

The Kettle offers great float fishing in small boats, as well as excellent bank fishing.

Canada
Washington

Laurier

33 mi.

32.2 mi.

Laurier Road

Deep Creek

29.4 mi.

Kettle River

Flow

Kerry Creek

Colville National Forest

Summit Lake

Rest Area
26.6 mi.

Sand Creek Road

Sand Creek

Sand Creek Road

Rock Cut Bridge
23.7 mi.

Jenny Creek

Goldstake

Rock Cut

Little Rock Creek Road

Hughes

Little Boulder Creek

Pierre Lake

22.3 mi.

Colville National Forest

Martin Creek

Pelky Creek

Roack Cut Road

Pierre Lake Road

19.3 mi.

Orient Cutoff Road

Orient

Deer Creek

Dulwich

N
W E
S

395

Boulder Creek

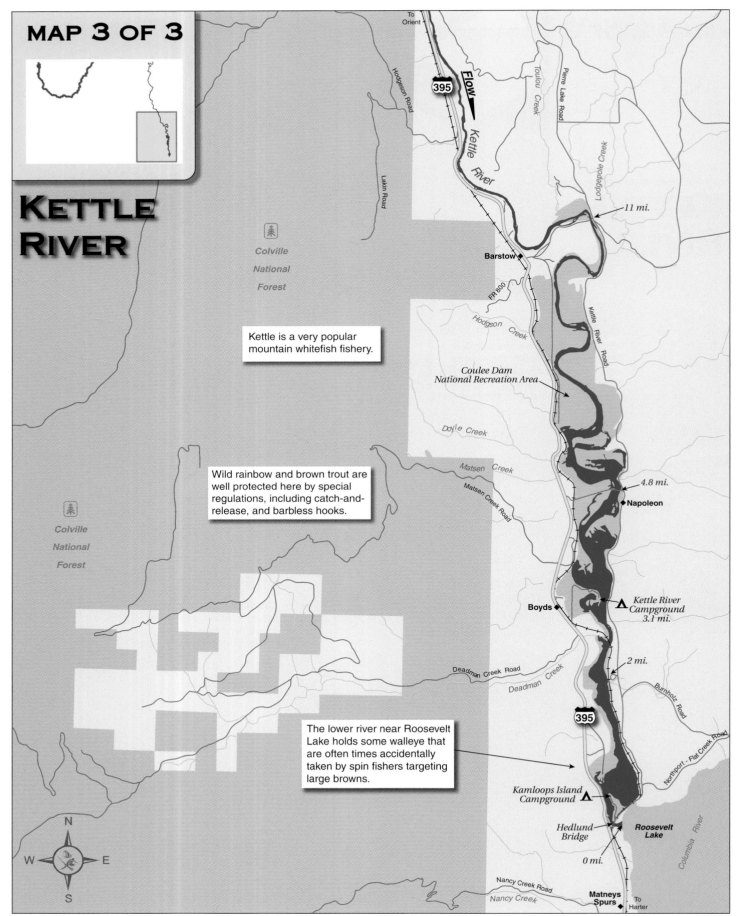

MAP 3 OF 3

KETTLE RIVER

Colville National Forest

Colville National Forest

Kettle is a very popular mountain whitefish fishery.

Wild rainbow and brown trout are well protected here by special regulations, including catch-and-release, and barbless hooks.

The lower river near Roosevelt Lake holds some walleye that are often times accidentally taken by spin fishers targeting large browns.

To Orient

Flow

Kettle River

Hodgson Road

Toulou Creek

Pierre Lake Road

Lodgepole Creek

Lakin Road

11 mi.

Barstow

FR 800

Hodgson Creek

Kettle River Road

Coulee Dam National Recreation Area

Doyle Creek

Matsen Creek

Matsen Creek Road

4.8 mi.

Napoleon

Kettle River Campground 3.1 mi.

Boyds

Deadman Creek Road

Deadman Creek

2 mi.

Burnholz Road

Northport - Flat Creek Road

Kamloops Island Campground

Hedlund Bridge

Roosevelt Lake

Columbia River

0 mi.

Nancy Creek Road

Nancy Creek

Matneys Spurs

To Harter

N
W   E
S

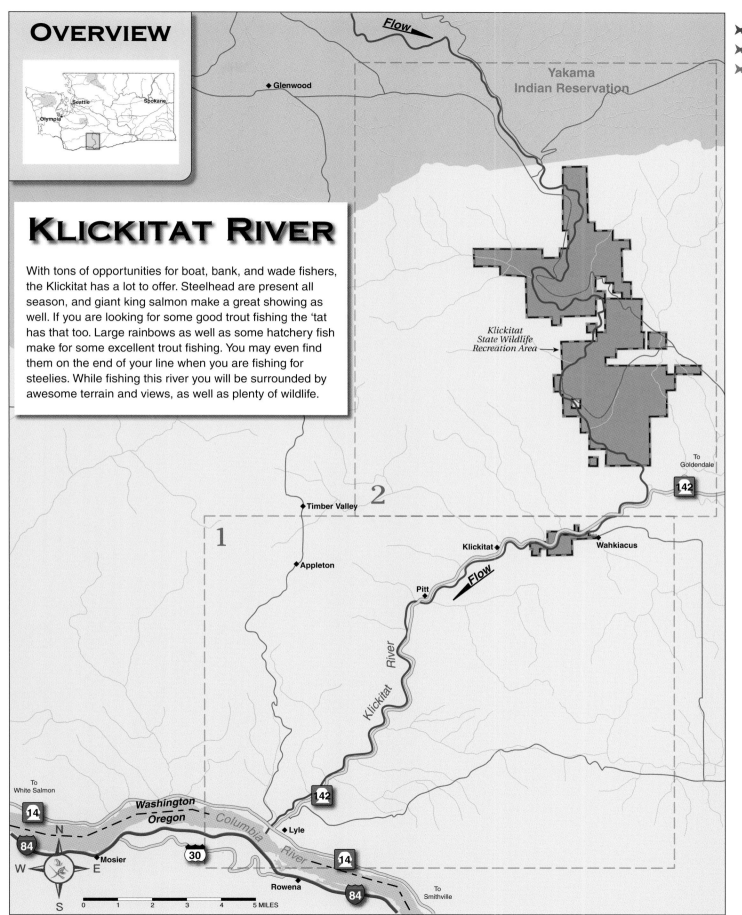

OVERVIEW

KLICKITAT RIVER

With tons of opportunities for boat, bank, and wade fishers, the Klickitat has a lot to offer. Steelhead are present all season, and giant king salmon make a great showing as well. If you are looking for some good trout fishing the 'tat has that too. Large rainbows as well as some hatchery fish make for some excellent trout fishing. You may even find them on the end of your line when you are fishing for steelies. While fishing this river you will be surrounded by awesome terrain and views, as well as plenty of wildlife.

Seattle
Olympia
Spokane

Flow

♦ Glenwood

Yakama
Indian Reservation

Klickitat
State Wildlife
Recreation Area

To
Goldendale

142

2

♦ Timber Valley

1

♦ Appleton

Klickitat

Wahkiacus

Pitt

Flow

Klickitat River

To
White Salmon

14

Washington
Oregon

Columbia River

142

84

30

♦ Lyle

14

N

W   E

S

♦ Mosier

♦ Rowena

84

To
Smithville

0   1   2   3   4   5 MILES

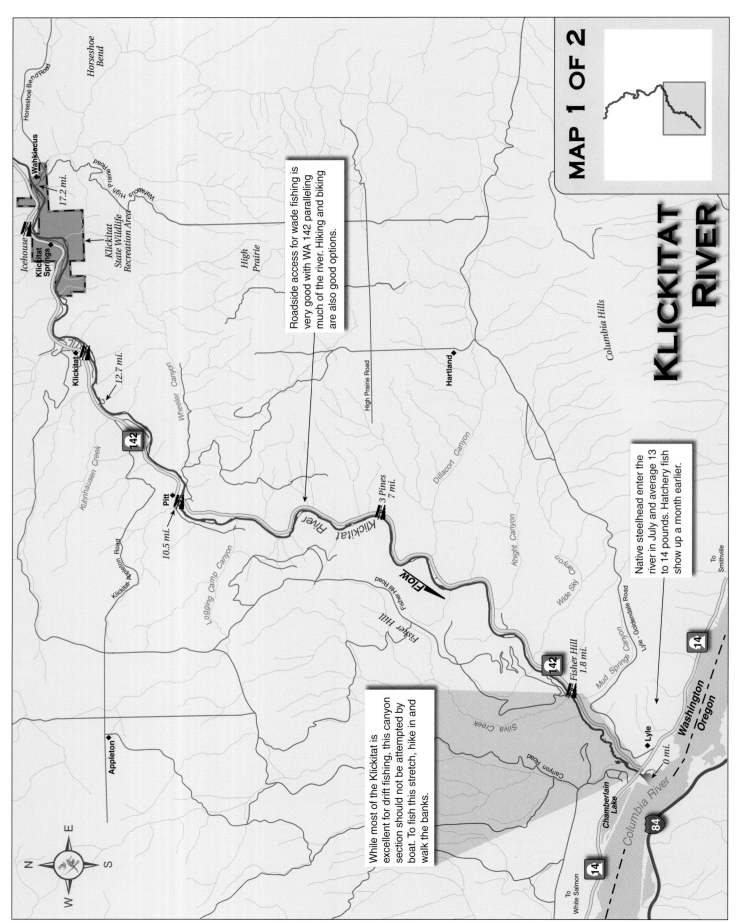

MAP 1 OF 2

KLICKITAT RIVER

Roadside access for wade fishing is very good with WA 142 paralleling much of the river. Hiking and biking are also good options.

Native steelhead enter the river in July and average 13 to 14 pounds. Hatchery fish show up a month earlier.

While most of the Klickitat is excellent for drift fishing, this canyon section should not be attempted by boat. To fish this stretch, hike in and walk the banks.

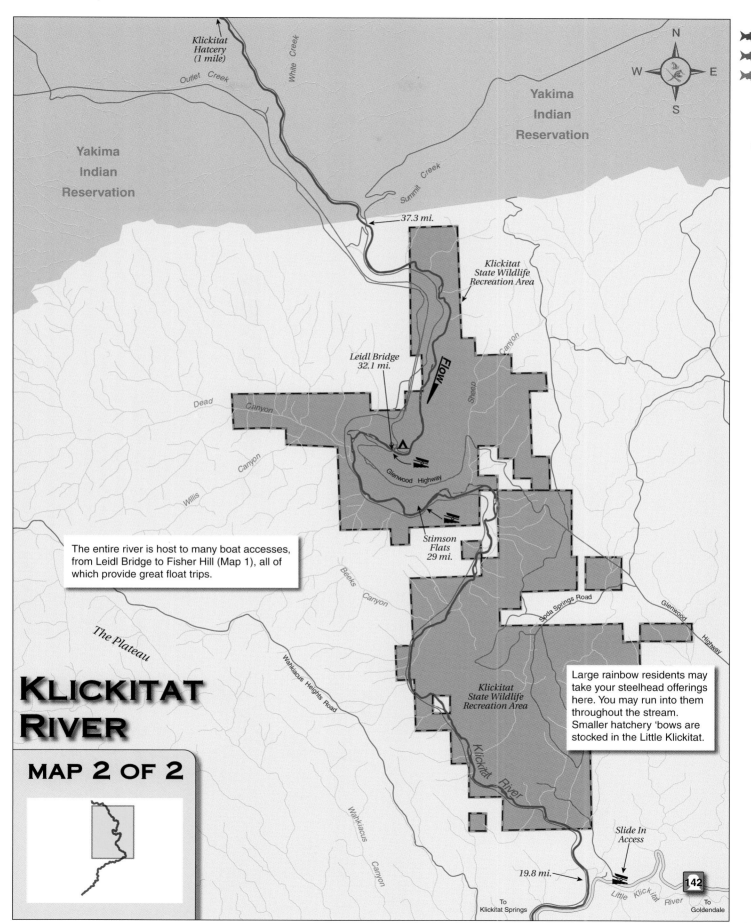

Klickitat Hatcery
(1 mile)

White Creek

Outlet Creek

Summit Creek

Yakima
Indian
Reservation

Yakima
Indian
Reservation

37.3 mi.

Klickitat
State Wildlife
Recreation Area

Sheep Canyon

Leidl Bridge
32.1 mi.

Flow

Dead Canyon

Canyon

Willis

Glenwood Highway

Stimson
Flats
29 mi.

The entire river is host to many boat accesses, from Leidl Bridge to Fisher Hill (Map 1), all of which provide great float trips.

Beeks Canyon

Soda Springs Road

Glenwood Highway

The Plateau

Wahkiacus Heights Road

KLICKITAT RIVER

Klickitat
State Wildlife
Recreation Area

Large rainbow residents may take your steelhead offerings here. You may run into them throughout the stream. Smaller hatchery 'bows are stocked in the Little Klickitat.

MAP 2 OF 2

Wahkiacus Canyon

Klickitat River

Slide In
Access

19.8 mi.

142

Little Klickitat River

To
Klickitat Springs

To
Goldendale

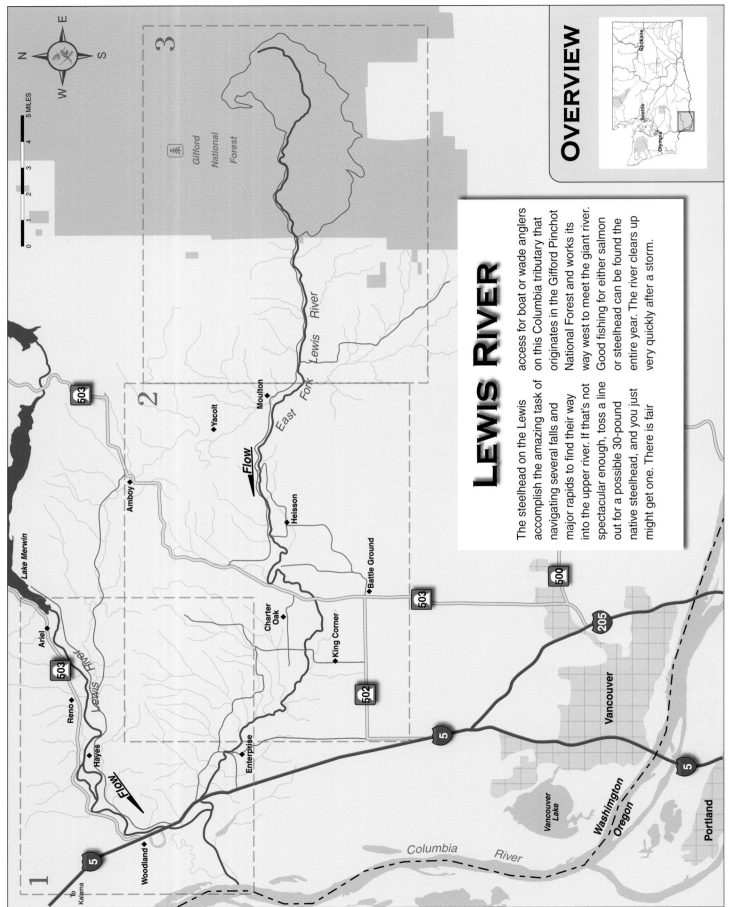

LEWIS RIVER

The steelhead on the Lewis accomplish the amazing task of navigating several falls and major rapids to find their way into the upper river. If that's not spectacular enough, toss a line out for a possible 30-pound native steelhead, and you just might get one. There is fair access for boat or wade anglers on this Columbia tributary that originates in the Gifford Pinchot National Forest and works its way west to meet the giant river. Good fishing for either salmon or steelhead can be found the entire year. The river clears up very quickly after a storm.

OVERVIEW

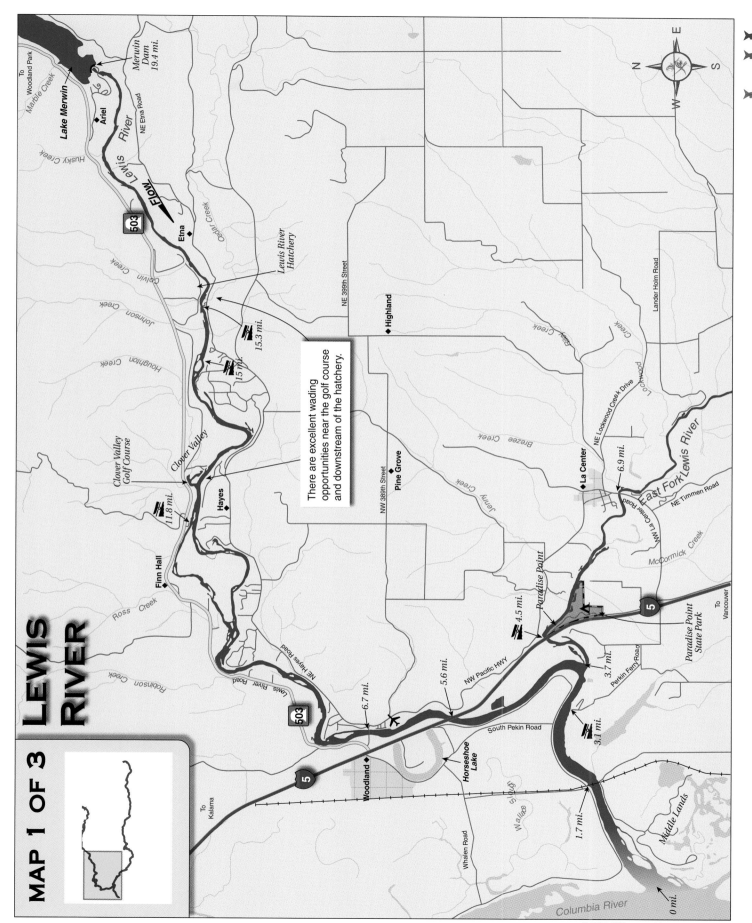

MAP 1 OF 3

LEWIS RIVER

There are excellent wading opportunities near the golf course and downstream of the hatchery.

Merwin Dam
19.4 mi.

Lake Merwin

Ariel

Woodland Park
To

Marble Creek

Husky Creek

Lewis River

Etna

503

FLOW

Cedar Creek

Colvin Creek

Johnson Creek

Houghton Creek

Lewis River Hatchery

15.3 mi.

15 mi.

Clover Valley Golf Course

Clover Valley

11.8 mi.

Hayes

Finn Hall

Ross Creek

Robinson Creek

Lewis River Road

NE Hayes Road

503

6.7 mi.

NE 399th Street

Highland

NW 389th Street

Pine Grove

Jenny Creek

Brezee Creek

Creek

La Center

NE Lockwood Creek Drive

Lockwood Creek

Lander Holm Road

East Fork Lewis River

6.9 mi.

NW La Center Road

NE Timmen Road

McCormick Creek

Paradise Point

4.5 mi.

5

Paradise Point State Park

To Vancouver

3.7 mi.

Perkin Fern Road

3.1 mi.

South Pekin Road

5.6 mi.

NW Pacific HWY

5

Woodland

Horseshoe Lake

Whalen Road

Wallace Slough

Lewis River Slough

1.7 mi.

Middle Lands

To Kalama

5

0 mi.

Columbia River

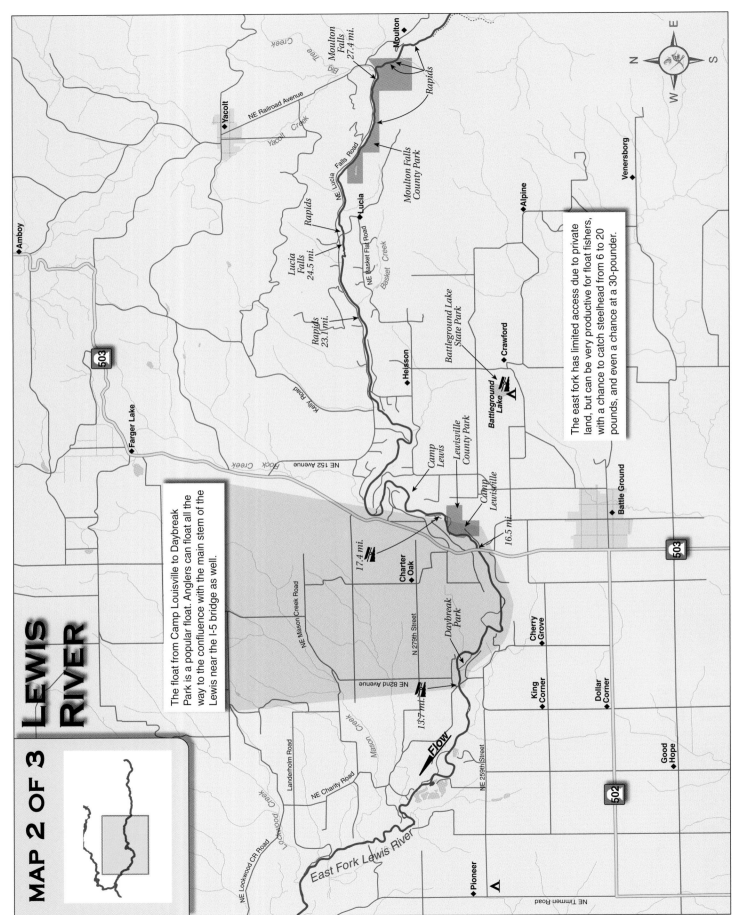

MAP 2 OF 3

LEWIS RIVER

The float from Camp Louisville to Daybreak Park is a popular float. Anglers can float all the way to the confluence with the main stem of the Lewis near the I-5 bridge as well.

The east fork has limited access due to private land, but can be very productive for float fishers, with a chance to catch steelhead from 6 to 20 pounds, and even a chance at a 30-pounder.

Moulton Falls 27.4 mi.

Rapids

Moulton

Yacolt

NE Railroad Avenue

Yacolt Creek

Big Tree Creek

Rapids

NE Lucia Falls Road

Lucia

Moulton Falls County Park

Amboy

NE Basket Flat Road

Basket Creek

Lucia Falls 24.5 mi.

Rapids

Rapids 23.1 mi.

Heisson

Kelly Road

Battleground Lake State Park

Alpine

Crawford

Venersborg

Battleground Lake

503

Farger Lake

Rock Creek

NE 152 Avenue

Camp Lewis

Lewisville County Park

Camp Lewisville

16.5 mi.

Battle Ground

503

17.4 mi.

Charter Oak

NE Mason Creek Road

N 279th Street

Daybreak Park

Cherry Grove

King Corner

Dollar Corner

Good Hope

502

NE 82nd Avenue

13.7 mi.

Flow

NE 259th Street

Mason Creek

Landerholm Road

NE Charity Road

East Fork Lewis River

Lockwood Creek

NE Lockwood CR Road

Pioneer

NE Timmen Road

© 2005 Wilderness Adventures Press, Inc.

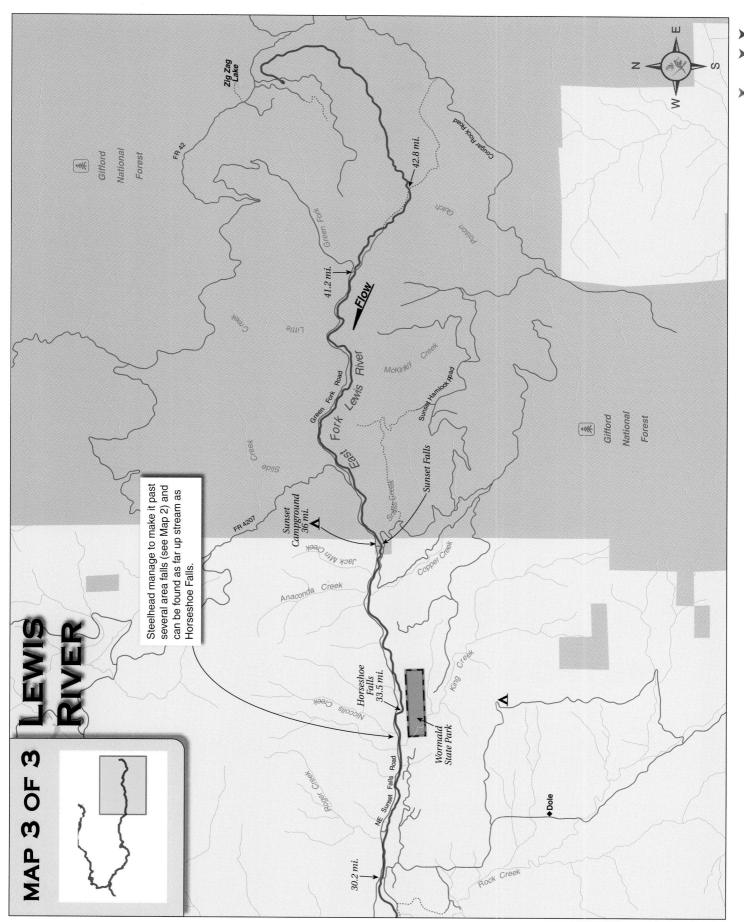

MAP 3 OF 3 **LEWIS RIVER**

Steelhead manage to make it past several area falls (see Map 2) and can be found as far up stream as Horseshoe Falls.

Zig Zag Lake

Gifford National Forest

FR 42

Green Fork

Cougar Rock Road

42.8 mi.

Poison Gulch

41.2 mi.

Flow

Little   Creek

McKinley   Creek

East Fork Lewis River

Green Fork Road

Sunset Hamlock Road

Slide   Creek

Sneoss Creek

Sunset Falls

Gifford National Forest

FR 4207

Sunset Campground 36 mi.

Jack Mtn Creek

Copper Creek

Anaconda   Creek

Niccolls Creek

Horseshoe Falls 33.5 mi.

King   Creek

Wormald State Park

Roger Creek

NE Sunset Falls Road

Dole

30.2 mi.

Rock Creek

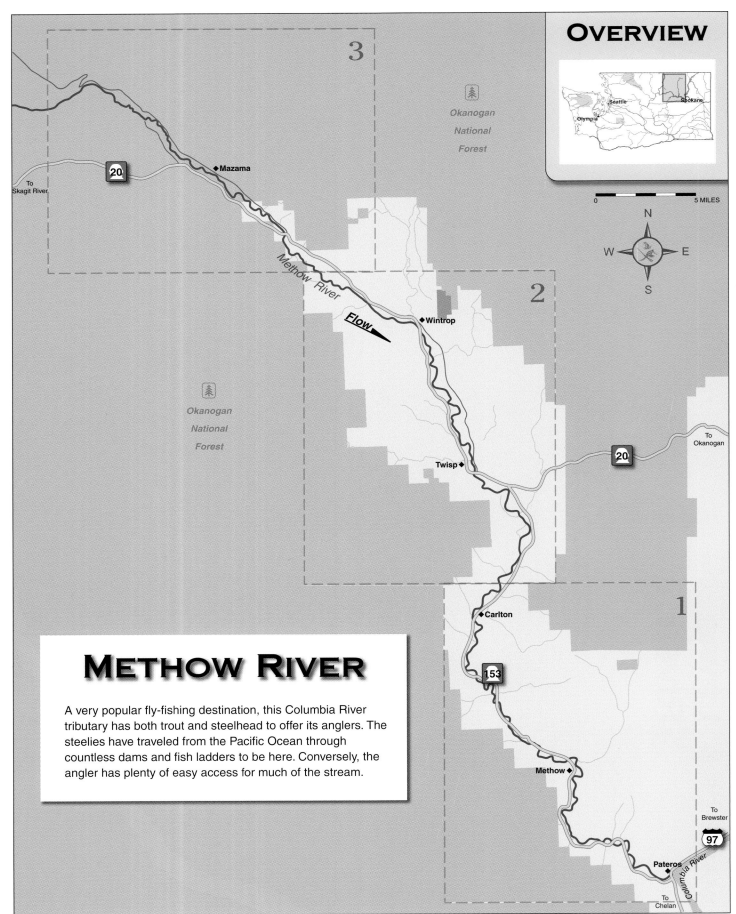

OVERVIEW

3

Okanogan
National
Forest

To
Skagit River

20 ◆Mazama

Methow River

Flow

◆Wintrop

2

N
W   E
S

0   5 MILES

To
Okanogan

20

Okanogan
National
Forest

Twisp ◆

◆Carlton

1

METHOW RIVER

A very popular fly-fishing destination, this Columbia River
tributary has both trout and steelhead to offer its anglers. The
steelies have traveled from the Pacific Ocean through
countless dams and fish ladders to be here. Conversely, the
angler has plenty of easy access for much of the stream.

153

Methow ◆

To
Brewster

97

Pateros ◆

To
Chelan

Columbia River

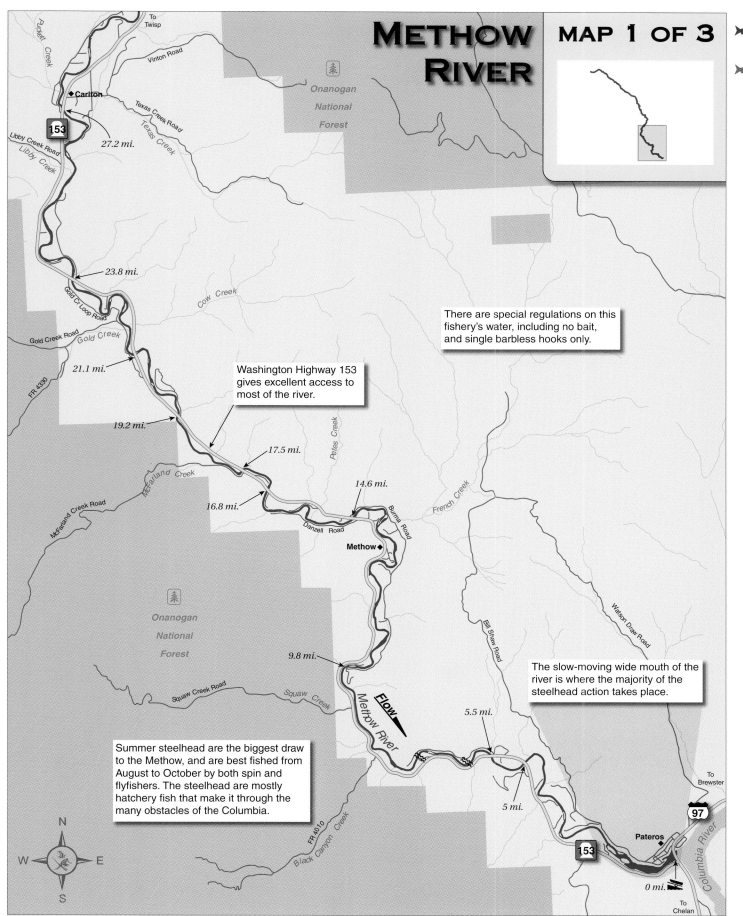

MAP 1 OF 3

METHOW RIVER

To Twisp

Vinton Road

Onanogan
National
Forest

◆Carlton

153

Libby Creek Road

Libby Creek

Texas Creek Road

Texas Creek

27.2 mi.

23.8 mi.

Gold Cr Loop Road

Cow Creek

Gold Creek Road

Gold Creek

FR 4330

21.1 mi.

There are special regulations on this fishery's water, including no bait, and single barbless hooks only.

Washington Highway 153 gives excellent access to most of the river.

19.2 mi.

Petes Creek

McFarland Creek

17.5 mi.

French Creek

14.6 mi.

McFarland Creek Road

16.8 mi.

Danzell Road

Burma Road

Methow ◆

Watson Draw Road

Onanogan
National
Forest

Bill Shaw Road

The slow-moving wide mouth of the river is where the majority of the steelhead action takes place.

9.8 mi.

Flow

Methow River

5.5 mi.

Squaw Creek Road

Squaw Creek

To Brewster

Summer steelhead are the biggest draw to the Methow, and are best fished from August to October by both spin and flyfishers. The steelhead are mostly hatchery fish that make it through the many obstacles of the Columbia.

5 mi.

97

N
W · E
S

FR 4010

Black Canyon Creek

Pateros ◆

153

Columbia River

0 mi.

To Chelan

© 2005 Wilderness Adventures Press, Inc.

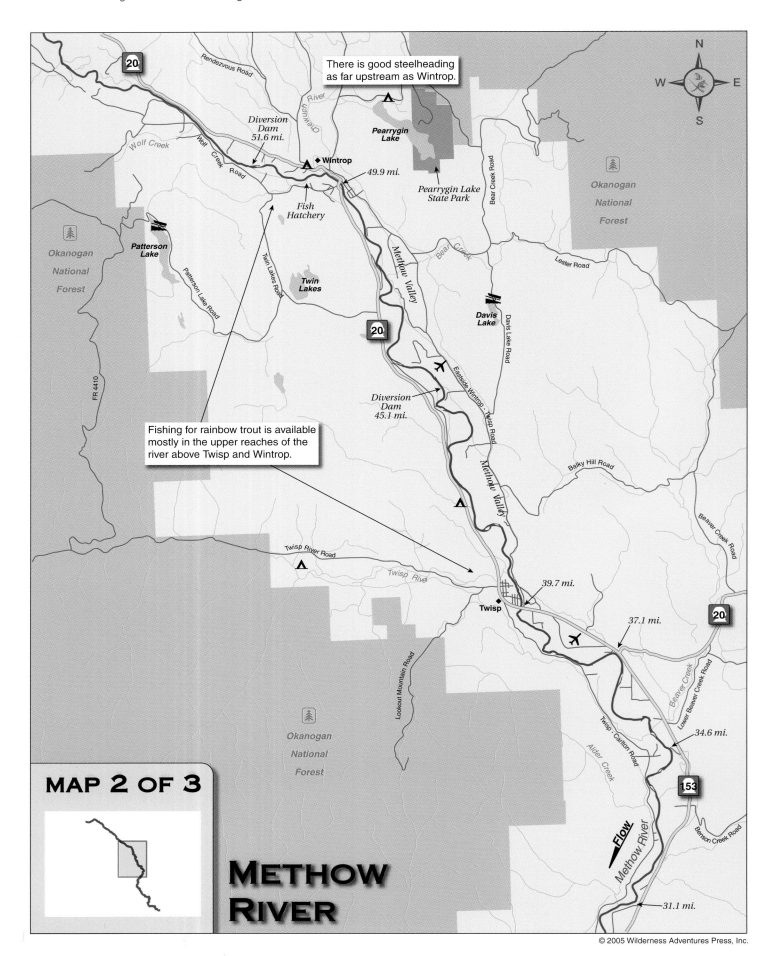

There is good steelheading as far upstream as Wintrop.

Fishing for rainbow trout is available mostly in the upper reaches of the river above Twisp and Wintrop.

Diversion Dam 51.6 mi.

49.9 mi.

Diversion Dam 45.1 mi.

39.7 mi.

37.1 mi.

34.6 mi.

31.1 mi.

Wolf Creek

Wolf Creek Road

Patterson Lake

Patterson Lake Road

Twin Lakes Road

Twin Lakes

Fish Hatchery

Wintrop

Rendezvous Road

Chewuch River

Pearrygin Lake

Pearrygin Lake State Park

Bear Creek Road

Bear Creek

Okanogan National Forest

Lester Road

Davis Lake

Davis Lake Road

Methow Valley

Methow Valley

Balky Hill Road

Eastside Wintrop - Twisp Road

Okanogan National Forest

FR 4410

Twisp River Road

Twisp River

Twisp

Lookout Mountain Road

Okanogan National Forest

Beaver Creek Road

Lower Beaver Creek Road

Beaver Creek

Twisp - Carlton Road

Alder Creek

Benson Creek Road

Flow

Methow River

MAP 2 OF 3

MÉTHOW RIVER

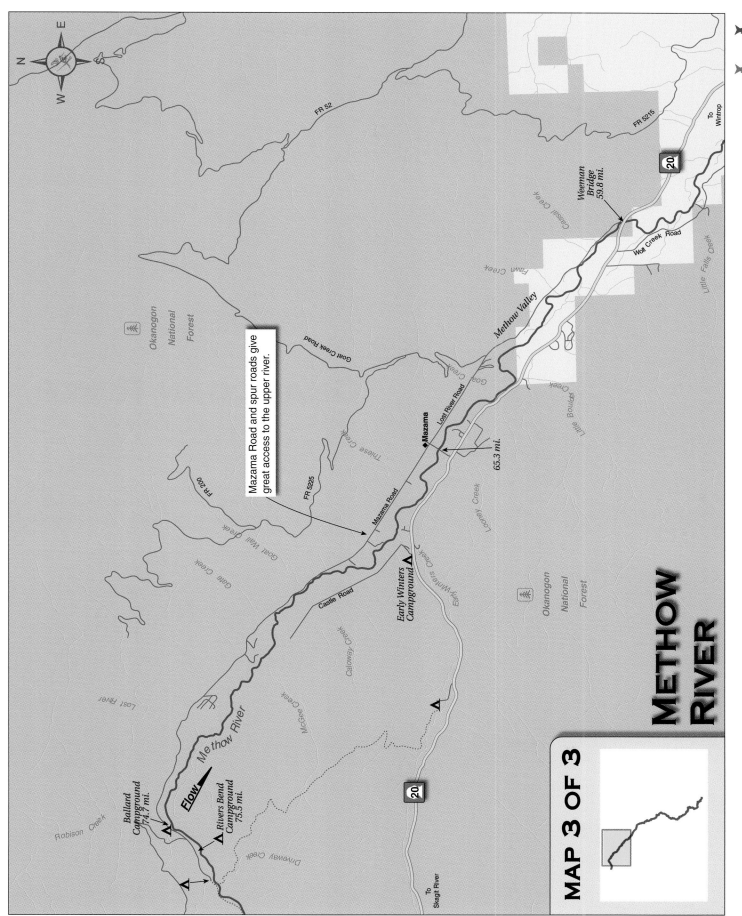

Mazama Road and spur roads give great access to the upper river.

Weeman Bridge 59.8 mi.

65.3 mi.

◆Mazama

Early Winters Campground △

Ballard Campground 74.7 mi. △

△ Rivers Bend Campground 75.5 mi.

Flow

Methow River

Okanogon National Forest

Okanogon National Forest

Methow Valley

To Winthrop

To Skagit River

FR 52

FR 5215

FR 5225

FR 200

Goat Creek Road

Lost River Road

Mazama Road

Castle Road

Wolf Creek Road

Cassal Creek

Fawn Creek

Goat Creek

Little Boulder Creek

Little Falls Creek

Looney Creek

Early Winters Creek

Caloway Creek

McGee Creek

Gate Creek

Goat Wall Creek

Trilese Creek

Lost River

Robison Creek

Driveway Creek

MAP 3 OF 3

METHOW RIVER

© 2005 Wilderness Adventures Press, Inc.

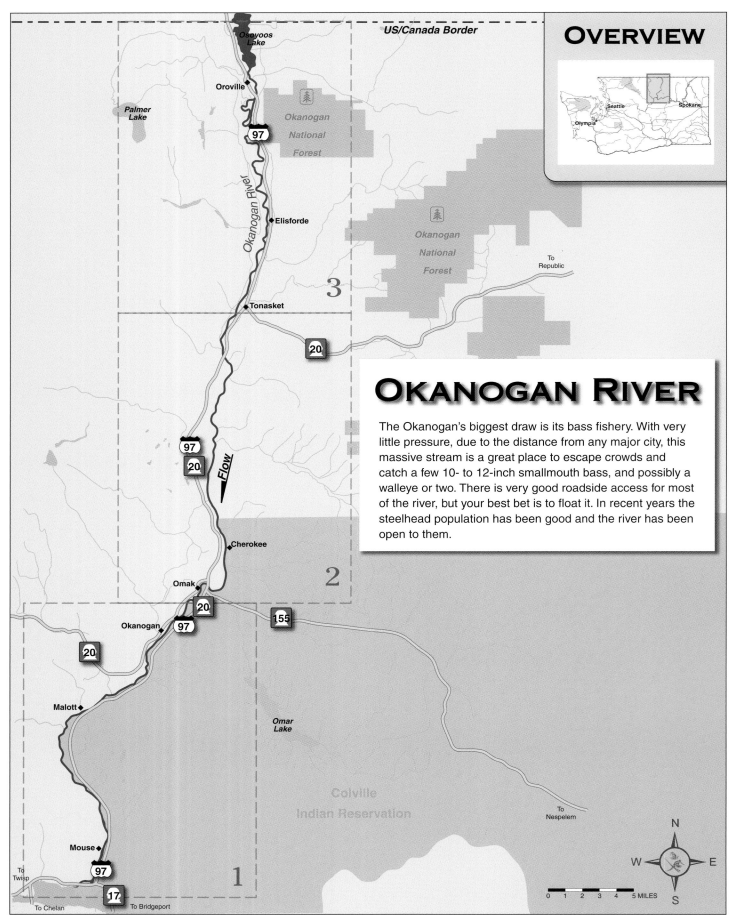

US/Canada Border

OVERVIEW

Osoyoos Lake

Oroville

Palmer Lake

97

Okanogan National Forest

Okanogan River

Elisforde

Okanogan National Forest

To Republic

3

Tonasket

20

OKANOGAN RIVER

The Okanogan's biggest draw is its bass fishery. With very little pressure, due to the distance from any major city, this massive stream is a great place to escape crowds and catch a few 10- to 12-inch smallmouth bass, and possibly a walleye or two. There is very good roadside access for most of the river, but your best bet is to float it. In recent years the steelhead population has been good and the river has been open to them.

97
20

Flow

Cherokee

2

Omak

20

155

Okanogan **97**

20

Malott

Omar Lake

Colville Indian Reservation

To Nespelem

Mouse

To Twisp

97

17

To Chelan   To Bridgeport

1

N
W — E
S

0 1 2 3 4 5 MILES

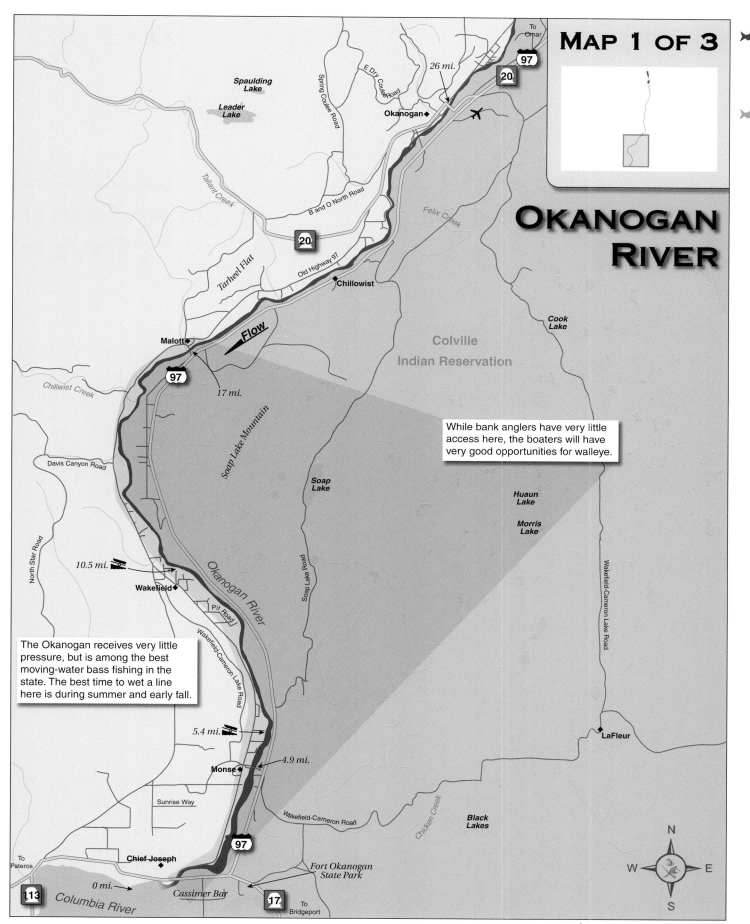

Spaulding Lake

Leader Lake

E Dry Coulee Road

Spring Coulee Road

26 mi.

To Omar

97

20

Okanogan

Tallant Creek

B and O North Road

Felix Creek

MAP 1 OF 3

OKANOGAN RIVER

20

Tarheel Flat

Old Highway 97

Chillowist

Cook Lake

Colville

Indian Reservation

Flow

Malott

97

17 mi.

Chiliwist Creek

Soap Lake Mountain

While bank anglers have very little access here, the boaters will have very good opportunities for walleye.

Soap Lake

Huaun Lake

Morris Lake

Davis Canyon Road

North Star Road

10.5 mi.

Wakefield

Okanogan River

Pit Road

Soap Lake Road

Wakefield-Cameron Lake Road

Wakefield-Cameron Lake Road

The Okanogan receives very little pressure, but is among the best moving-water bass fishing in the state. The best time to wet a line here is during summer and early fall.

5.4 mi.

LaFleur

4.9 mi.

Monse

Sunrise Way

Wakefield-Cameron Road

Chicken Creek

Black Lakes

97

N

Chief Joseph

Fort Okanogan State Park

W E

113

To Pateros

0 mi.

Cassimer Bar

17

To Bridgeport

S

© 2005 Wilderness Adventures Press, Inc.

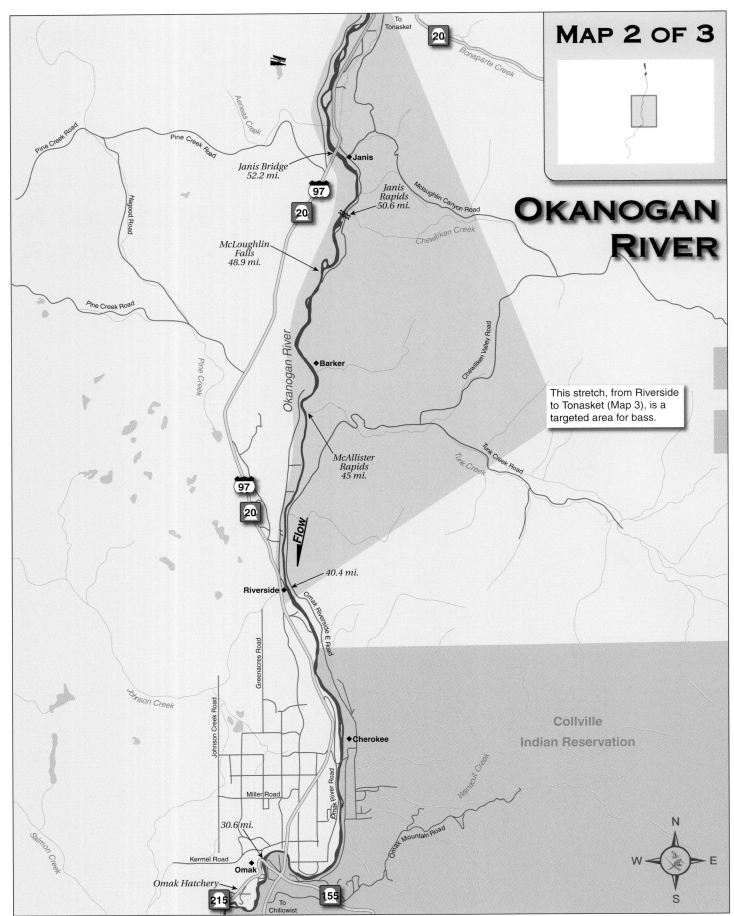

MAP 2 OF 3

OKANOGAN RIVER

This stretch, from Riverside to Tonasket (Map 3), is a targeted area for bass.

To Tonasket

Bonaparte Creek

Aeneas Creek

Pine Creek Road

Pine Creek Road

Hagood Road

Pine Creek Road

Janis Bridge
52.2 mi.

◆ Janis

Janis Rapids
50.6 mi.

Mclaughlin Canyon Road

McLoughlin Falls
48.9 mi.

Chewiliken Creek

Pine Creek

Okanogan River

◆ Barker

Chewiliken Valley Road

McAllister Rapids
45 mi.

Tunk Creek

Tunk Creek Road

Flow

40.4 mi.

Riverside ◆

Omak Riverside E Road

Greenacres Road

Johnson Creek

Johnson Creek Road

Collville

Indian Reservation

◆ Cherokee

Wanacut Creek

Omak River Road

Miller Road

30.6 mi.

Kermel Road

Omak Mountain Road

Omak ◆

Omak Hatchery

215

To Chillowist

155

N
W E
S

© 2005 Wilderness Adventures Press, Inc.

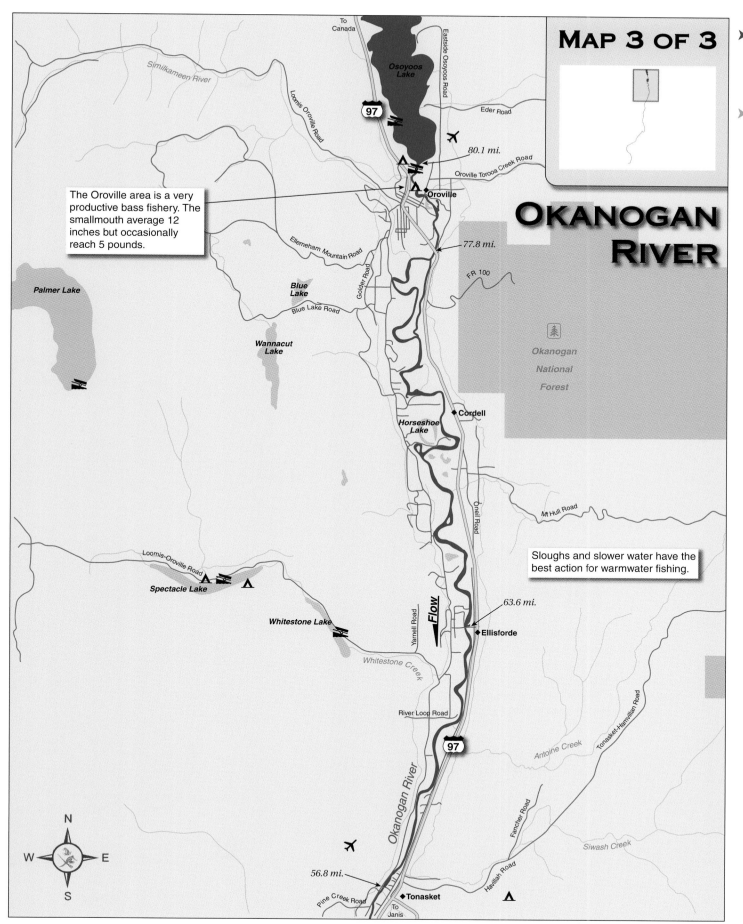

The Oroville area is a very productive bass fishery. The smallmouth average 12 inches but occasionally reach 5 pounds.

Sloughs and slower water have the best action for warmwater fishing.

MAP 3 OF 3

OKANOGAN RIVER

Similkameen River

Osoyoos Lake

To Canada

Eastside Osoyoos Road

97

Eder Road

80.1 mi.

Oroville Torooa Creek Road

Oroville

77.8 mi.

Ellemeham Mountain Road

Golder Road

FR 100

Blue Lake

Blue Lake Road

Loomis Oroville Road

Palmer Lake

Wannacut Lake

Okanogan National Forest

Horseshoe Lake

Cordell

Mt Hull Road

Oneil Road

Loomis-Oroville Road

Spectacle Lake

Whitestone Lake

Yarnell Road

Flow

63.6 mi.

Ellisforde

Whitestone Creek

River Loop Road

97

Antoine Creek

Tonasket-Hamvillan Road

Fancher Road

Okanogan River

Havillah Road

Siwash Creek

N
W E
S

56.8 mi.

Pine Creek Road

Tonasket

To Janis

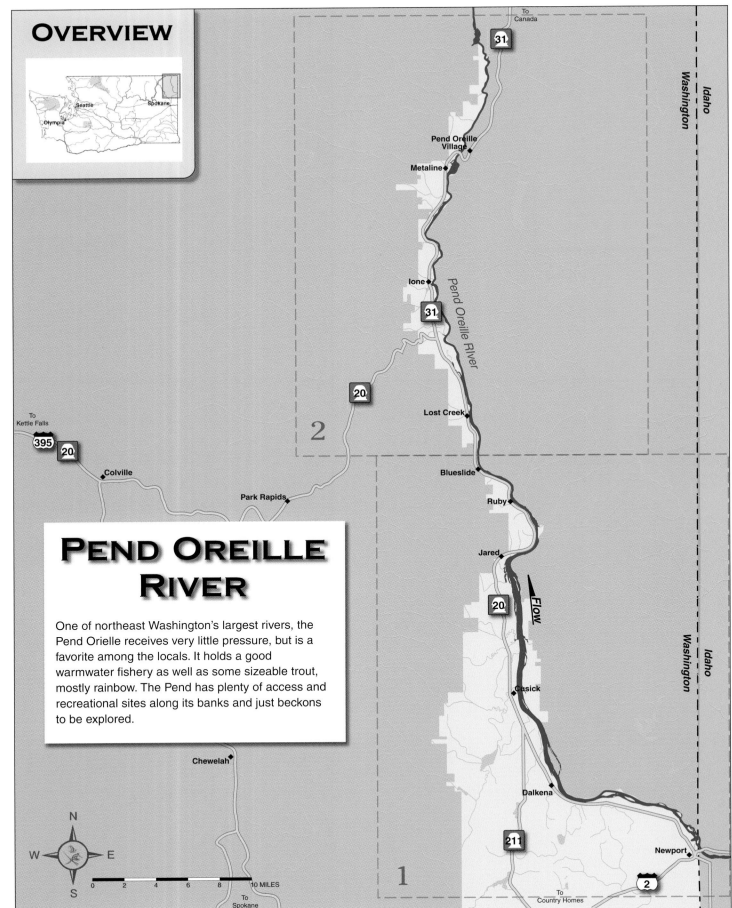

OVERVIEW

To
Canada

31

Washington | Idaho

Pend Oreille
Village

Metaline

Pend Oreille River

Ione

31

20

Lost Creek

2

To
Kettle Falls

395 20

Colville

Park Rapids

Blueslide

Ruby

Jared

Flow

20

PEND OREILLE RIVER

One of northeast Washington's largest rivers, the Pend Orielle receives very little pressure, but is a favorite among the locals. It holds a good warmwater fishery as well as some sizeable trout, mostly rainbow. The Pend has plenty of access and recreational sites along its banks and just beckons to be explored.

Cusick

Chewelah

Dalkena

Washington | Idaho

N
W   E
S

211

Newport

0   2   4   6   8   10 MILES

To
Spokane

1

2

To
Country Homes

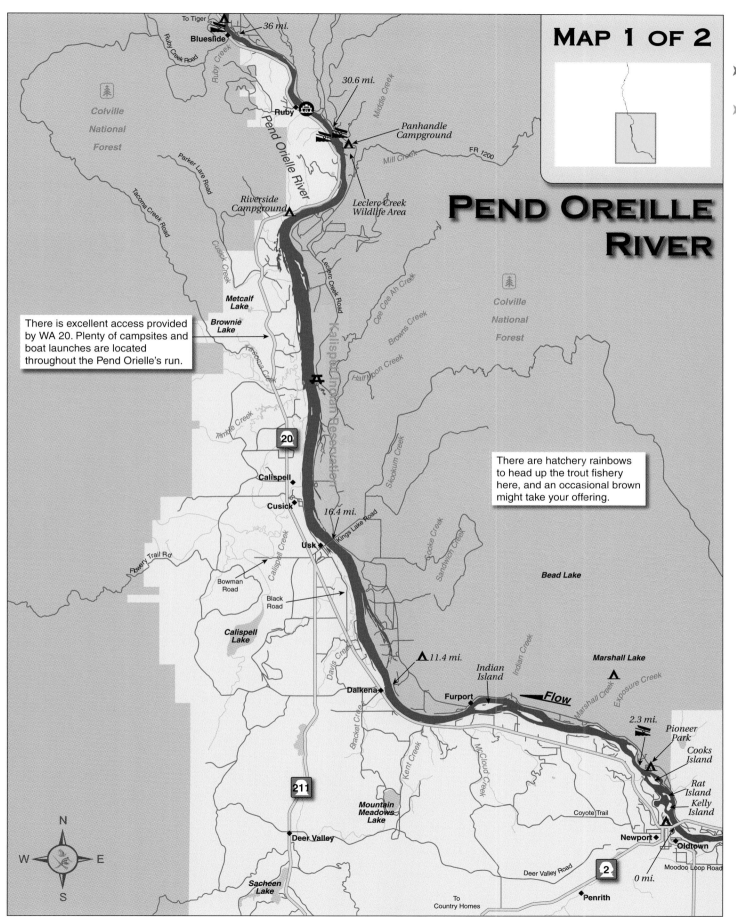

MAP 1 OF 2

PEND OREILLE RIVER

To Tiger

36 mi.

Blueslide

Ruby Creek Road

Colville
National
Forest

Parker Lake Road

Tacoma Creek Road

Ruby

Pend Orielle River

30.6 mi.

Middle Creek

Panhandle
Campground

Leclerc Creek
Wildlife Area

FR 1200

Mill Creek

Cusick Creek

Riverside
Campground

Leclerc Creek Road

Cee Cee Ah Creek

Browns Creek

Colville
National
Forest

Metcalf
Lake

Brownie
Lake

There is excellent access provided
by WA 20. Plenty of campsites and
boat launches are located
throughout the Pend Orielle's run.

Tacoma Creek

Half Moon Creek

Kalispel Indian Reservation

Trimble Creek

20

There are hatchery rainbows
to head up the trout fishery
here, and an occasional brown
might take your offering.

Skookum Creek

Calispell

Cusick

16.4 mi.

Kings Lake Road

Usk

Bead Lake

Flowery Trail Rd

Calispell Creek

Bowman
Road

Black
Road

Cooke Creek

Sandwich Creek

Calispell
Lake

11.4 mi.

Indian Creek

Marshall Lake

Exposure Creek

Davis Creek

Dalkena

Furport

Indian
Island

Flow

Marshall Creek

2.3 mi.

Pioneer
Park

Cooks
Island

Bracket Creek

211

Kent Creek

McCloud Creek

Rat
Island

Kelly
Island

Mountain
Meadows
Lake

Coyote Trail

Newport

Oldtown

N
W   E
S

Deer Valley

Moodoo Loop Road

2

Deer Valley Road

0 mi.

Sacheen
Lake

To
Country Homes

Penrith

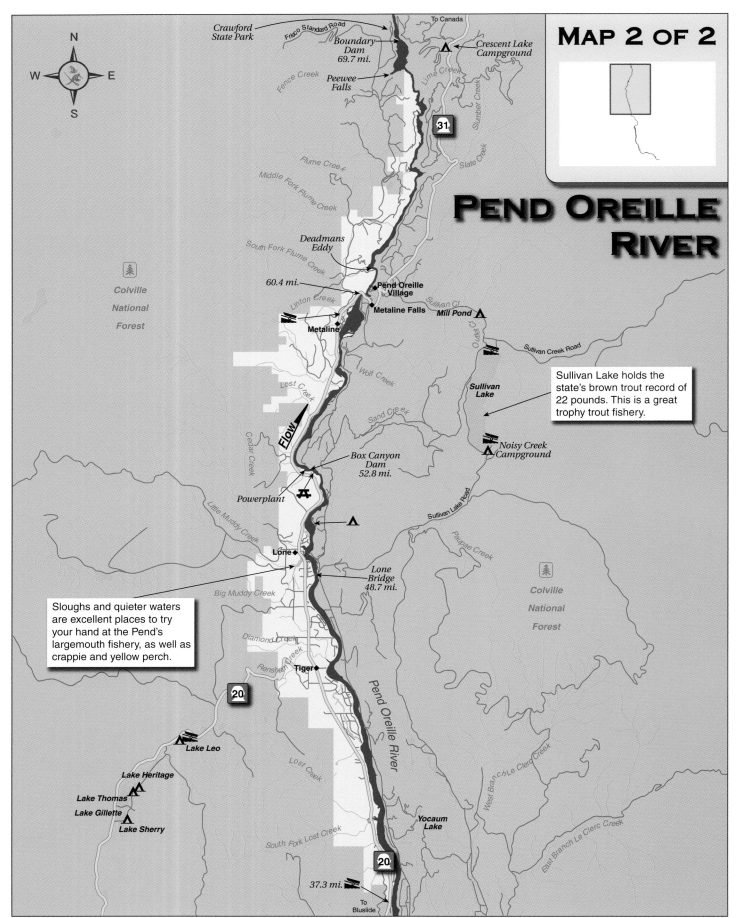

N
W E
S

Crawford State Park
Frisco Standard Road
To Canada
Boundary Dam 69.7 mi.
Crescent Lake Campground
Peewee Falls
Fence Creek
Lime Creek
Slumber Creek
Slate Creek

MAP 2 OF 2

Flume Creek
Middle Fork Flume Creek
South Fork Flume Creek

31

Deadmans Eddy
60.4 mi.
Pend Oreille Village
Metaline Falls
Metaline
Mill Pond
Sullivan Cr.
Linton Creek

PEND OREILLE RIVER

Colville National Forest

Wolf Creek
Sand Creek
Outlet Cr.
Sullivan Creek Road
Sullivan Lake

Lost Creek
Flow
Cedar Creek

Sullivan Lake holds the state's brown trout record of 22 pounds. This is a great trophy trout fishery.

Noisy Creek Campground

Box Canyon Dam 52.8 mi.
Powerplant
Little Muddy Creek
Sullivan Lake Road
Paupac Creek

Lone
Lone Bridge 48.7 mi.
Big Muddy Creek

Colville National Forest

Sloughs and quieter waters are excellent places to try your hand at the Pend's largemouth fishery, as well as crappie and yellow perch.

Diamond Creek
Renshaw Creek
Tiger

20

Pend Oreille River

Lost Creek

Lake Leo
Lake Heritage
Lake Thomas
Lake Gillette
Lake Sherry

West Branch Le Clerc Creek
East Branch Le Clerc Creek

South Fork Lost Creek
Yocaum Lake

20

37.3 mi.
To Bluslide

© 2005 Wilderness Adventures Press, Inc.

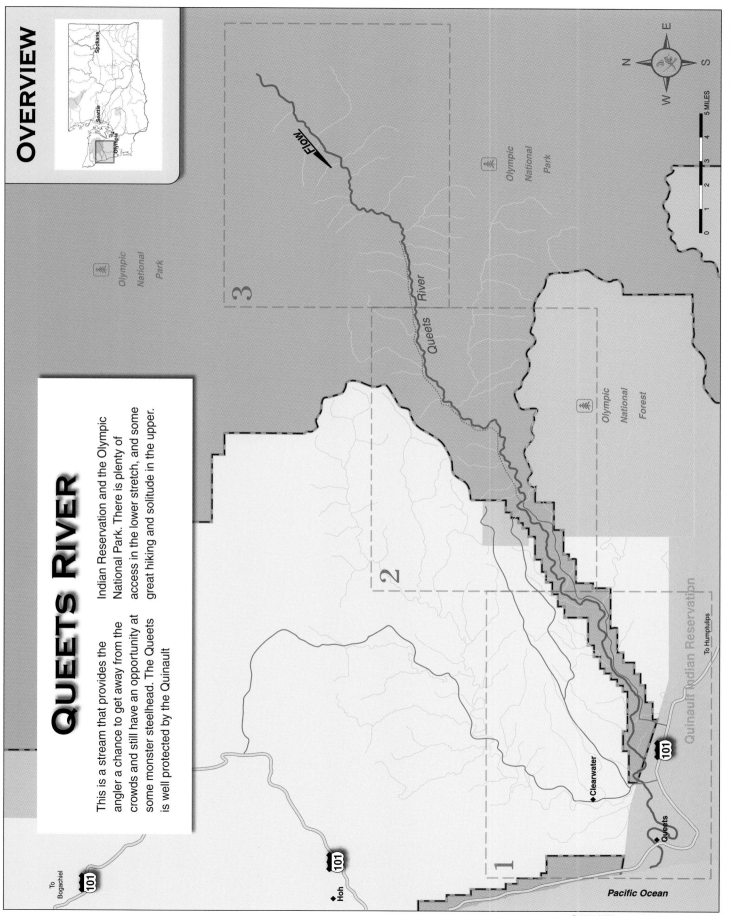

OVERVIEW

QUEETS RIVER

This is a stream that provides the angler a chance to get away from the crowds and still have an opportunity at some monster steelhead. The Queets is well protected by the Quinault Indian Reservation and the Olympic National Park. There is plenty of access in the lower stretch, and some great hiking and solitude in the upper.

FLOW

Olympic National Park

Olympic National Park

Queets River

Olympic National Forest

3

2

1

To Bogachiel

101

Hoh

101

Clearwater

Queets

101

Quinault Indian Reservation

To Humptulips

Pacific Ocean

N E S W

5 MILES
0 1 2 3 4

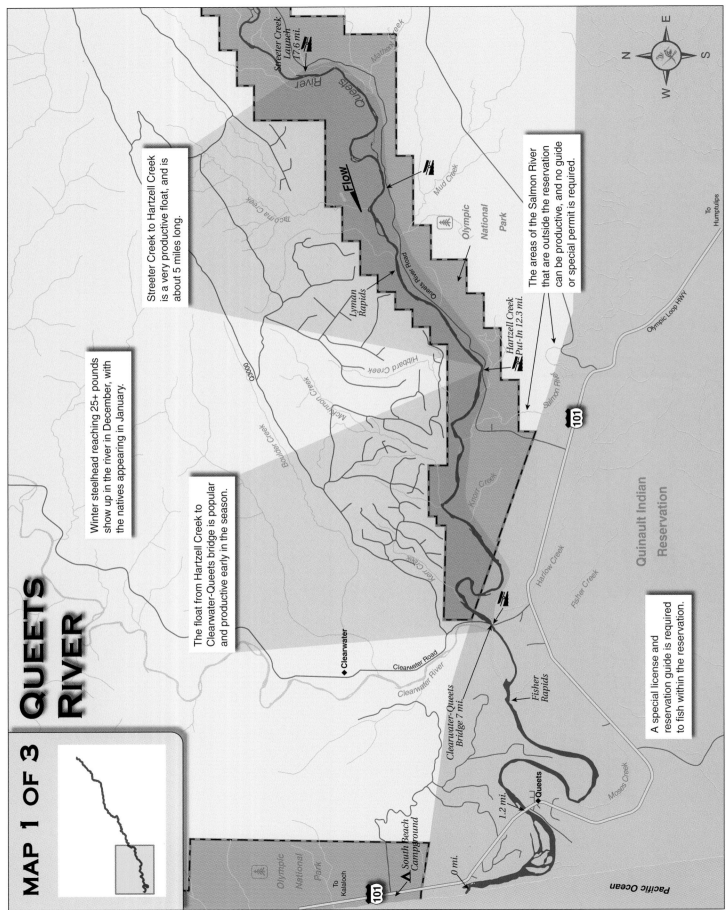

MAP 1 OF 3

QUEETS RIVER

Winter steelhead reaching 25+ pounds show up in the river in December, with the natives appearing in January.

Streeter Creek to Hartzell Creek is a very productive float, and is about 5 miles long.

The float from Hartzell Creek to Clearwater-Queets bridge is popular and productive early in the season.

The areas of the Salmon River that are outside the reservation can be productive, and no guide or special permit is required.

A special license and reservation guide is required to fish within the reservation.

Streeter Creek Launch 17.6 mi.

FLOW

Mathews Creek

Mud Creek

Olympic National Park

Queets River

Tacoma Creek

Lyman Rapids

Queets River Road

Hartzell Creek Put-In 12.3 mi.

Salmon River

Hibbard Creek

McKinnon Creek

Boulder Creek

Q3000

Knott Creek

101

Olympic Loop HWY

To Humptulips

Kerr Creek

Harlow Creek

Fisher Creek

Quinault Indian Reservation

Clearwater

Clearwater Road

Clearwater River

Clearwater-Queets Bridge 7 mi.

Fisher Rapids

Moses Creek

1.2 mi.

Queets

0 mi.

South Beach Campground

Olympic National Park

To Kalaloch

101

Pacific Ocean

© 2005 Wilderness Adventures Press, Inc.

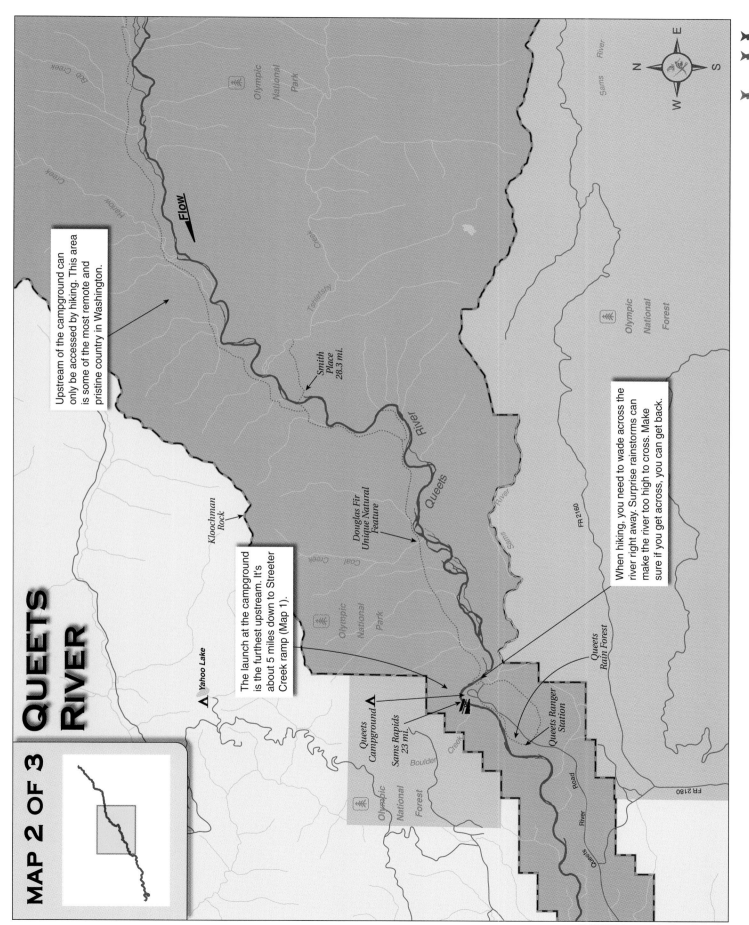

MAP 2 OF 3 | QUEETS RIVER

Upstream of the campground can only be accessed by hiking. This area is some of the most remote and pristine country in Washington.

FLOW

Smith Place 28.3 mi.

Kloochman Rock

The launch at the campground is the furthest upstream. It's about 5 miles down to Streeter Creek ramp (Map 1).

Yahoo Lake

Douglas Fir Unique Natural Feature

Queets River

When hiking, you need to wade across the river right away. Surprise rainstorms can make the river too high to cross. Make sure if you get across, you can get back.

Queets Campground

Sams Rapids 23 mi.

Queets Ranger Station

Queets Rain Forest

Olympic National Forest

Olympic National Park

Olympic National Park

Olympic National Forest

Sams River

Coal Creek

Tshletshy Creek

Bob Creek

Harlow Creek

Boulder Creek

FR 2160

FR 2180

Queets River

River Road

N E S W

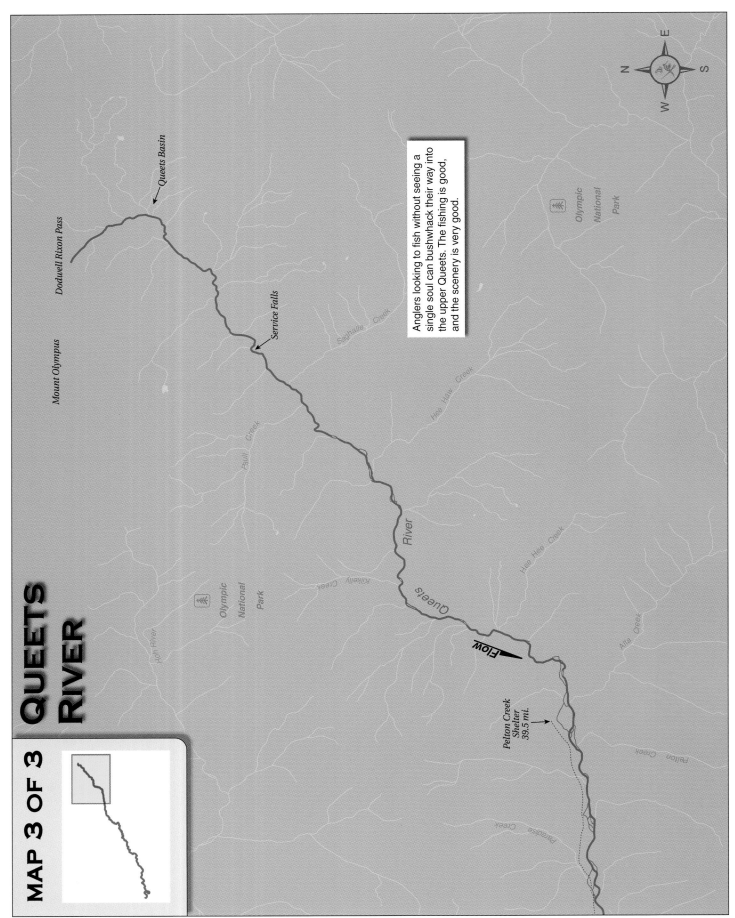

MAP 3 OF 3

QUEETS RIVER

Mount Olympus

Doduwell Rixon Pass

Queets Basin

Service Falls

Saghalie Creek

Hee Haw Creek

Hee Hee Creek

Olympic National Park

Paull Creek

Klikeally Creek

River

Queets

Flow

Alta Creek

Pelton Creek Shelter 39.5 mi.

Pelton Creek

Paradise Creek

Olympic National Park

Hoh River

Anglers looking to fish without seeing a single soul can bushwhack their way into the upper Queets. The fishing is good, and the scenery is very good.

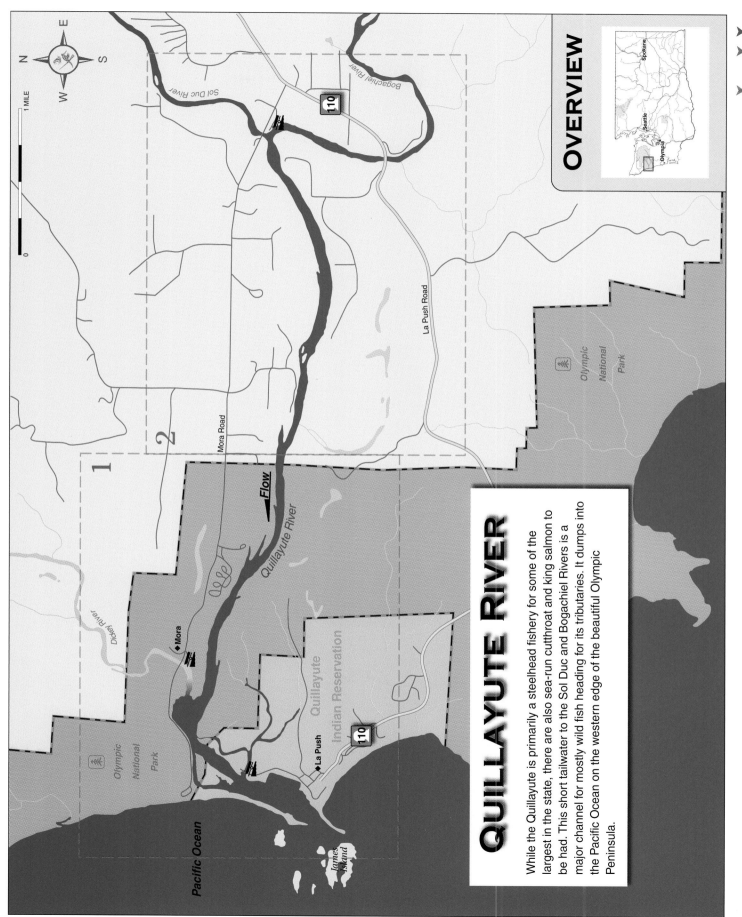

QUILLAYUTE RIVER

While the Quillayute is primarily a steelhead fishery for some of the largest in the state, there are also sea-run cutthroat and king salmon to be had. This short tailwater to the Sol Duc and Bogachiel Rivers is a major channel for mostly wild fish heading for its tributaries. It dumps into the Pacific Ocean on the western edge of the beautiful Olympic Peninsula.

OVERVIEW

Pacific Ocean

James Island

La Push

Quillayute Indian Reservation

Olympic National Park

Mora

Dickey River

Quillayute River

Flow

Mora Road

La Push Road

Sol Duc River

Bogachiel River

Olympic National Park

1 MILE

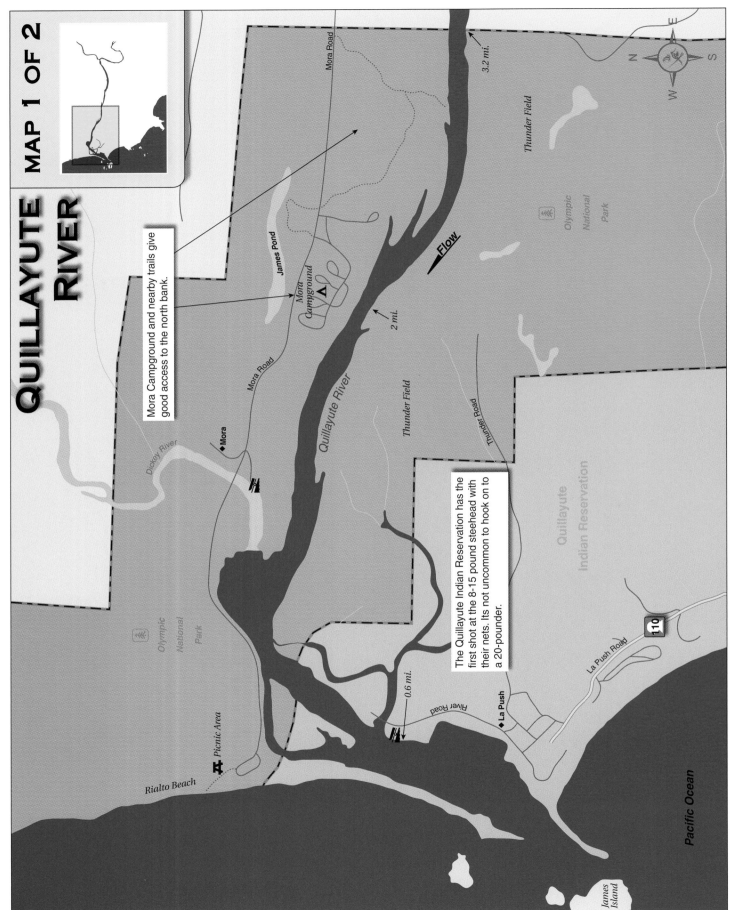

MAP 1 OF 2

QUILLAYUTE RIVER

Mora Campground and nearby trails give good access to the north bank.

The Quillayute Indian Reservation has the first shot at the 8-15 pound steelhead with their nets. Its not uncommon to hook on to a 20-pounder.

Mora Road

Thunder Field

Olympic National Park

3.2 mi.

Flow

2 mi.

James Pond

Mora Campground

Quillayute River

Thunder Field

Thunder Road

Mora Road

Mora

Dickey River

Olympic National Park

Quillayute Indian Reservation

0.6 mi.

River Road

La Push

La Push Road

110

Picnic Area

Rialto Beach

Pacific Ocean

James Island

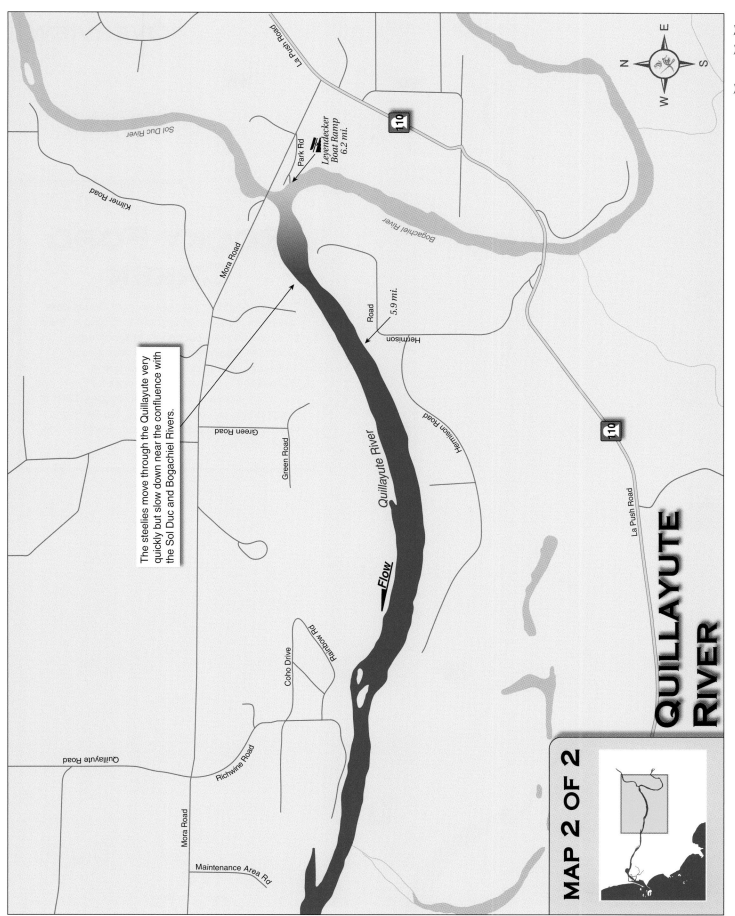

The steelies move through the Quillayute very quickly but slow down near the confluence with the Sol Duc and Bogachiel Rivers.

Sol Duc River

La Push Road

Park Rd

Leyendecker
Boat Ramp
6.2 mi.

101

Bogachiel River

Kilmer Road

Mora Road

Road

5.9 mi.

Hermison

Green Road

Green Road

Quillayute River

Hermison Road

Flow

101

La Push Road

Rainbow Rd

Coho Drive

Quillayute Road

Richwine Road

Mora Road

Maintenance Area Rd

**QUILLAYUTE
RIVER**

MAP 2 OF 2

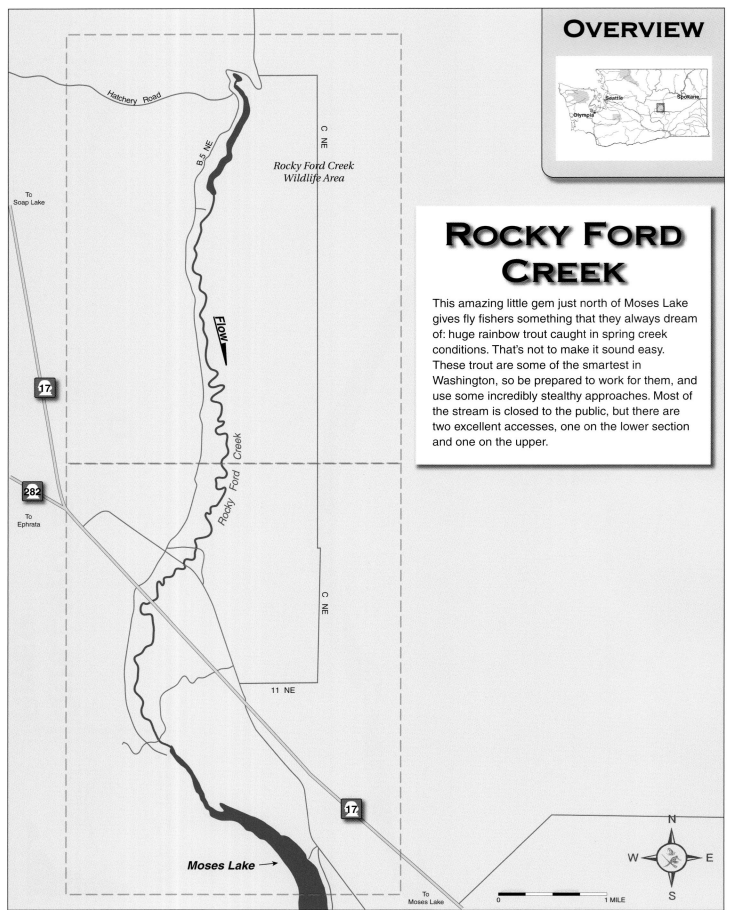

OVERVIEW

ROCKY FORD CREEK

This amazing little gem just north of Moses Lake gives fly fishers something that they always dream of: huge rainbow trout caught in spring creek conditions. That's not to make it sound easy. These trout are some of the smartest in Washington, so be prepared to work for them, and use some incredibly stealthy approaches. Most of the stream is closed to the public, but there are two excellent accesses, one on the lower section and one on the upper.

Hatchery Road

B 5 NE

C NE

Rocky Ford Creek Wildlife Area

To Soap Lake

FLOW

17

Rocky Ford Creek

282

To Ephrata

C NE

11 NE

17

Moses Lake →

To Moses Lake

N

W E

S

0   1 MILE

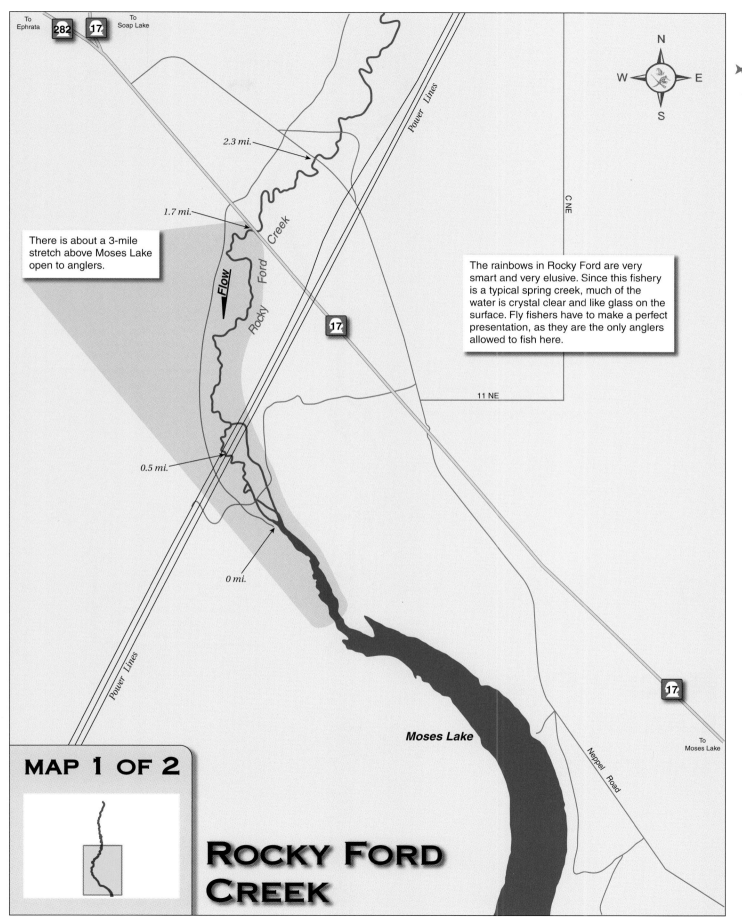

To
Ephrata
282
17
To
Soap Lake

N
W E
S

Power Lines

C NE

2.3 mi.

1.7 mi.

Flow

Rocky Ford Creek

There is about a 3-mile stretch above Moses Lake open to anglers.

The rainbows in Rocky Ford are very smart and very elusive. Since this fishery is a typical spring creek, much of the water is crystal clear and like glass on the surface. Fly fishers have to make a perfect presentation, as they are the only anglers allowed to fish here.

17

11 NE

0.5 mi.

0 mi.

17

To
Moses Lake

Moses Lake

Power Lines

Neppel Road

MAP 1 OF 2

ROCKY FORD
CREEK

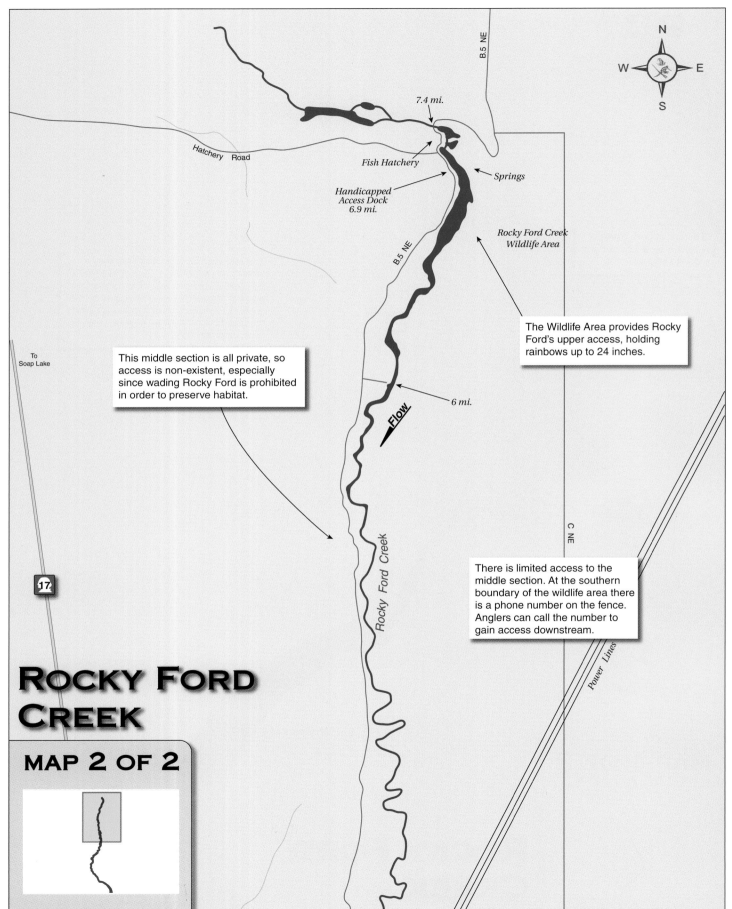

N
W E
S

7.4 mi.

B.5 NE

Hatchery Road

Fish Hatchery

Handicapped
Access Dock
6.9 mi.

Springs

Rocky Ford Creek
Wildlife Area

B.5 NE

To
Soap Lake

This middle section is all private, so
access is non-existent, especially
since wading Rocky Ford is prohibited
in order to preserve habitat.

The Wildlife Area provides Rocky
Ford's upper access, holding
rainbows up to 24 inches.

6 mi.

Flow

17

Rocky Ford Creek

C NE

There is limited access to the
middle section. At the southern
boundary of the wildlife area there
is a phone number on the fence.
Anglers can call the number to
gain access downstream.

Power Lines

ROCKY FORD
CREEK

MAP 2 OF 2

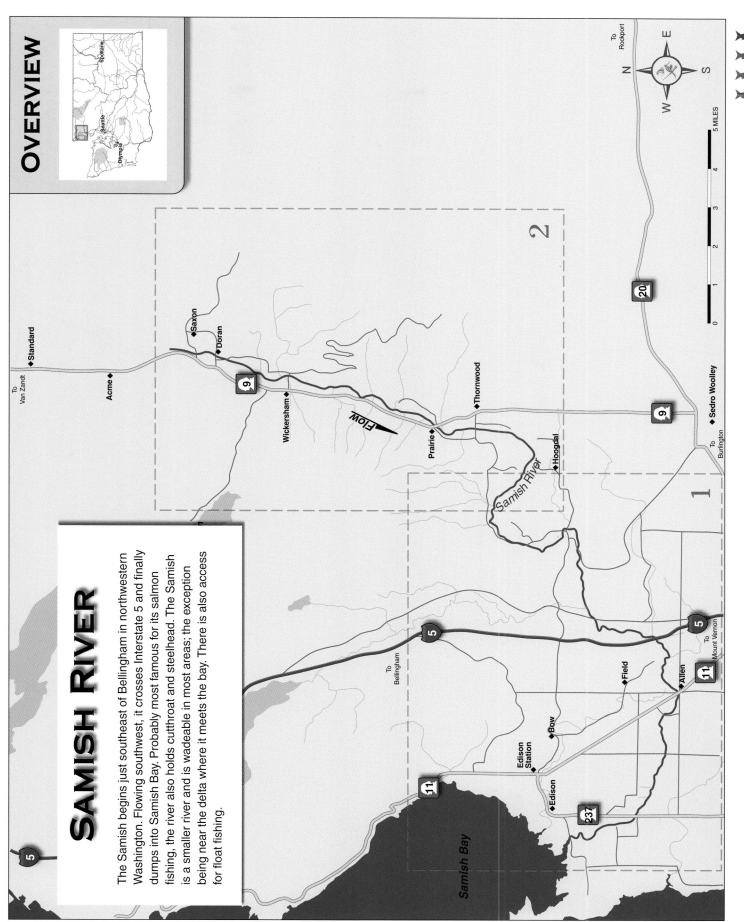

OVERVIEW

SAMISH RIVER

The Samish begins just southeast of Bellingham in northwestern Washington. Flowing southwest, it crosses Interstate 5 and finally dumps into Samish Bay. Probably most famous for its salmon fishing, the river also holds cutthroat and steelhead. The Samish is a smaller river and is wadeable in most areas; the exception being near the delta where it meets the bay. There is also access for float fishing.

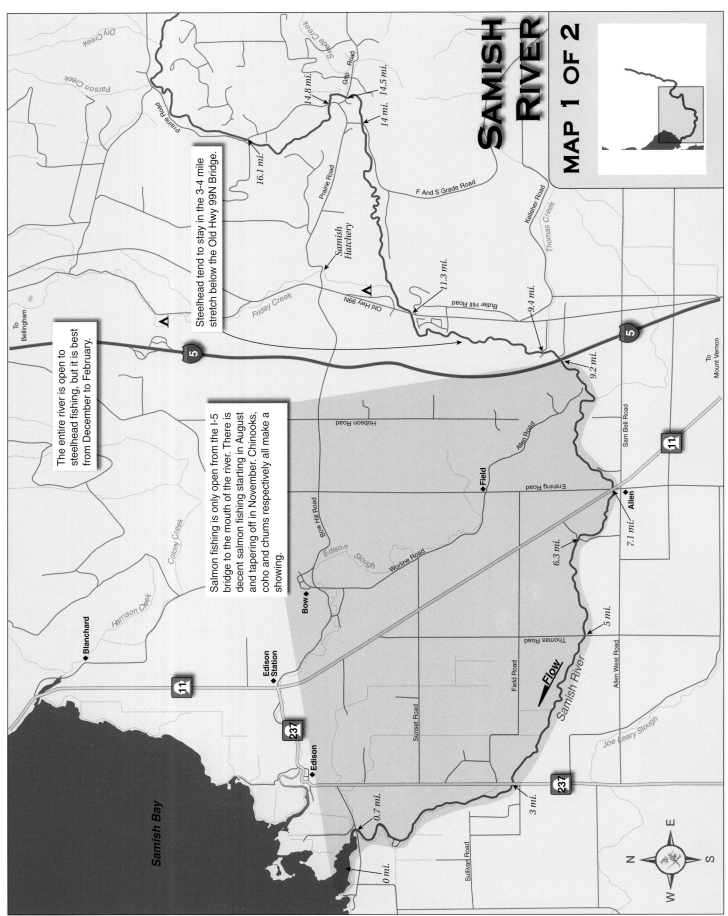

SAMISH RIVER

MAP 1 OF 2

Steelhead tend to stay in the 3-4 mile stretch below the Old Hwy 99N Bridge.

The entire river is open to steelhead fishing, but it is best from December to February.

Salmon fishing is only open from the I-5 bridge to the mouth of the river. There is decent salmon fishing starting in August and tapering off in November. Chinooks, coho and chums respectively all make a showing.

16.1 mi.
14.8 mi.
14 mi. 14.5 mi.
11.3 mi.
9.4 mi.
9.2 mi.
7.1 mi.
6.3 mi.
5 mi.
3 mi.
0.7 mi.
0 mi.

Samish Hatchery

F And S Grade Road
Kelleher Road
Thomas Creek
Butler Hill Road
Old Hwy 99N
Friday Creek
Prairie Road
Grip Road
Shale Creek
Parson Creek
Dry Creek
Prairie Road

To Bellingham

To Mount Vernon

Sam Bell Road
Hobson Road
Allen Road
Ershing Road
Field
Allen
Bow Hill Road
Edison Slough
Worline Road
Bow
Thomas Road
Field Road
Sunset Road
Allen West Road
Joe Leary Slough
Sullivan Road
Samish River
Flow

Blanchard
Harrison Creek
Colony Creek

Edison Station
Edison

Samish Bay

N
E
W
S

© 2005 Wilderness Adventures Press, Inc.

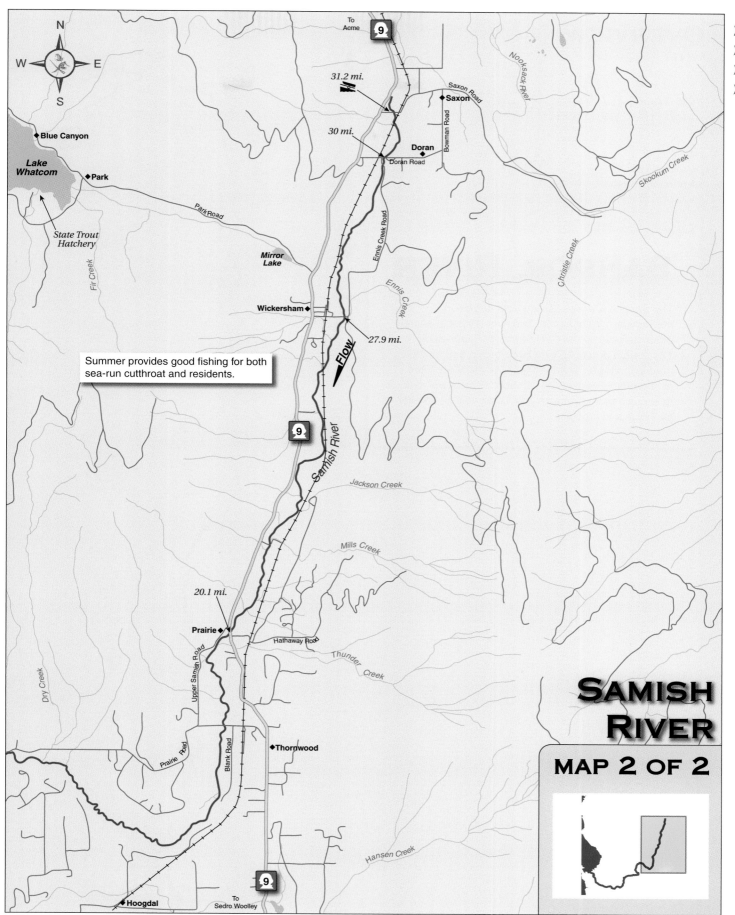

N
W · E
S

To Acme

9

31.2 mi.

Saxon Road

◆ **Saxon**

Bowman Road

Nooksack River

Skookum Creek

◆ Blue Canyon

30 mi.

Doran

Lake Whatcom

◆ Park

Doran Road

Park Road

State Trout Hatchery

Ennis Creek Road

Christie Creek

Fir Creek

Mirror Lake

Ennis Creek

Wickersham ◆

27.9 mi.

Summer provides good fishing for both sea-run cutthroat and residents.

Flow

Samish River

9

Jackson Creek

Mills Creek

20.1 mi.

Prairie ◆

Hathaway Road

Upper Samish Road

Thunder Creek

Dry Creek

Prairie Road

Blank Road

◆ **Thornwood**

SAMISH RIVER

MAP 2 OF 2

9

◆ Hoogdal

To Sedro Woolley

Hansen Creek

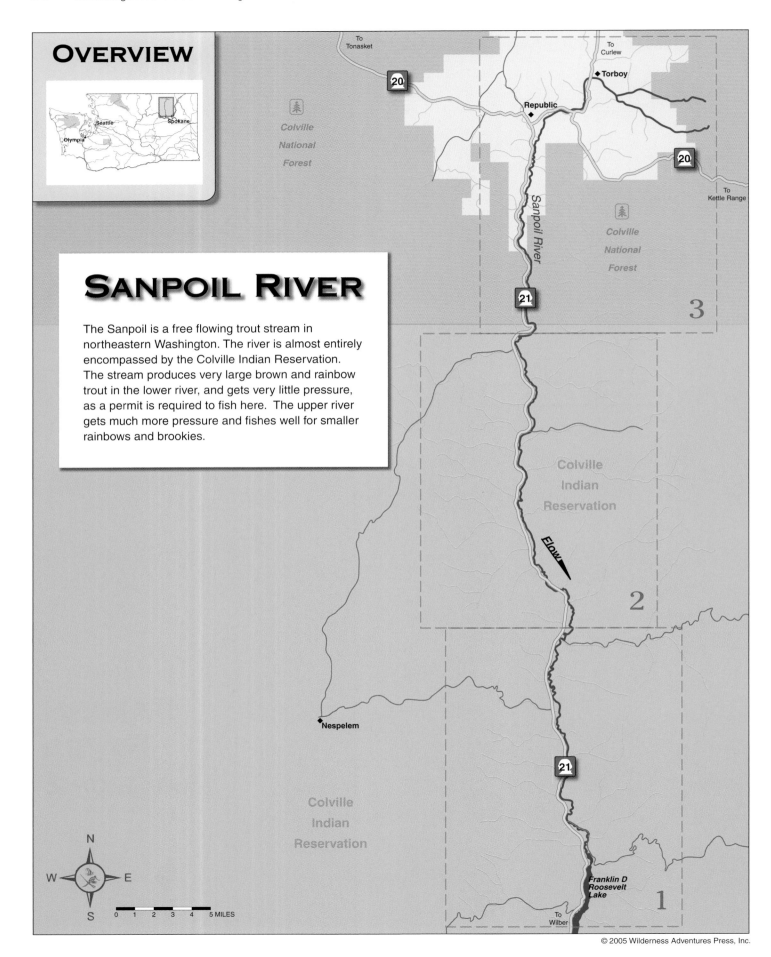

OVERVIEW

SANPOIL RIVER

The Sanpoil is a free flowing trout stream in northeastern Washington. The river is almost entirely encompassed by the Colville Indian Reservation. The stream produces very large brown and rainbow trout in the lower river, and gets very little pressure, as a permit is required to fish here. The upper river gets much more pressure and fishes well for smaller rainbows and brookies.

To Tonasket

To Curlew

20

Torboy

Republic

Colville

National

Forest

20

To
Kettle Range

Sanpoil River

Colville

National

Forest

21

3

Colville

Indian

Reservation

Flow

2

Nespelem

Colville

Indian

Reservation

21

N

W   E

S

0   1   2   3   4   5 MILES

Franklin D
Roosevelt
Lake

1

To
Wilber

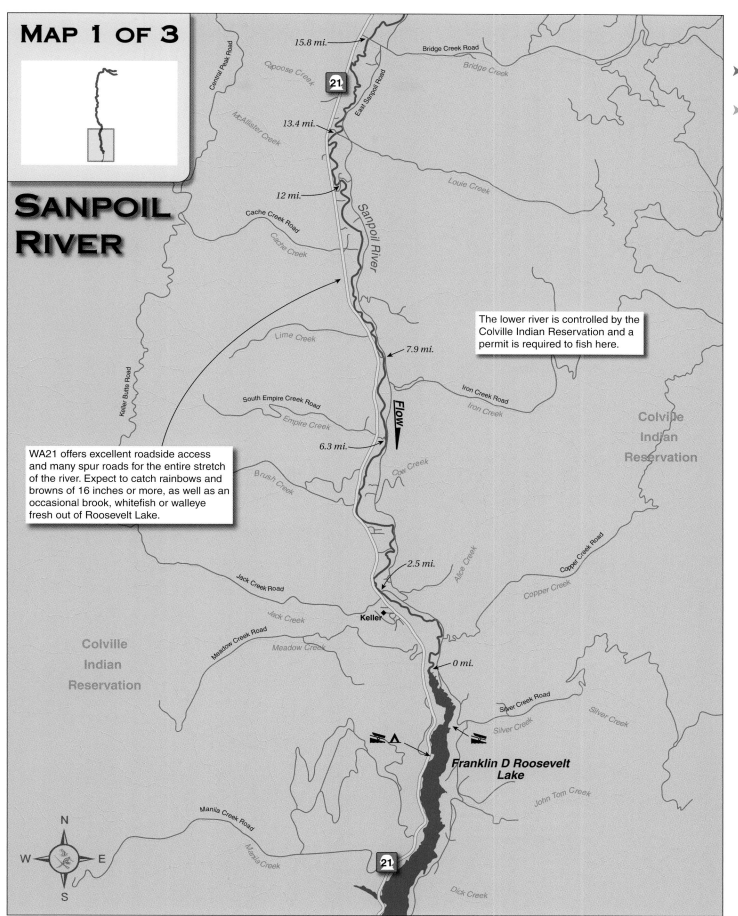

MAP 1 OF 3

SANPOIL RIVER

15.8 mi.

Bridge Creek Road

Bridge Creek

Central Peak Road

Capoose Creek

21

East Sanpoil Road

13.4 mi.

McAllister Creek

Louie Creek

12 mi.

Cache Creek Road

Sanpoil River

Cache Creek

The lower river is controlled by the Colville Indian Reservation and a permit is required to fish here.

Lime Creek

7.9 mi.

Keller Butte Road

South Empire Creek Road

Iron Creek Road

Iron Creek

Colville
Indian
Reservation

Empire Creek

Flow

WA21 offers excellent roadside access and many spur roads for the entire stretch of the river. Expect to catch rainbows and browns of 16 inches or more, as well as an occasional brook, whitefish or walleye fresh out of Roosevelt Lake.

6.3 mi.

Brush Creek

Cow Creek

Copper Creek Road

2.5 mi.

Alice Creek

Copper Creek

Jack Creek Road

Jack Creek

Keller

Colville
Indian
Reservation

Meadow Creek Road

Meadow Creek

0 mi.

Silver Creek Road

Silver Creek

Silver Creek

Franklin D Roosevelt Lake

N
W   E
S

Manila Creek Road

John Tom Creek

Manila Creek

21

Dick Creek

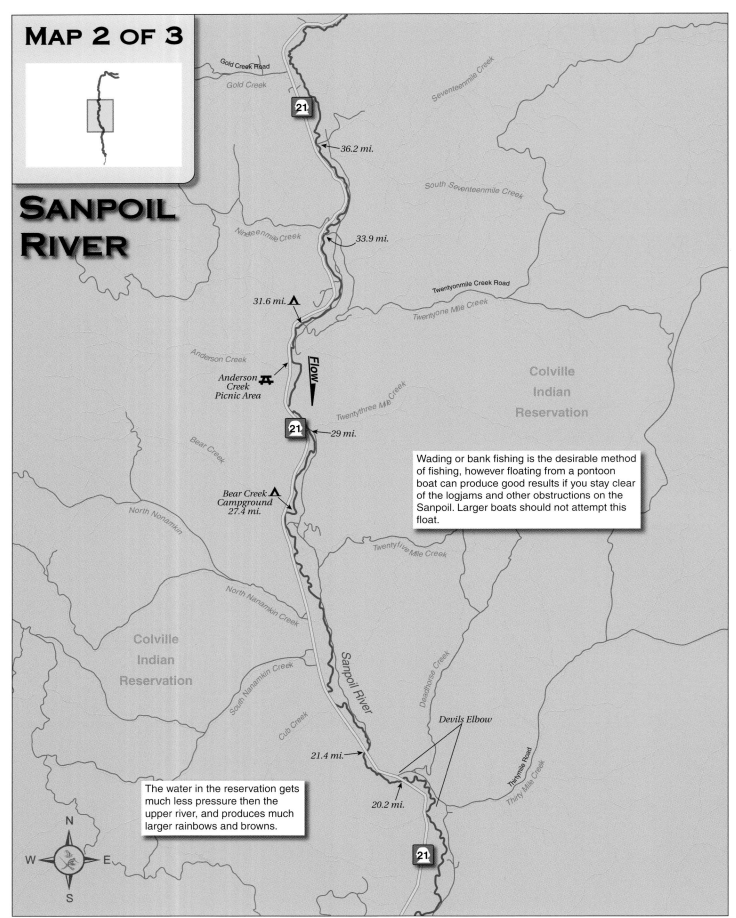

MAP 2 OF 3

SANPOIL RIVER

Gold Creek Road

Gold Creek

21

36.2 mi.

Seventeenmile Creek

South Seventeenmile Creek

Nineteenmile Creek

33.9 mi.

Twentyonmile Creek Road

31.6 mi.

Twentyone Mile Creek

Anderson Creek

Flow

Anderson Creek Picnic Area

Colville Indian Reservation

Bear Creek

21

29 mi.

Twentythree Mile Creek

Bear Creek Campground 27.4 mi.

Wading or bank fishing is the desirable method of fishing, however floating from a pontoon boat can produce good results if you stay clear of the logjams and other obstructions on the Sanpoil. Larger boats should not attempt this float.

North Nonamkin

Twentyfive Mile Creek

North Nanamkin Creek

Colville Indian Reservation

Sanpoil River

Deadhorse Creek

South Nanamkin Creek

Devils Elbow

Cub Creek

21.4 mi.

Thirtymile Road

Thirty Mile Creek

The water in the reservation gets much less pressure then the upper river, and produces much larger rainbows and browns.

20.2 mi.

N
W E
S

21

© 2005 Wilderness Adventures Press, Inc.

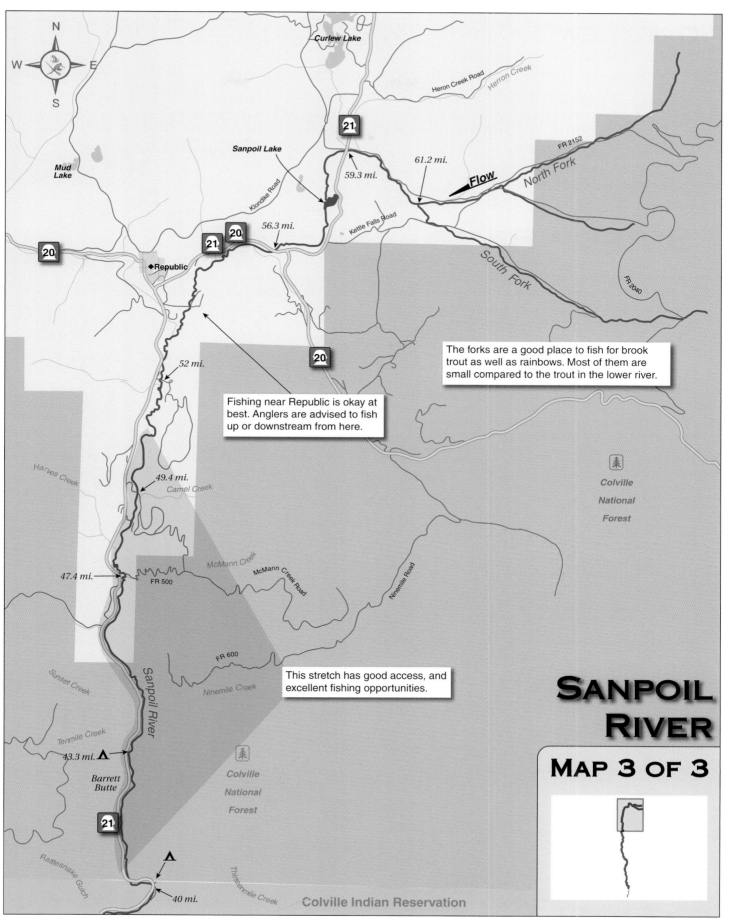

Curlew Lake

Heron Creek Road

Herron Creek

FR 2152

21

Sanpoil Lake

59.3 mi.

61.2 mi.

Flow

North Fork

Klondike Road

56.3 mi.

Kettle Falls Road

Mud Lake

20

21

20

South Fork

FR 2040

◆Republic

20

The forks are a good place to fish for brook trout as well as rainbows. Most of them are small compared to the trout in the lower river.

52 mi.

Fishing near Republic is okay at best. Anglers are advised to fish up or downstream from here.

Harves Creek

Colville

National

Forest

49.4 mi.

Camel Creek

47.4 mi.

FR 500

McMann Creek

McMann Creek Road

Ninemile Road

Sanpoil River

FR 600

Ninemile Creek

This stretch has good access, and excellent fishing opportunities.

Sunset Creek

SANPOIL
RIVER

Tenmile Creek

43.3 mi. ▲

Barrett Butte

Colville

National

Forest

MAP 3 OF 3

21

▲

Rattlesnake Gulch

40 mi.

Thirteenmile Creek

Colville Indian Reservation

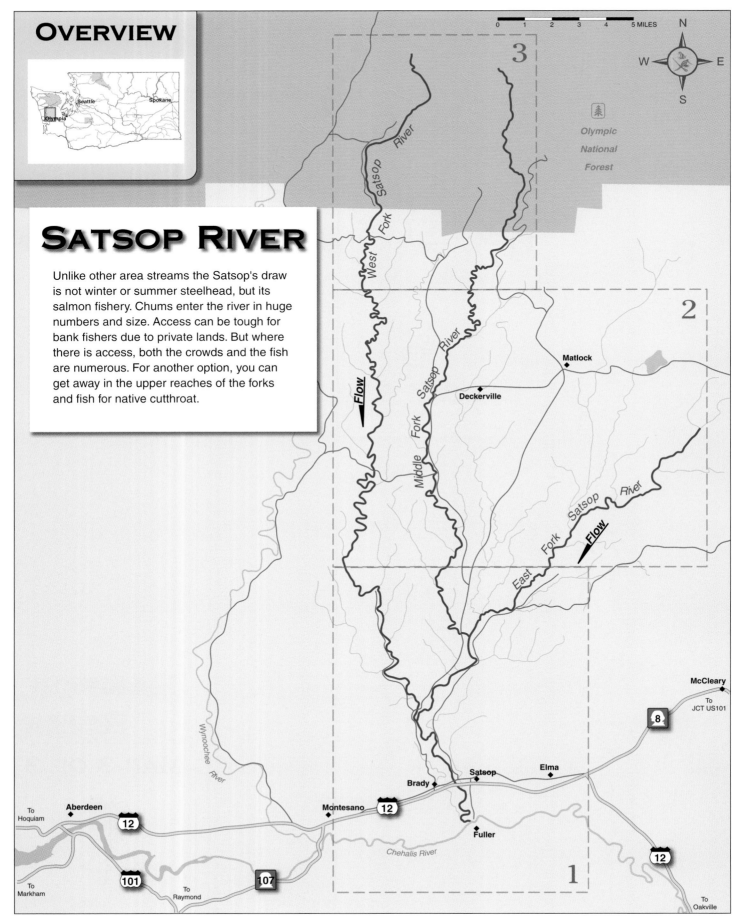

OVERVIEW

SATSOP RIVER

Unlike other area streams the Satsop's draw is not winter or summer steelhead, but its salmon fishery. Chums enter the river in huge numbers and size. Access can be tough for bank fishers due to private lands. But where there is access, both the crowds and the fish are numerous. For another option, you can get away in the upper reaches of the forks and fish for native cutthroat.

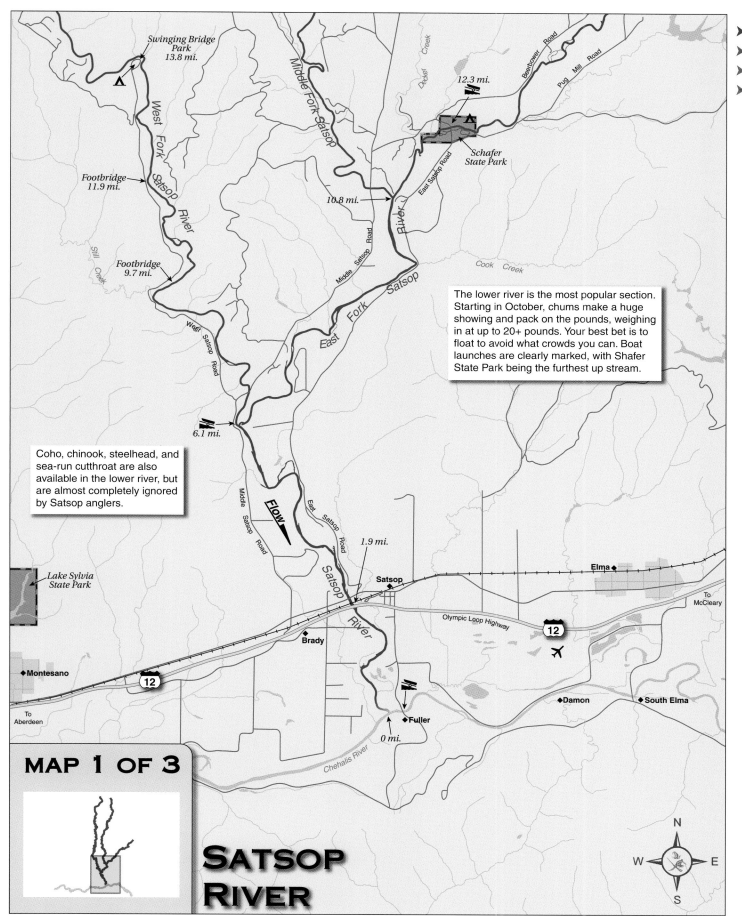

Swinging Bridge
Park
13.8 mi.

West Fork Satsop River

Middle Fork Satsop

Decker Creek

Beetbower Road

Pug Mill Road

12.3 mi.

Schafer
State Park

East Satsop Road

Footbridge
11.9 mi.

Still Creek

10.8 mi.

East Fork Satsop

Cook Creek

Footbridge
9.7 mi.

Middle Satsop Road

The lower river is the most popular section. Starting in October, chums make a huge showing and pack on the pounds, weighing in at up to 20+ pounds. Your best bet is to float to avoid what crowds you can. Boat launches are clearly marked, with Shafer State Park being the furthest up stream.

West Satsop Road

6.1 mi.

Coho, chinook, steelhead, and sea-run cutthroat are also available in the lower river, but are almost completely ignored by Satsop anglers.

Middle Satsop Road

Flow

1.9 mi.

Lake Sylvia
State Park

Satsop

East Satsop Road

Elma

To McCleary

Olympic Loop Highway

12

Montesano

Satsop River

Brady

12

To Aberdeen

Damon

South Elma

Fuller

0 mi.

Chehalis River

MAP 1 OF 3

SATSOP RIVER

N
W   E
S

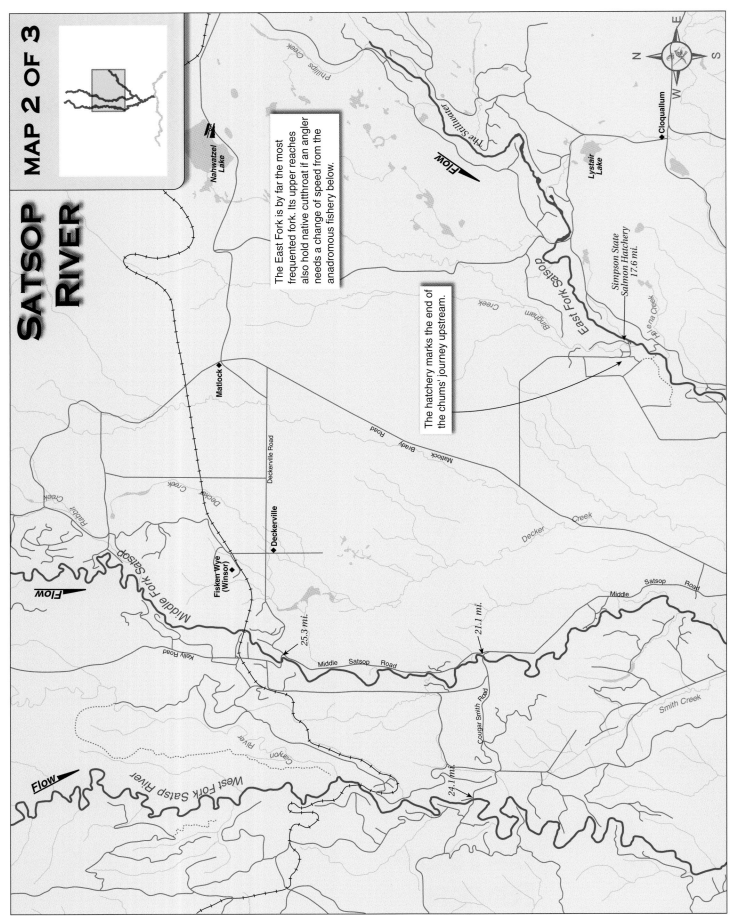

SATSOP RIVER

MAP 2 OF 3

The East Fork is by far the most frequented fork. Its upper reaches also hold native cutthroat if an angler needs a change of speed from the anadromous fishery below.

The hatchery marks the end of the chums' journey upstream.

Simpson State Salmon Hatchery 17.6 mi.

Cloquallum

Lystair Lake

Nahwatzel Lake

Matlock

Deckerville

Fisken Wye (Winsor)

25.3 mi.

21.1 mi.

24.1 mi.

Middle Satsop Road

West Fork Satsop River

Middle Fork Satsop

Canyon River

Smith Creek

Decker Creek

Bingham Creek

Helena Creek

East Fork Satsop

The Stillwater

Phillips Creek

Rabbit Creek

Decker Creek

Deckerville Road

Matlock Brady Road

Kelly Road

Cougar Smith Road

Middle Satsop Road

Flow

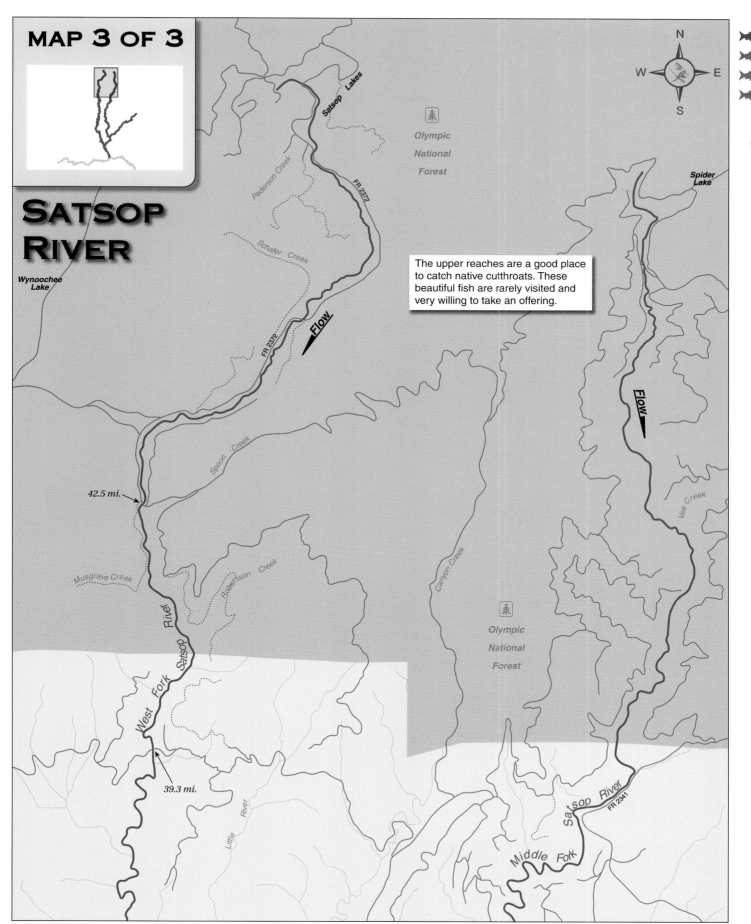

MAP 3 OF 3

SATSOP RIVER

Wynoochee Lake

Olympic National Forest

Satsop Lakes

Pederson Creek

Schafer Creek

FR 2372

FR 2372

Flow

The upper reaches are a good place to catch native cutthroats. These beautiful fish are rarely visited and very willing to take an offering.

Spider Lake

Flow

Vee Creek

Spoon Creek

42.5 mi.

Musgrave Creek

Robertson Creek

West Fork Satsop River

Canyon Creek

Olympic National Forest

39.3 mi.

Little River

Satsop River

FR 2341

Middle Fork

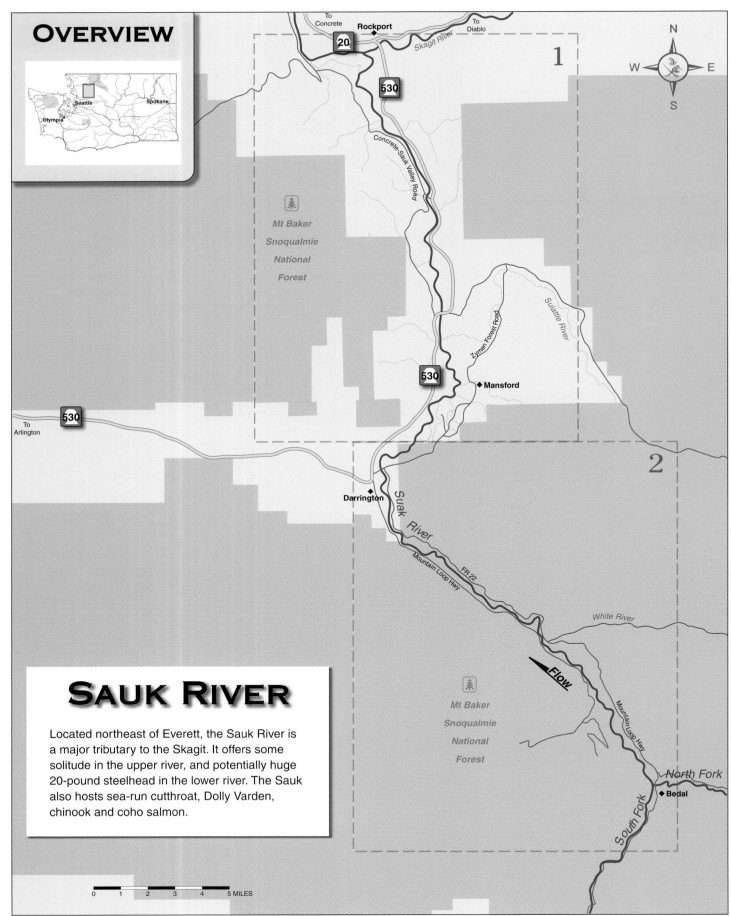

OVERVIEW

To Concrete
Rockport
To Diablo
20
530
1

N
W E
S

Skagit River

Concrete-Sauk Valley Road

Mt Baker
Snoqualmie
National
Forest

Suiattle River

Zyman Forest Road

530
Mansford

530
To Arlington

2

Suak River

Darrington

Mountain Loop Hwy
FR 22

White River

Flow

Mt Baker
Snoqualmie
National
Forest

Mountain Loop Hwy

North Fork

South Fork
Bedal

SAUK RIVER

Located northeast of Everett, the Sauk River is a major tributary to the Skagit. It offers some solitude in the upper river, and potentially huge 20-pound steelhead in the lower river. The Sauk also hosts sea-run cutthroat, Dolly Varden, chinook and coho salmon.

0 1 2 3 4 5 MILES

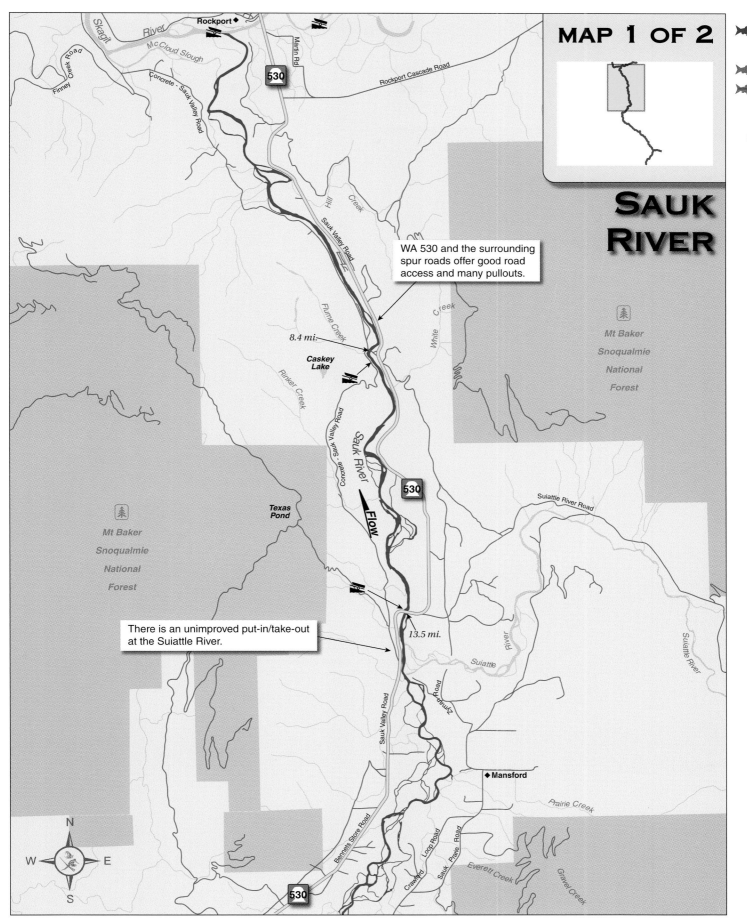

MAP 1 OF 2

SAUK RIVER

Rockport

Skagit River

McCloud Slough

Finney Creek Road

Concrete - Sauk Valley Road

Martin Rd.

530

Rockport Cascade Road

Hill Creek

Sauk Valley Road

WA 530 and the surrounding spur roads offer good road access and many pullouts.

Flume Creek

White Creek

8.4 mi.

Caskey Lake

Rinker Creek

Concrete - Sauk Valley Road

Sauk River

FLOW

530

Mt Baker
Snoqualmie
National
Forest

Suiattle River Road

Texas Pond

Mt Baker
Snoqualmie
National
Forest

Suiattle River

13.5 mi.

Suiattle River

There is an unimproved put-in/take-out at the Suiattle River.

Sauk Valley Road

Zyman Road

Mansford

Prairie Creek

Bennets Store Road

Crawford Loop Road

Sauk Prarie Road

Everett Creek

Gravel Creek

530

N
W   E
S

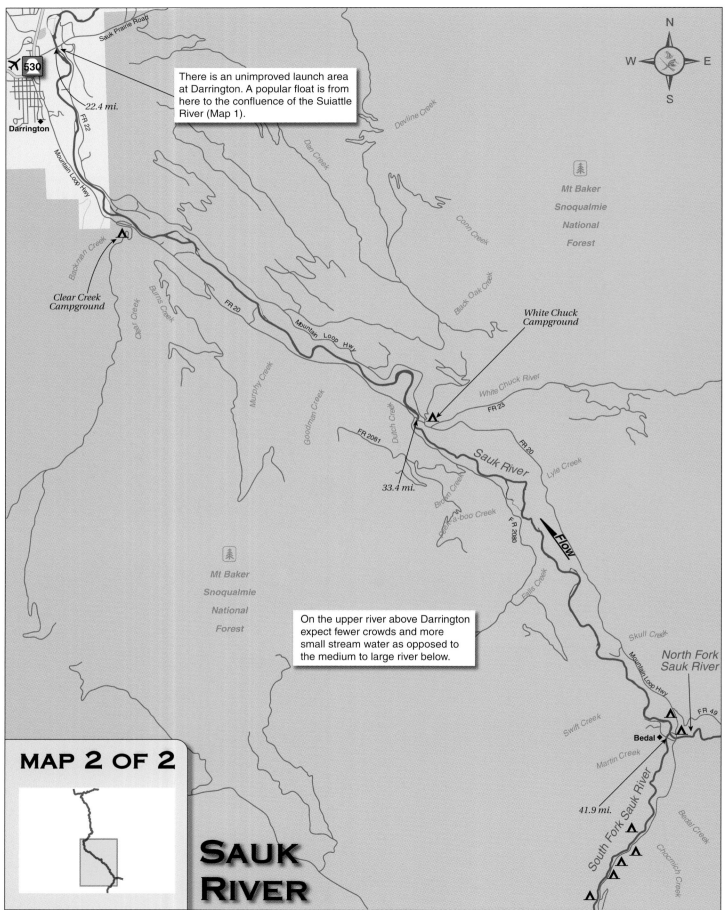

There is an unimproved launch area at Darrington. A popular float is from here to the confluence of the Suiattle River (Map 1).

Darrington

Sauk Prairie Road

530

22.4 mi.

FR 22

Mountain Loop Hwy

Backman Creek

Clear Creek Campground

Clear Creek

Burns Creek

FR 20

Mountain Loop Hwy

Murphy Creek

Goodman Creek

Dutch Creek

FR 2081

33.4 mi.

Brown Creek

Peek-a-boo Creek

Dan Creek

Devline Creek

Conn Creek

Black Oak Creek

Mt Baker Snoqualmie National Forest

White Chuck Campground

White Chuck River

FR 23

Sauk River

Lyle Creek

FR 20

F.R 2080

Flow

Falls Creek

Mt Baker Snoqualmie National Forest

On the upper river above Darrington expect fewer crowds and more small stream water as opposed to the medium to large river below.

Skull Creek

Mountain Loop Hwy

North Fork Sauk River

FR 49

Swift Creek

Bedal

Martin Creek

41.9 mi.

South Fork Sauk River

Bedal Creek

Chocwich Creek

MAP 2 OF 2

SAUK RIVER

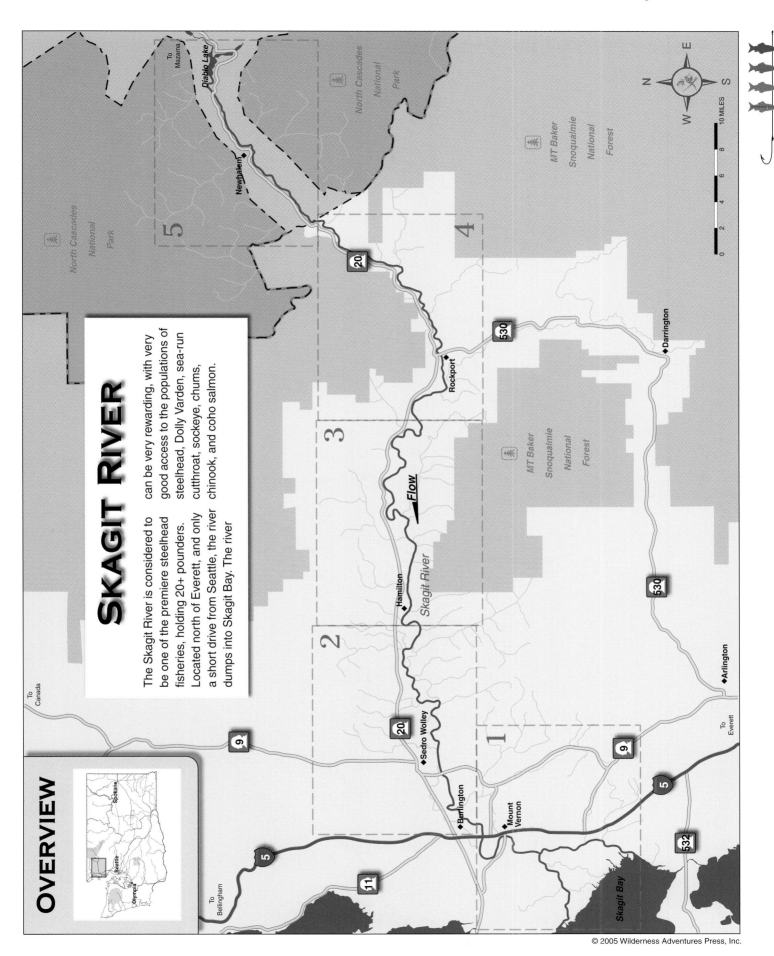

OVERVIEW

SKAGIT RIVER

The Skagit River is considered to be one of the premiere steelhead fisheries, holding 20+ pounders. Located north of Everett, and only a short drive from Seattle, the river dumps into Skagit Bay. The river can be very rewarding, with very good access to the populations of steelhead, Dolly Varden, sea-run cutthroat, sockeye, chums, chinook, and coho salmon.

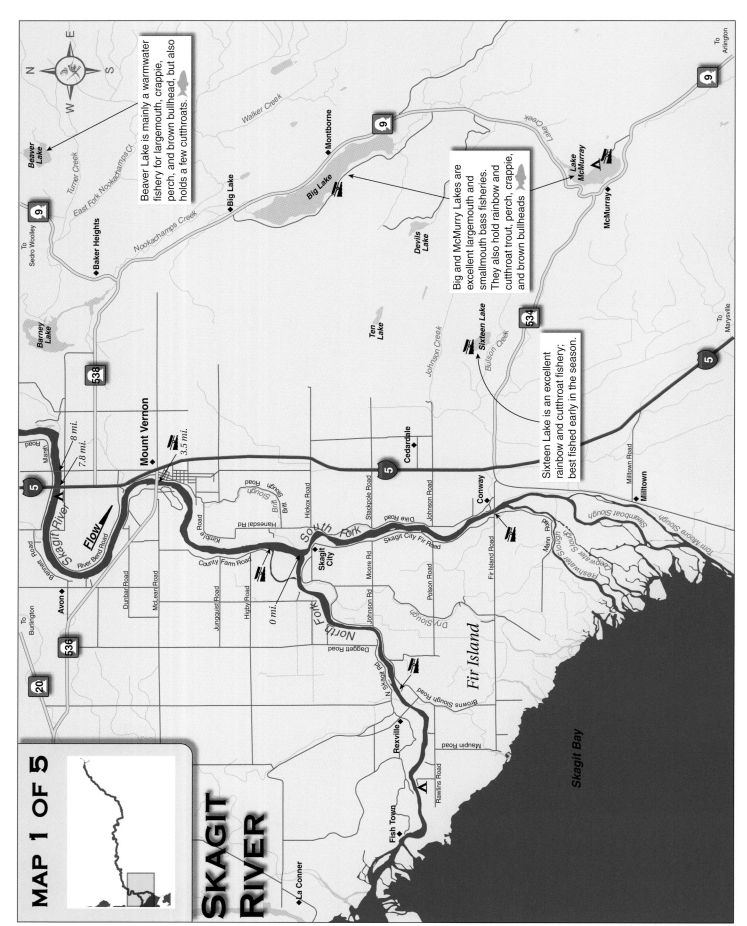

Beaver Lake is mainly a warmwater fishery for largemouth, crappie, perch, and brown bullhead, but also holds a few cutthroats.

Big and McMurry Lakes are excellent largemouth and smallmouth bass fisheries. They also hold rainbow and cutthroat trout, perch, crappie, and brown bullheads

Sixteen Lake is an excellent rainbow and cutthroat fishery; best fished early in the season.

MAP 1 OF 5

SKAGIT RIVER

© 2005 Wilderness Adventures Press, Inc.

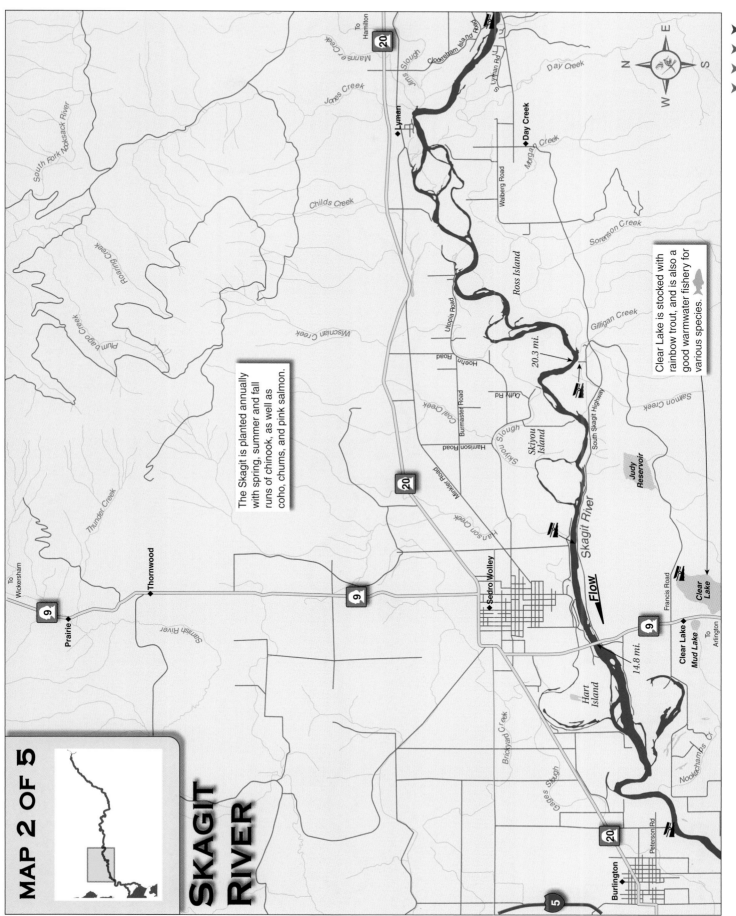

The Skagit is planted annually with spring, summer and fall runs of chinook, as well as coho, chums, and pink salmon.

Clear Lake is stocked with rainbow trout, and is also a good warmwater fishery for various species.

MAP 2 OF 5

SKAGIT RIVER

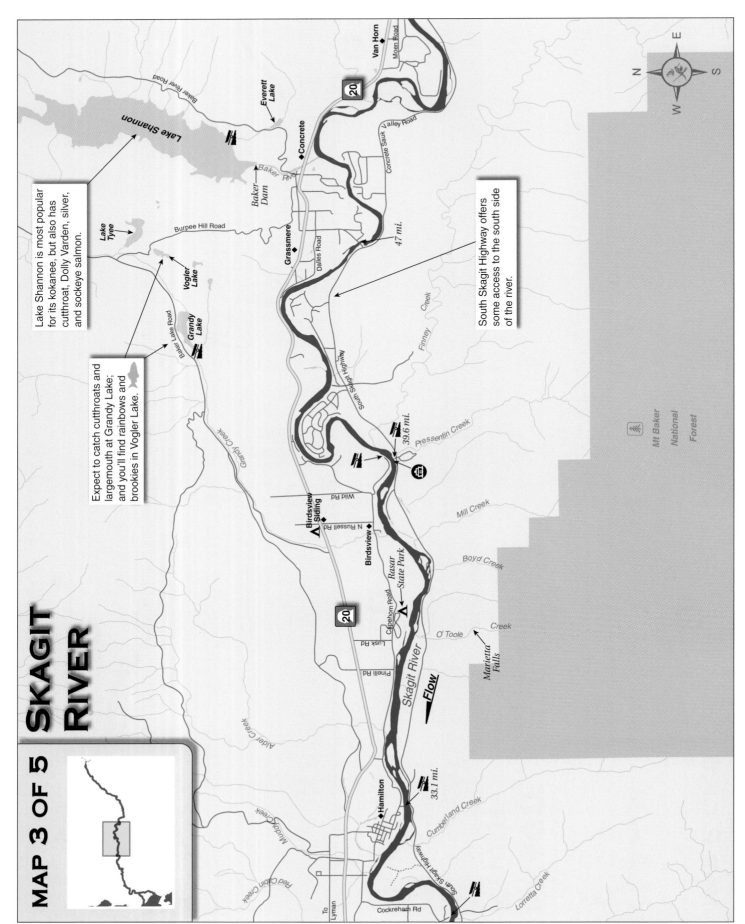

MAP 3 OF 5 | SKAGIT RIVER

Lake Shannon is most popular for its kokanee, but also has cutthroat, Dolly Varden, silver, and sockeye salmon.

Expect to catch cutthroats and largemouth at Grandy Lake; and you'll find rainbows and brookies in Vogler Lake.

South Skagit Highway offers some access to the south side of the river.

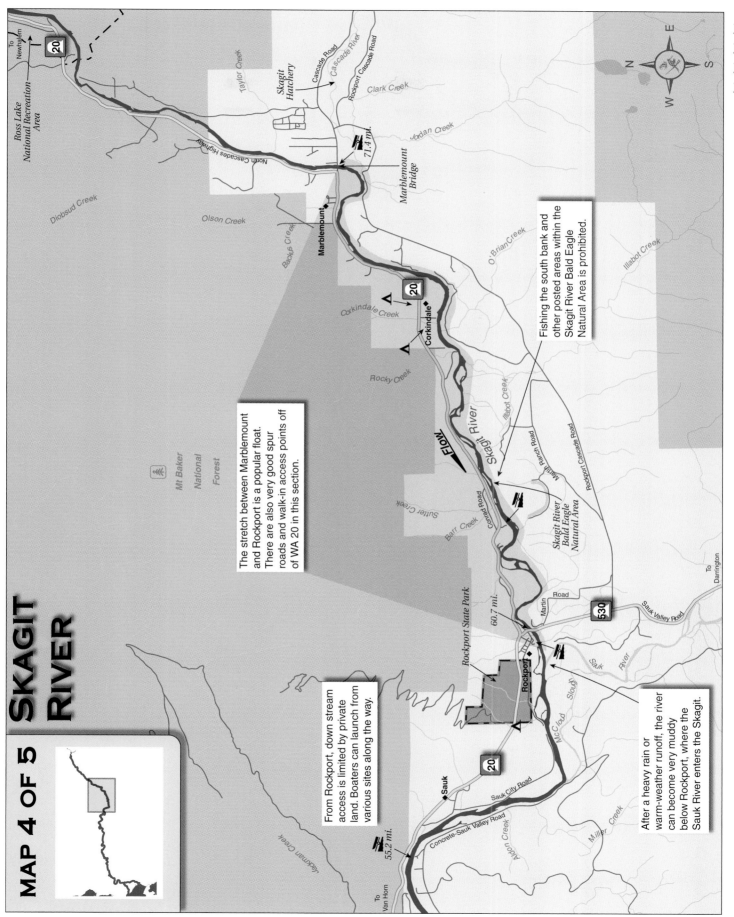

MAP 4 OF 5

SKAGIT RIVER

The stretch between Marblemount and Rockport is a popular float. There are also very good spur roads and walk-in access points off of WA 20 in this section.

From Rockport, down stream access is limited by private land. Boaters can launch from various sites along the way.

Fishing the south bank and other posted areas within the Skagit River Bald Eagle Natural Area is prohibited.

After a heavy rain or warm-weather runoff, the river can become very muddy below Rockport, where the Sauk River enters the Skagit.

FLOW

71.4 mi.

60.7 mi.

55.2 mi.

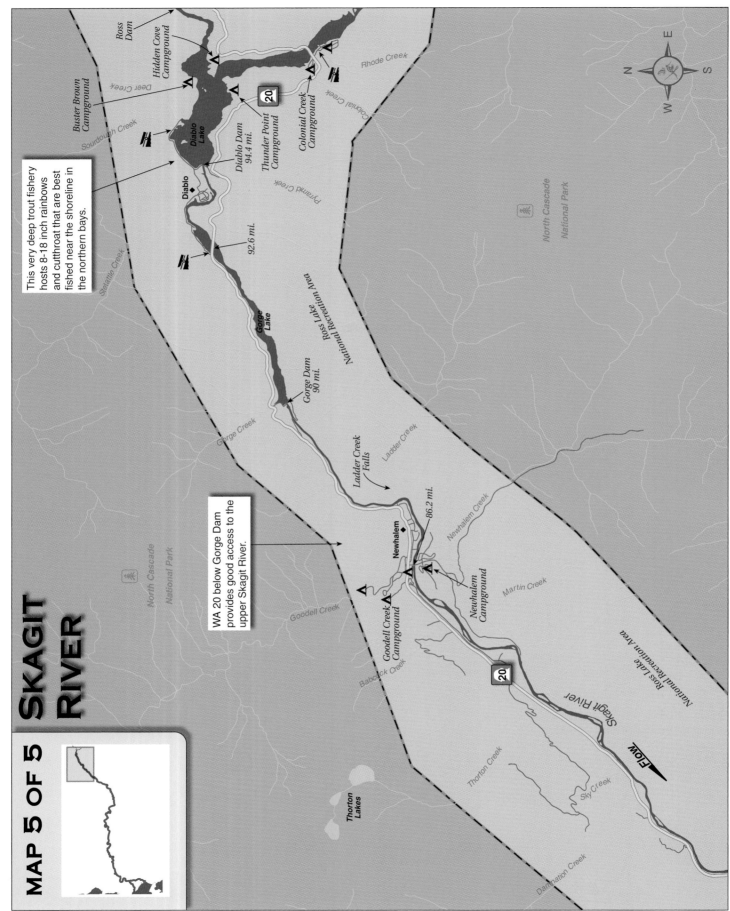

MAP 5 OF 5

SKAGIT RIVER

This very deep trout fishery hosts 8-18 inch rainbows and cutthroat that are best fished near the shoreline in the northern bays.

WA 20 below Gorge Dam provides good access to the upper Skagit River.

Ross Dam

Hidden Cove Campground

Buster Brown Campground

Deer Creek

Sourdough Creek

Diablo Lake

Diablo

Diablo Dam 94.4 mi.

Thunder Point Campground

Colonial Creek Campground

Colonial Creek

Rhode Creek

20

Stetattle Creek

92.6 mi.

Pyramid Creek

North Cascade National Park

Gorge Lake

Ross Lake National Recreation Area

Gorge Dam 90 mi.

Gorge Creek

Ladder Creek Falls

Ladder Creek

Newhalem Creek

North Cascade National Park

Newhalem

86.2 mi.

Goodell Creek

Goodell Creek Campground

Newhalem Campground

Martin Creek

Babcock Creek

20

Skagit River

Thorton Creek

Sky Creek

Thorton Lakes

Ross Lake National Recreation Area

FLOW

Damnation Creek

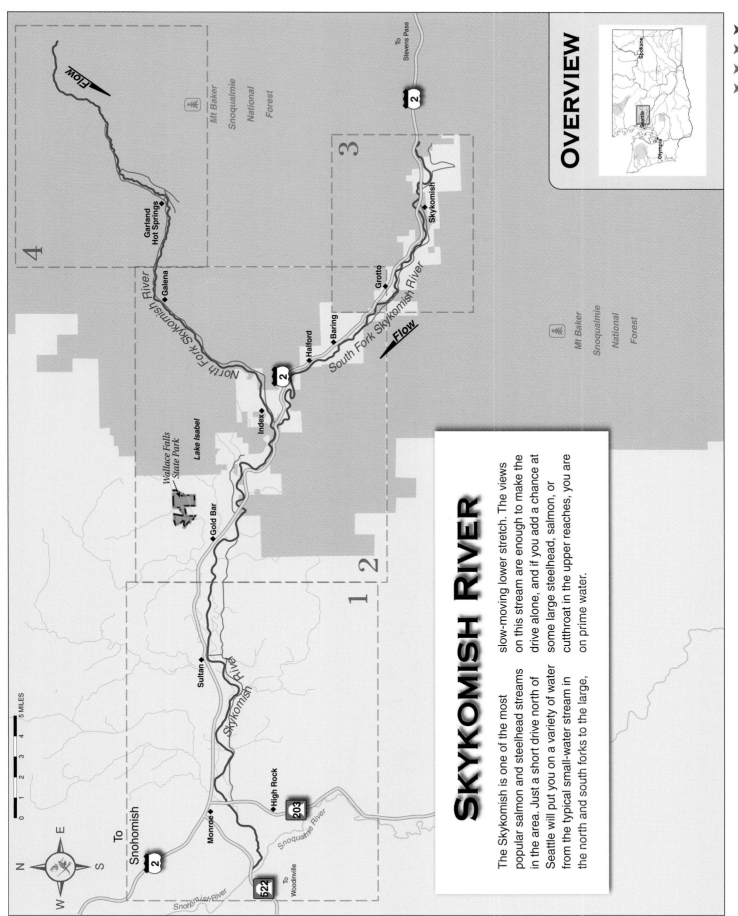

SKYKOMISH RIVER

The Skykomish is one of the most popular salmon and steelhead streams in the area. Just a short drive north of Seattle will put you on a variety of water from the typical small-water stream in the north and south forks to the large, slow-moving lower stretch. The views on this stream are enough to make the drive alone, and if you add a chance at some large steelhead, salmon, or cutthroat in the upper reaches, you are on prime water.

OVERVIEW

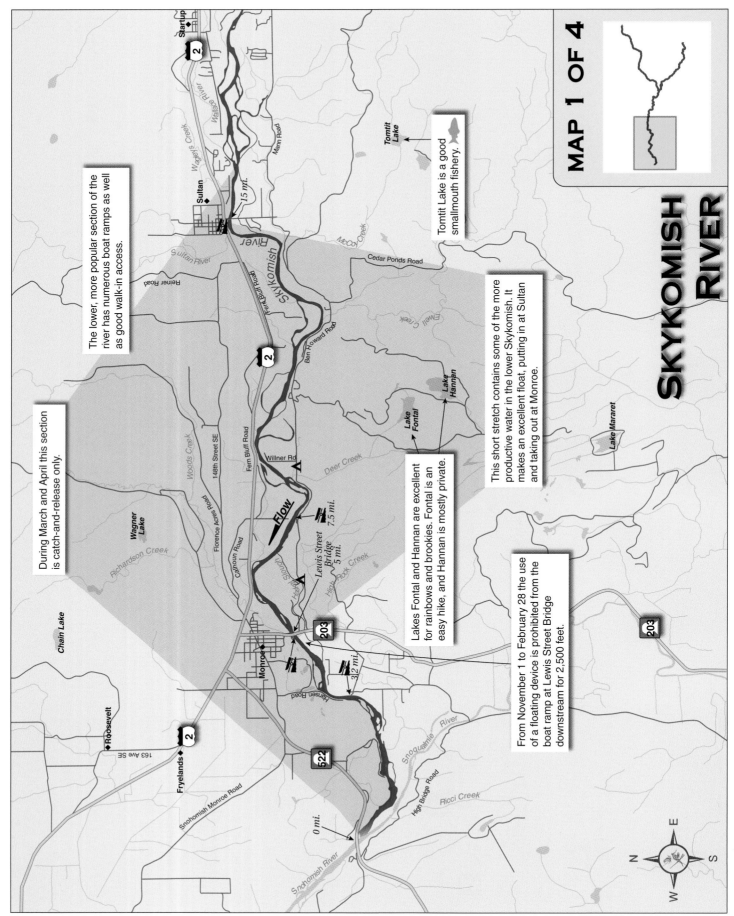

MAP 1 OF 4

SKYKOMISH RIVER

Tomtit Lake is a good smallmouth fishery.

The lower, more popular section of the river has numerous boat ramps as well as good walk-in access.

During March and April this section is catch-and-release only.

This short stretch contains some of the more productive water in the lower Skykomish. It makes an excellent float, putting in at Sultan and taking out at Monroe.

Lakes Fontal and Hannan are excellent for rainbows and brookies. Fontal is an easy hike, and Hannan is mostly private.

From November 1 to February 28 the use of a floating device is prohibited from the boat ramp at Lewis Street Bridge downstream for 2,500 feet.

Startup

Sultan

Monroe

Roosevelt

Fryelands

Wallace River

Wagley's Creek

Mann Road

Sultan River

Reiner Road

Fern Bluff Road

Skykomish River

Cedar Ponds Road

McCoy Creek

Ewell Creek

Lake Hannan

Lake Fontal

Lake Mararet

Ben Howard Road

148th Street SE

Woods Creek

Florence Acres Road

Wagner Lake

Richardson Creek

Chain Lake

Calhoun Road

Willner Rd

Deer Creek

Elwell Slough

High Rock Creek

Lewis Street Bridge

Flow

Hansen Road

163 Ave SE

Snohomish Monroe Road

Snoqualmie River

High Bridge Road

Ricci Creek

Snohomish River

Tomtit Lake

15 mi.

7.5 mi.

5 mi.

3.2 mi.

0 mi.

N E S W

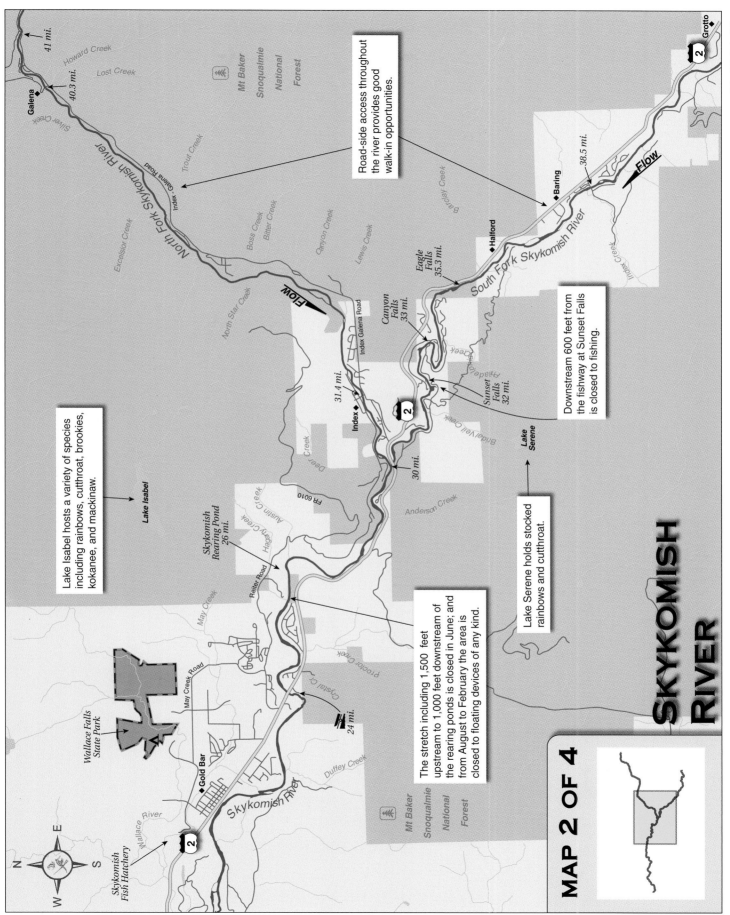

Road-side access throughout the river provides good walk-in opportunities.

Lake Isabel hosts a variety of species including rainbows, cutthroat, brookies, kokanee, and mackinaw.

Downstream 600 feet from the fishway at Sunset Falls is closed to fishing.

Lake Serene holds stocked rainbows and cutthroat.

The stretch including 1,500 feet upstream to 1,000 feet downstream of the rearing ponds is closed in June; and from August to February the area is closed to floating devices of any kind.

Mt Baker Snoqualmie National Forest

North Fork Skykomish River

South Fork Skykomish River

Skykomish River

Wallace River

Skykomish Fish Hatchery

Wallace Falls State Park

Lake Isabel

Lake Serene

Skykomish Rearing Pond 26 mi.

Eagle Falls 35.3 mi.

Canyon Falls 33 mi.

Sunset Falls 32 mi.

Galena

Grotto

Baring

Halford

Index

Gold Bar

41 mi.
40.3 mi.
38.5 mi.
31.4 mi.
30 mi.
24 mi.

Flow

Howard Creek
Lost Creek
Silver Creek
Trout Creek
Excelsior Creek
Boss Creek
Bitter Creek
Canyon Creek
Lewis Creek
North Star Creek
Barclay Creek
Index Creek
Philadelphia Creek
Bridal Veil Creek
Anderson Creek
Deer Creek
Austin Creek
Haggy Creek
May Creek
Proctor Creek
Crystal Cr.
Duffey Creek

Galena Road
Index Galena Road
Reiter Road
May Creek Road
FR 6010

N
E
S
W

SKYKOMISH RIVER

MAP 2 OF 4

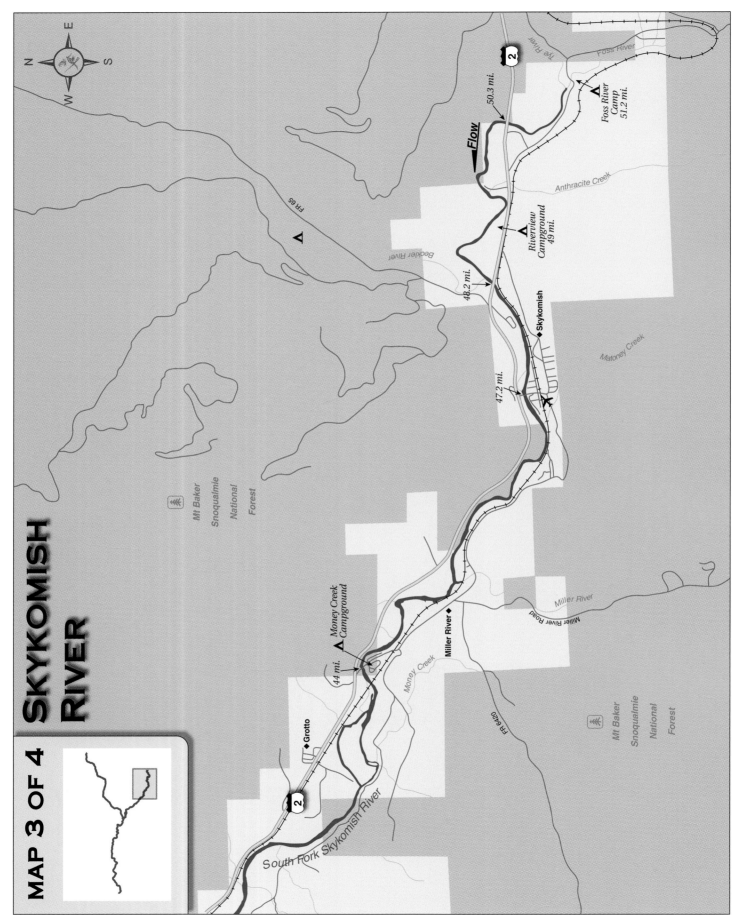

MAP **3** OF **4**

SKYKOMISH RIVER

Flow

50.3 mi.

Foss River Camp 51.2 mi.

Anthracite Creek

Riverview Campground 49 mi.

48.2 mi.

Becker River

Skykomish

Matoney Creek

47.2 mi.

Mt Baker Snoqualmie National Forest

Miller River

Miller River

Miller River Road

Money Creek Campground

44 mi.

Miller River

Money Creek

FR 020

Mt Baker Snoqualmie National Forest

Grotto

South Fork Skykomish River

FR 65

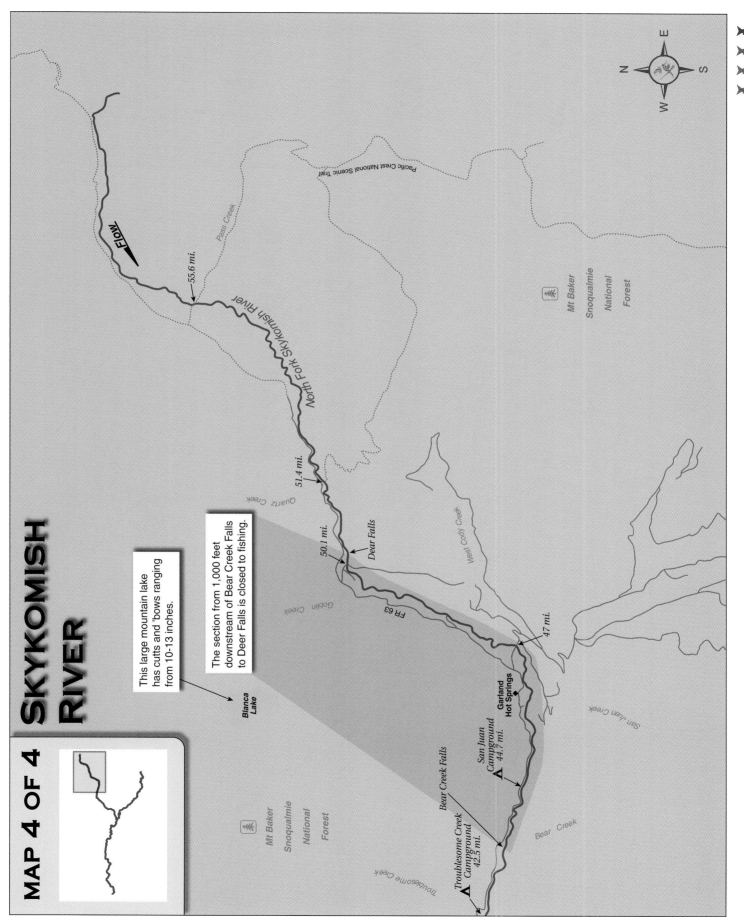

MAP 4 OF 4

SKYKOMISH RIVER

This large mountain lake has cutts and 'bows ranging from 10-13 inches.

The section from 1,000 feet downstream of Bear Creek Falls to Deer Falls is closed to fishing.

Blanca Lake

FLOW

55.6 mi.

51.4 mi.

North Fork Skykomish River

Pass Creek

Pacific Crest National Scenic Trail

Quartz Creek

50.1 mi.

Dear Falls

Goblin Creek

FR 63

47 mi.

West Cady Creek

Mt Baker Snoqualmie National Forest

San Juan Creek

Garland Hot Springs

San Juan Campground △ 44.7 mi.

Bear Creek Falls

Bear Creek

Troublesome Creek Campground △ 42.5 mi.

Troublesome Creek

Mt Baker Snoqualmie National Forest

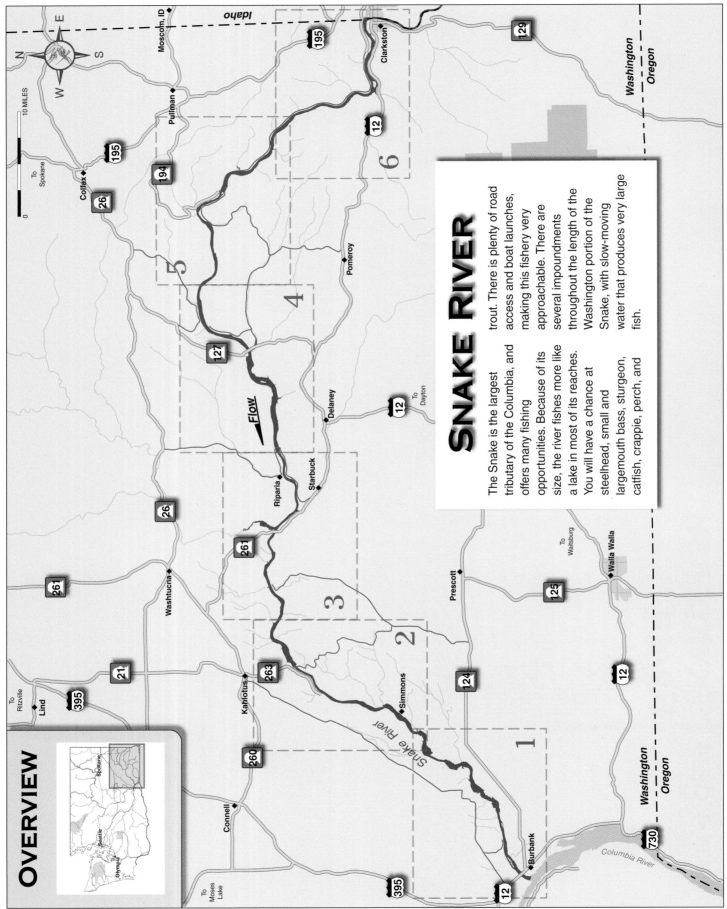

Snake River

The Snake is the largest tributary of the Columbia, and offers many fishing opportunities. Because of its size, the river fishes more like a lake in most of its reaches. You will have a chance at steelhead, small and largemouth bass, sturgeon, catfish, crappie, perch, and trout. There is plenty of road access and boat launches, making this fishery very approachable. There are several impoundments throughout the length of the Washington portion of the Snake, with slow-moving water that produces very large fish.

OVERVIEW

Flow

Snake River

Columbia River

Washington
Oregon

Idaho

Moscow, ID
Pullman
Colfax
Clarkston
Pomeroy
Delaney
Starbuck
Riparia
Washtucna
Kahlotus
Simmons
Prescott
Walla Walla
Connell
Lind
Burbank

To Spokane
To Ritzville
To Moses Lake
To Waitsburg
To Dayton

10 MILES

Seattle
Spokane
Olympia

195 · 129 · 12 · 194 · 26 · 127 · 261 · 26 · 261 · 21 · 395 · 263 · 260 · 124 · 125 · 12 · 730 · 395

1 · 2 · 3 · 4 · 5 · 6

MAP 1 OF 6

SNAKE RIVER

The Snake has two primary draws: smallmouth fishing in the spring and summer, and steelhead fishing in the fall and winter.

Votaw

Page

Snake River

FLOW

Fishhook Park 19.5 mi.

Redd

Emma Lake

McClenny Road

Page Road

Kikkundt Road

Pasco - Kahlotus Road

Murphy Road

Herman Road

Delton Lake

15 mi.

Levey Park 13.5 mi.

Levey

Lake Sacajawea

Ash

Charbonneau Park

Columbia Plateau Trail State Park

Ice Harbor Road

Ice Harbor Dam Fish Ladder 9.6 mi.

Ice Harbor Drive

Adkins

Welland

124

Adkins Road

Slater Road

Slater

Humorist

Burbank Slough

Dam

Lake Wallula

Sand Dunes

Martindale

Martindale Road

Pasco - Kahlotus Road

124

McNary National Wildlife Refuge

Burbank Heights

Burbank

2.1 mi.

Ainsworth

To Pasco

12

12

To Wallula

0 mi.

Columbia River

Sacajawea State Park

N E S W

© 2005 Wilderness Adventures Press, Inc.

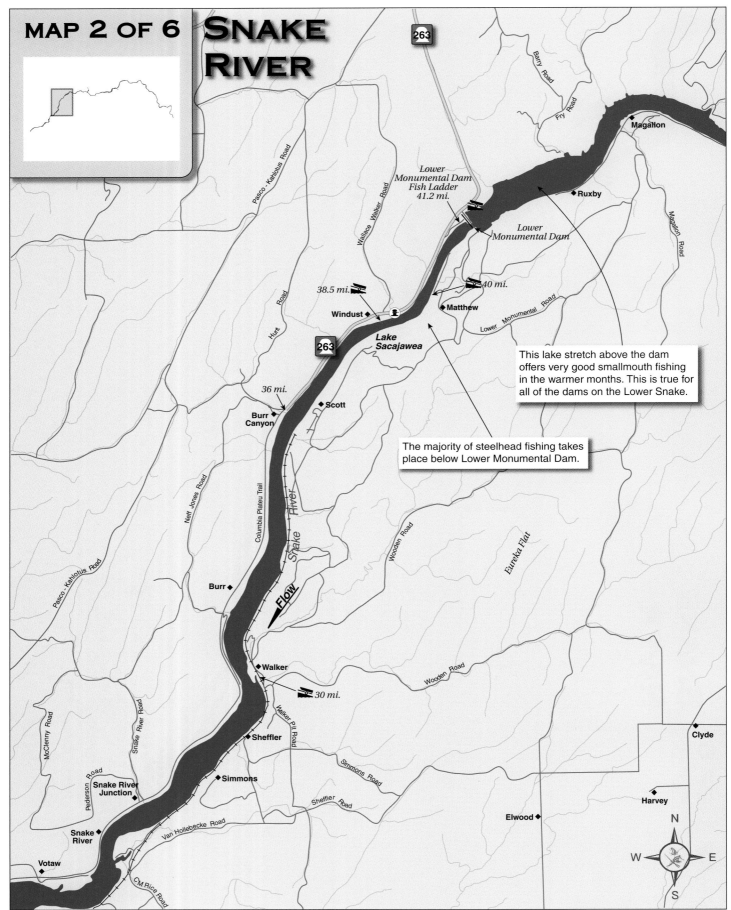

MAP 2 OF 6 **SNAKE RIVER**

263

Magallon

Fry Road

Barry Road

Ruxby

Lower Monumental Dam Fish Ladder 41.2 mi.

Lower Monumental Dam

Magallon Road

Pasco - Kahlotus Road

Wallace Walker Road

38.5 mi.

40 mi.

Windust

Matthew

Lower Monumental Road

Road

Hunt

263

Lake Sacajawea

This lake stretch above the dam offers very good smallmouth fishing in the warmer months. This is true for all of the dams on the Lower Snake.

36 mi.

Scott

Burr Canyon

The majority of steelhead fishing takes place below Lower Monumental Dam.

Neff Jones Road

Columbia Plateau Trail

Snake River

Wooden Road

Eureka Flat

Burr

Flow

Pasco - Kahlotus Road

Walker

30 mi.

Wooden Road

Clyde

McClenny Road

Walker Pit Road

Sheffler

Simmons Road

Simmons

Pederson Road

Snake River Road

Harvey

Snake River Junction

Sheffler Road

Elwood

Snake River

Van Hollebecke Road

Votaw

CM Rice Road

N
W E
S

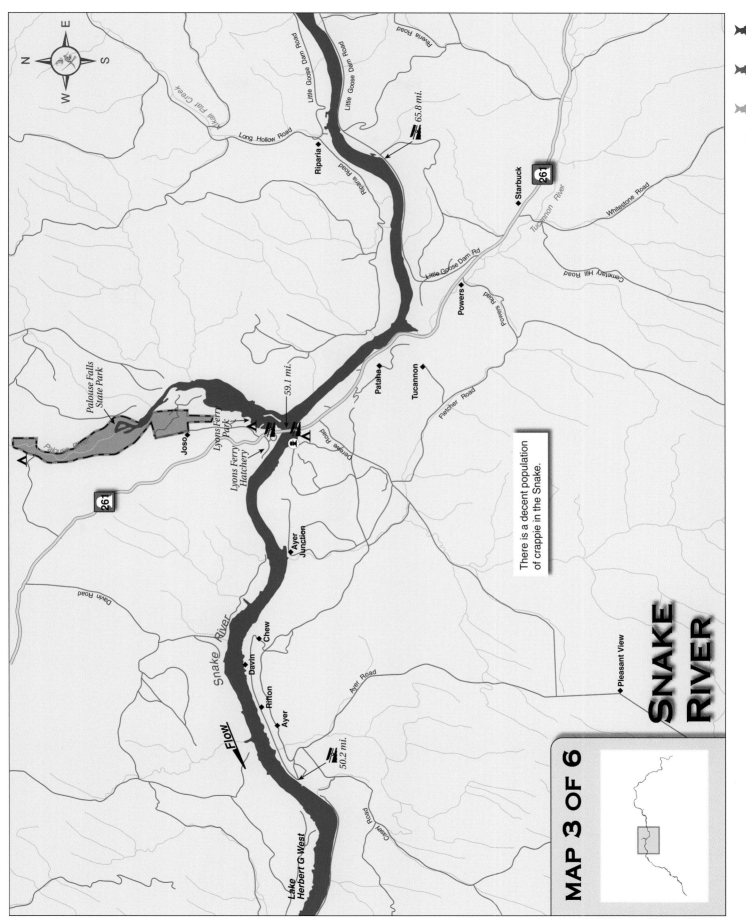

There is a decent population of crappie in the Snake.

MAP 3 OF 6

SNAKE
RIVER

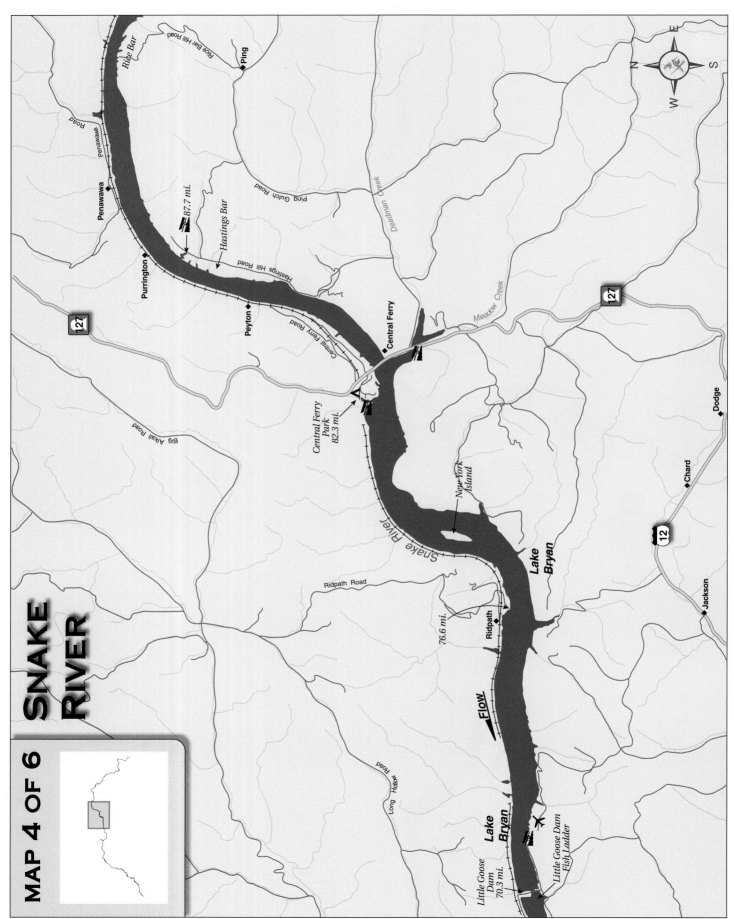

MAP 4 OF 6

SNAKE RIVER

© 2005 Wilderness Adventures Press, Inc.

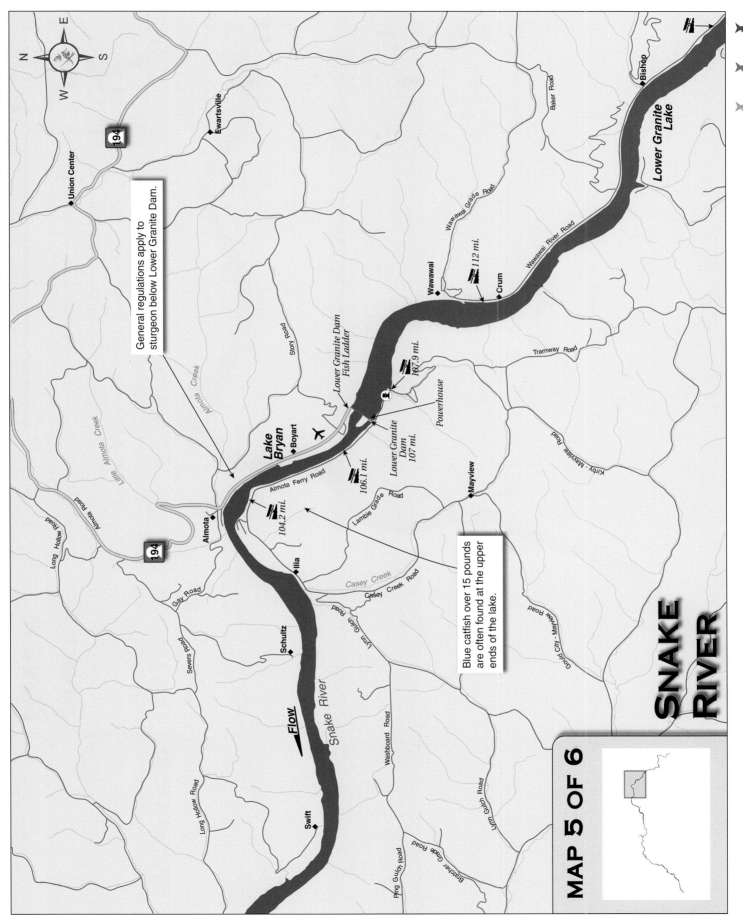

General regulations apply to sturgeon below Lower Granite Dam.

Blue catfish over 15 pounds are often found at the upper ends of the lake.

Lower Granite Lake

Bishop

Baker Road

112 mi.

Wawawai Grade Road

Wawawai

Crum

Wawawai River Road

Tramway Road

107.9 mi.

Lower Granite Dam Fish Ladder

Powerhouse

Kirby - Mayview Road

Story Road

Ewartsville

194

Union Center

Almota Creek

Little Almota Creek

Lake Bryan

Boyart

106.1 mi.

Lower Granite Dam 107 mi.

Mayview

Almota Ferry Road

Lambie Grade Road

Almota Road

Long Hollow Road

Almota

104.2 mi.

194

Illia

Gay Road

Casey Creek

Casey Creek

Casey Creek Road

Sewers Road

Lynn Gulch Road

Gould City - Mayview Road

Schultz

Flow

Snake River

Washboard Road

Long Hollow Road

Swift

Ping Gulch Road

Blatcher Grade Road

Lynn Gulch Road

SNAKE RIVER

MAP 5 OF 6

© 2005 Wilderness Adventures Press, Inc.

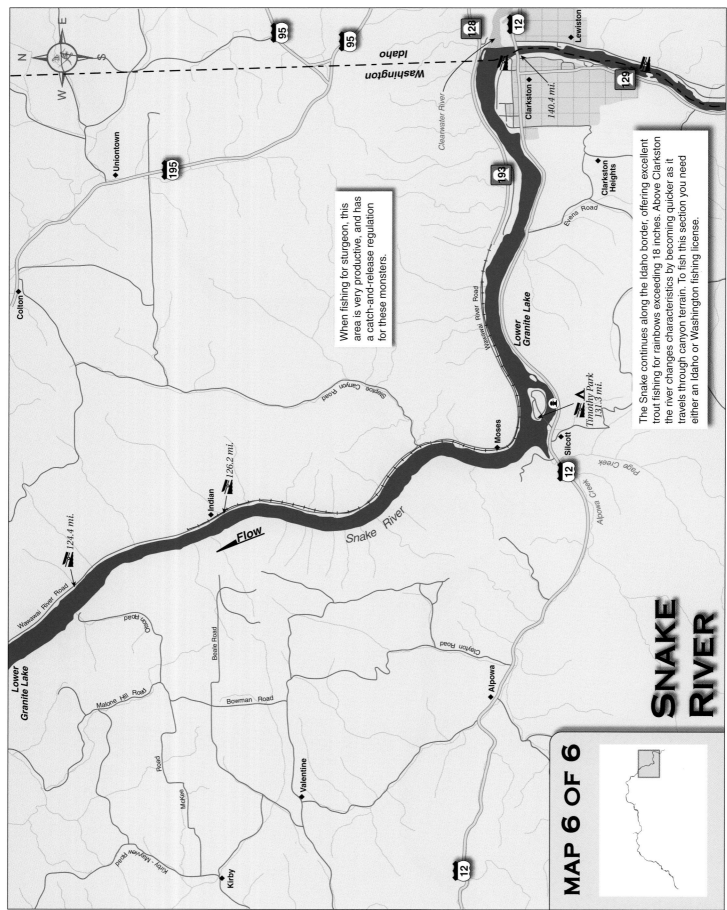

When fishing for sturgeon, this area is very productive, and has a catch-and-release regulation for these monsters.

The Snake continues along the Idaho border, offering excellent trout fishing for rainbows exceeding 18 inches. Above Clarkston the river changes characteristics by becoming quicker as it travels through canyon terrain. To fish this section you need either an Idaho or Washington fishing license.

SNAKE RIVER

MAP 6 OF 6

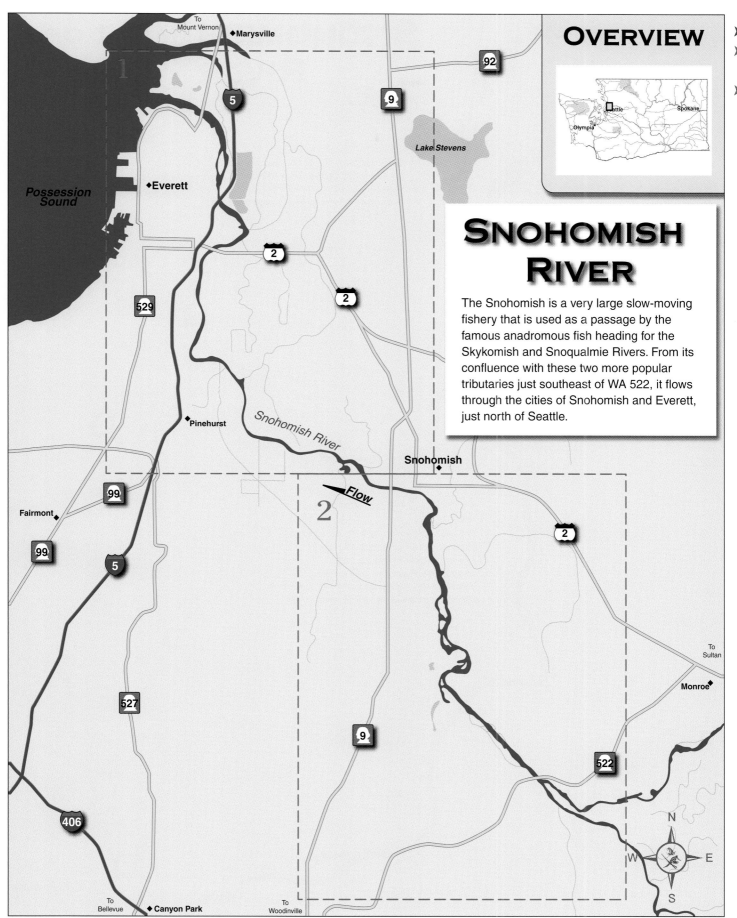

OVERVIEW

SNOHOMISH RIVER

The Snohomish is a very large slow-moving fishery that is used as a passage by the famous anadromous fish heading for the Skykomish and Snoqualmie Rivers. From its confluence with these two more popular tributaries just southeast of WA 522, it flows through the cities of Snohomish and Everett, just north of Seattle.

Possession Sound

◆Everett

Marysville

To Mount Vernon

Lake Stevens

Snohomish River

◆Pinehurst

Snohomish

Fairmont

Flow

2

To Sultan

Monroe◆

To Bellevue ◆Canyon Park

To Woodinville

N
W   E
S

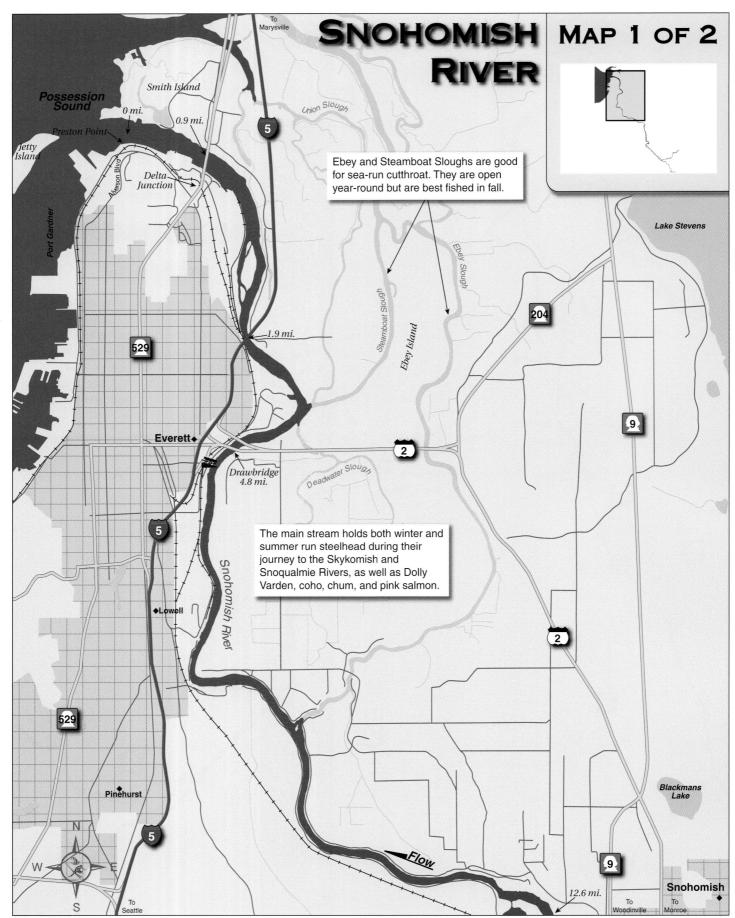

SNOHOMISH RIVER MAP 1 OF 2

Ebey and Steamboat Sloughs are good for sea-run cutthroat. They are open year-round but are best fished in fall.

The main stream holds both winter and summer run steelhead during their journey to the Skykomish and Snoqualmie Rivers, as well as Dolly Varden, coho, chum, and pink salmon.

© 2005 Wilderness Adventures Press, Inc.

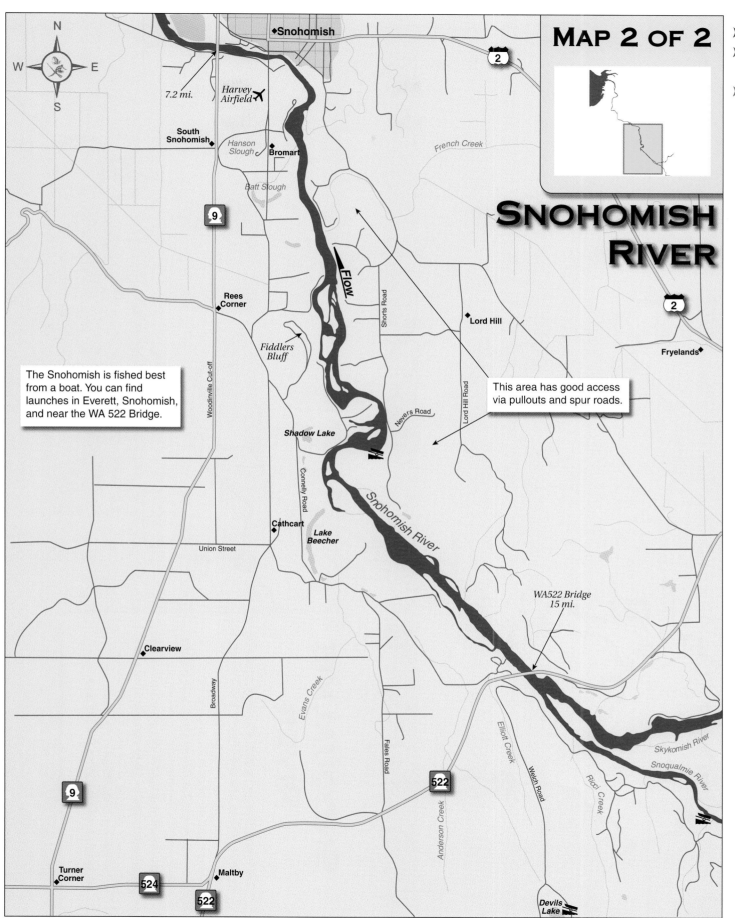

MAP 2 OF 2

SNOHOMISH
RIVER

The Snohomish is fished best from a boat. You can find launches in Everett, Snohomish, and near the WA 522 Bridge.

This area has good access via pullouts and spur roads.

Snohomish

7.2 mi.

Harvey Airfield

South Snohomish

Hanson Slough

Bromart

Batt Slough

French Creek

Rees Corner

Fiddlers Bluff

Shorts Road

Lord Hill

Fryelands

Woodinville Cut-off

Neyer's Road

Lord Hill Road

Shadow Lake

Connelly Road

Snohomish River

Cathcart

Lake Beecher

Union Street

WA522 Bridge 15 mi.

Clearview

Evans Creek

Broadway

Fales Road

Elliott Creek

Welch Road

Skykomish River

Snoqualmie River

Ricci Creek

Anderson Creek

Turner Corner

Maltby

Devils Lake

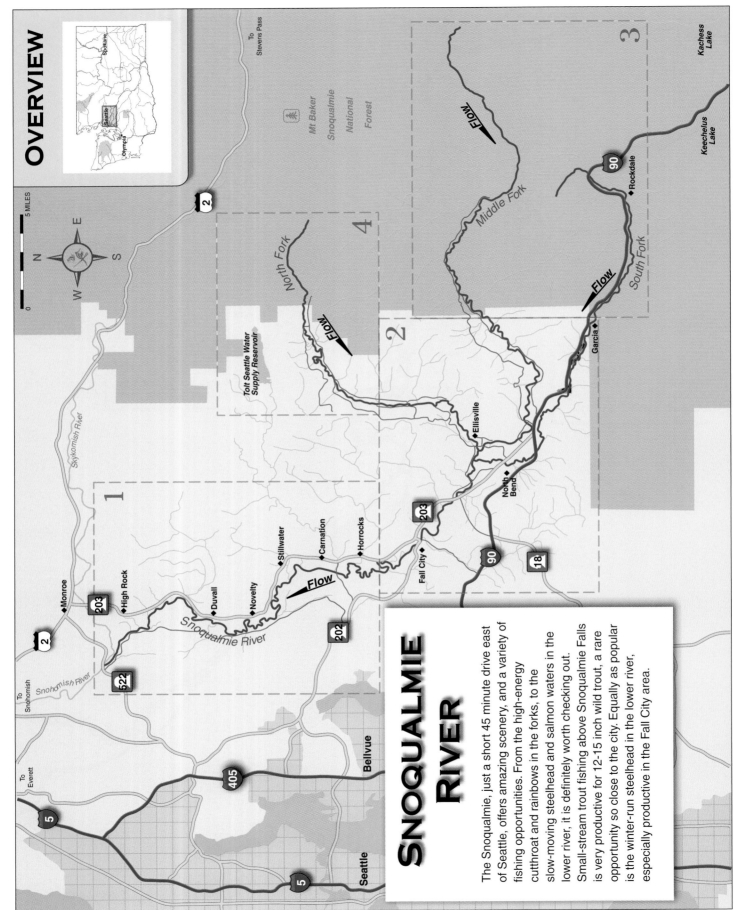

OVERVIEW

SNOQUALMIE RIVER

The Snoqualmie, just a short 45 minute drive east of Seattle, offers amazing scenery, and a variety of fishing opportunities. From the high-energy cutthroat and rainbows in the forks, to the slow-moving steelhead and salmon waters in the lower river, it is definitely worth checking out. Small-stream trout fishing above Snoqualmie Falls is very productive for 12-15 inch wild trout, a rare opportunity so close to the city. Equally as popular is the winter-run steelhead in the lower river, especially productive in the Fall City area.

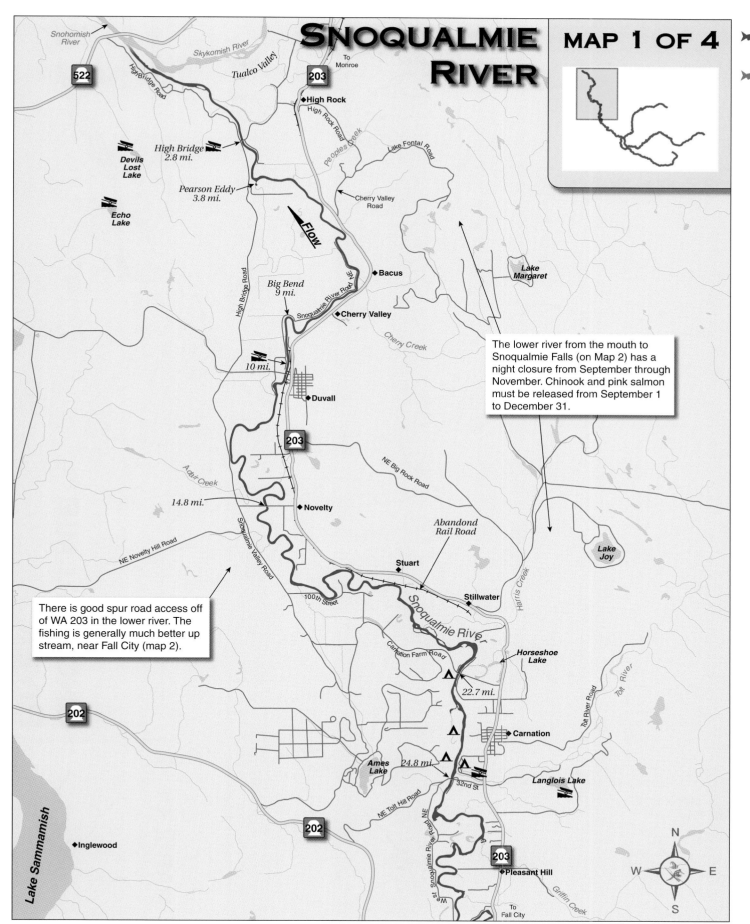

SNOQUALMIE RIVER

MAP 1 OF 4

To Monroe

High Rock

High Bridge
2.8 mi.

**Devils
Lost
Lake**

Pearson Eddy
3.8 mi.

**Echo
Lake**

Flow

Bacus

Big Bend
9 mi.

Cherry Valley

**Lake
Margaret**

The lower river from the mouth to Snoqualmie Falls (on Map 2) has a night closure from September through November. Chinook and pink salmon must be released from September 1 to December 31.

10 mi.

Duvall

14.8 mi.

Novelty

*Abandond
Rail Road*

**Lake
Joy**

There is good spur road access off of WA 203 in the lower river. The fishing is generally much better up stream, near Fall City (map 2).

Stuart

Stillwater

100th Street

*Horseshoe
Lake*

22.7 mi.

24.8 mi.

Carnation

**Ames
Lake**

32nd St.

Langlois Lake

Inglewood

Pleasant Hill

To Fall City

N
W E
S

© 2005 Wilderness Adventures Press, Inc.

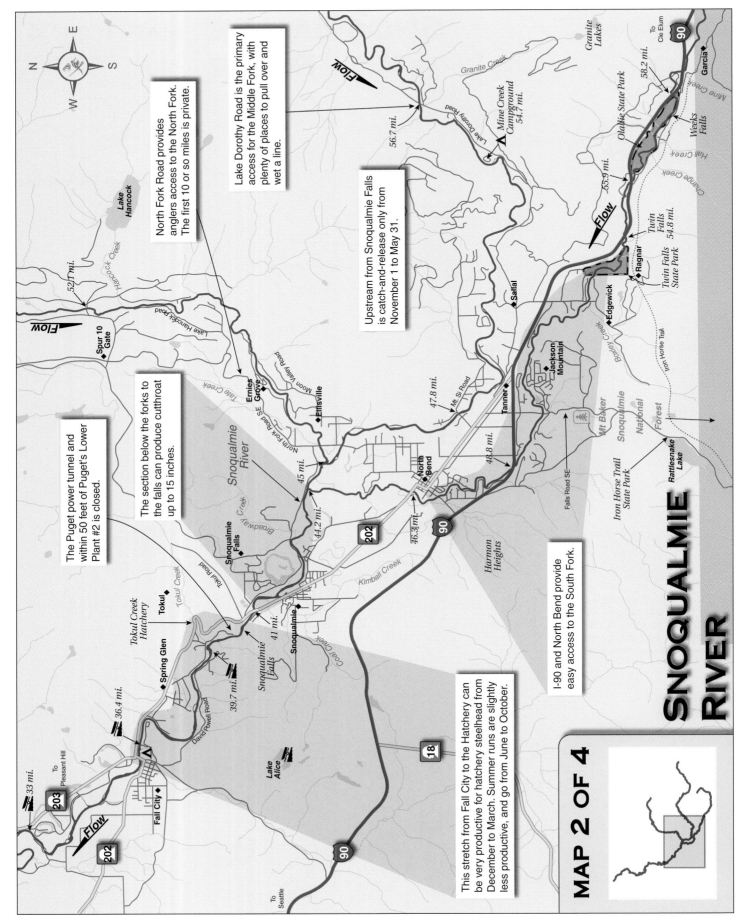

North Fork Road provides anglers access to the North Fork. The first 10 or so miles is private.

Lake Dorothy Road is the primary access for the Middle Fork, with plenty of places to pull over and wet a line.

Upstream from Snoqualmie Falls is catch-and-release only from November 1 to May 31.

The section below the forks to the falls can produce cutthroat up to 15 inches.

The Puget power tunnel and within 50 feet of Puget's Lower Plant #2 is closed.

This stretch from Fall City to the Hatchery can be very productive for hatchery steelhead from December to March. Summer runs are slightly less productive, and go from June to October.

I-90 and North Bend provide easy access to the South Fork.

SNOQUALMIE RIVER

MAP 2 OF 4

© 2005 Wilderness Adventures Press, Inc.

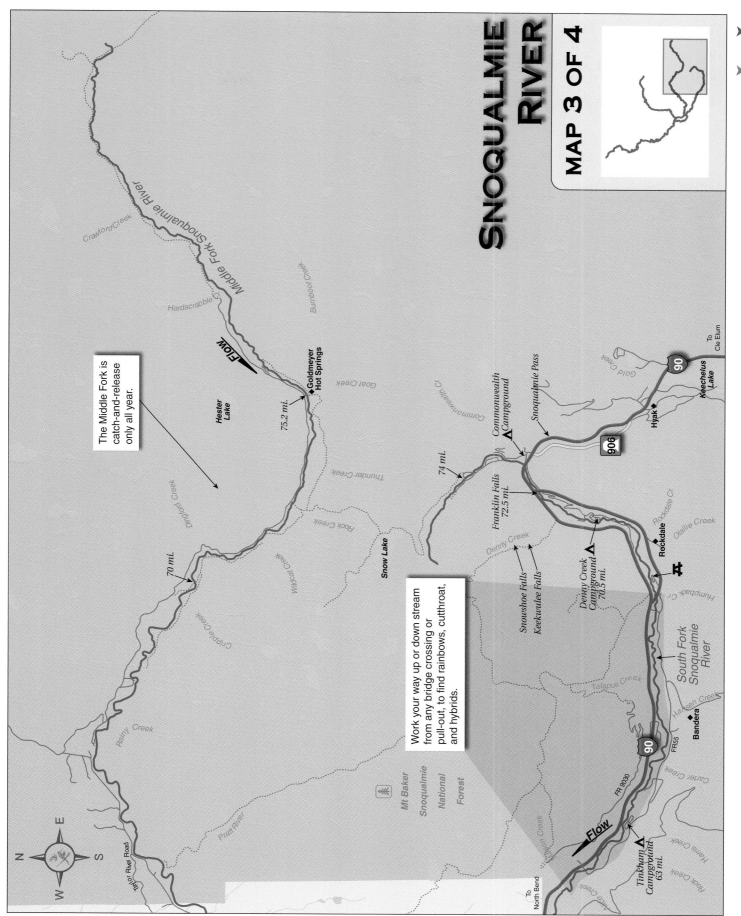

SNOQUALMIE RIVER

MAP 3 OF 4

The Middle Fork is catch-and-release only all year.

Work your way up or down stream from any bridge crossing or pull-out, to find rainbows, cutthroat, and hybrids.

Middle Fork Snoqualmie River

Crawford Creek

Hardscrabble Cr.

Burnboot Creek

Flow

Goldmeyer Hot Springs

75.2 mi.

Hester Lake

Goat Creek

Diablold Creek

Thunder Creek

Rock Creek

Commonwealth Cr

Commonwealth Campground

Snoqualmie Pass

To Cle Elum

90

Gold Creek

Hyak

Keechelus Lake

906

74 mi.

Franklin Falls
72.5 mi.

Denny Creek

Snowshoe Falls

Keekwulee Falls

Rockdale Cr

Rockdale

Olallie Creek

Denny Creek Campground
70.5 mi.

70 mi.

Wildcat Cr

Snow Lake

Cripple Creek

Humpback Cr.

South Fork Snoqualmie River

Rainy Creek

Talapus Creek

Hansen Creek

Bandera

90

FR55

FR 9030

Carter Creek

Mt Baker Snoqualmie National Forest

Pratt River

Taylor River Road

N
E
S
W

Talpus Creek

Flow

Tinkham Campground
63 mi.

To North Bend

Rock Creek

Harris Creek

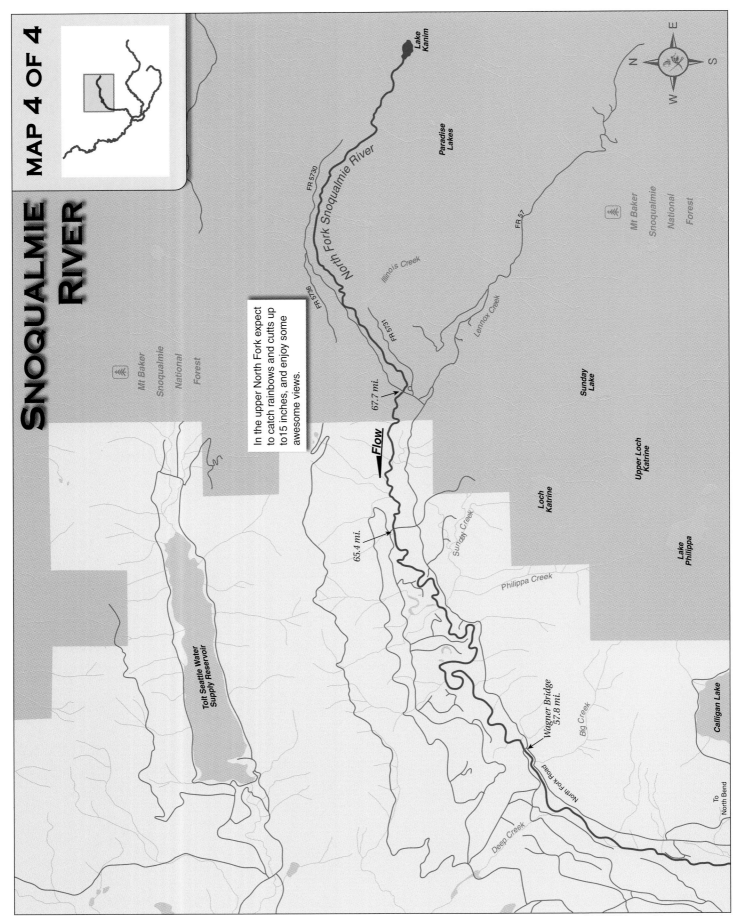

SNOQUALMIE RIVER

MAP 4 OF 4

In the upper North Fork expect to catch rainbows and cutts up to15 inches, and enjoy some awesome views.

North Fork Snoqualmie River

Lake Kanim

Paradise Lakes

FR 5730

FR 5736

FR 5731

Illinois Creek

Lennox Creek

FR 57

Mt Baker Snoqualmie National Forest

Mt Baker Snoqualmie National Forest

67.7 mi.

Flow

65.4 mi.

Sunday Creek

Sunday Lake

Upper Loch Katrine

Loch Katrine

Lake Philippa

Philippa Creek

Tolt Seattle Water Supply Reservoir

Wagner Bridge 57.8 mi.

Big Creek

North Fork Road

Deep Creek

Calligan Lake

To North Bend

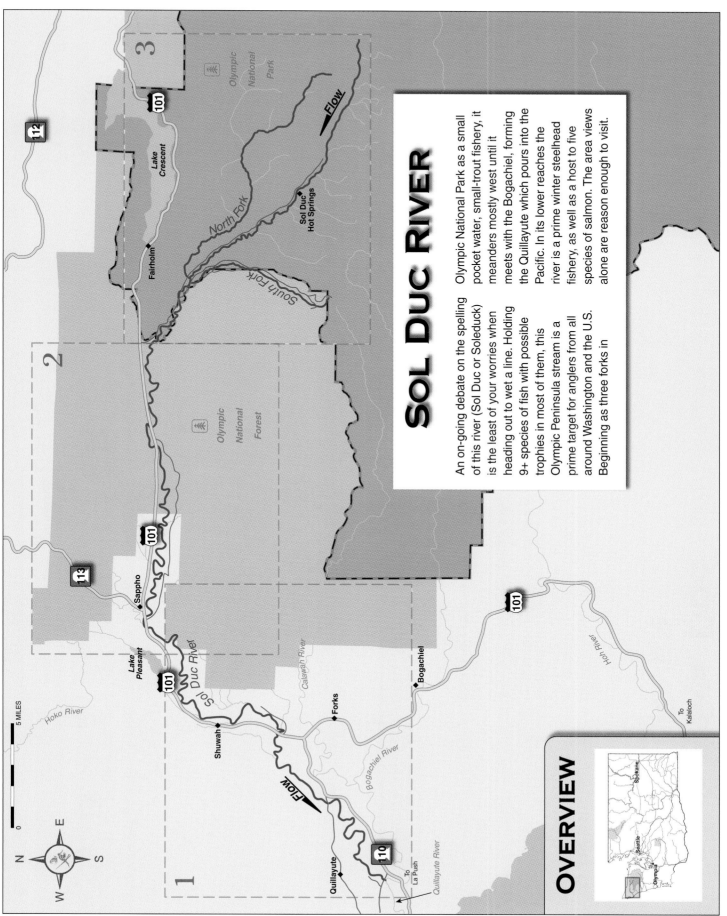

SOL DUC RIVER

An on-going debate on the spelling of this river (Sol Duc or Soleduck) is the least of your worries when heading out to wet a line. Holding 9+ species of fish with possible trophies in most of them, this Olympic Peninsula stream is a prime target for anglers from all around Washington and the U.S. Beginning as three forks in

Olympic National Park as a small pocket water, small-trout fishery, it meanders mostly west until it meets with the Bogachiel, forming the Quillayute which pours into the Pacific. In its lower reaches the river is a prime winter steelhead fishery, as well as a host to five species of salmon. The area views alone are reason enough to visit.

OVERVIEW

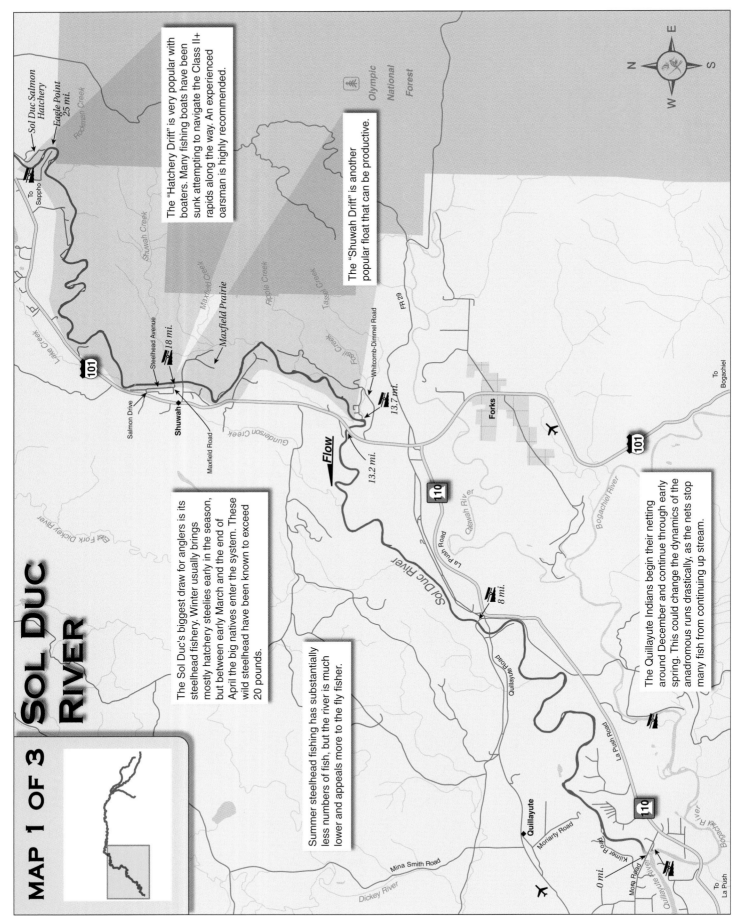

MAP 1 OF 3 | SOL DUC RIVER

The "Hatchery Drift" is very popular with boaters. Many fishing boats have been sunk attempting to navigate the Class II+ rapids along the way. An experienced oarsman is highly recommended.

The "Shuwah Drift" is another popular float that can be productive.

The Sol Duc's biggest draw for anglers is its steelhead fishery. Winter usually brings mostly hatchery steelies early in the season, but between early March and the end of April the big natives enter the system. These wild steelhead have been known to exceed 20 pounds.

Summer steelhead fishing has substantially less numbers of fish, but the river is much lower and appeals more to the fly fisher.

The Quillayute Indians begin their netting around December and continue through early spring. This could change the dynamics of the anadromous runs drastically, as the nets stop many fish from continuing up stream.

Sol Duc Salmon Hatchery
Eagle Point 25 mi.
To Sappho
Rockman Creek
Lake Creek
Steelhead Avenue
18 mi.
Salmon Drive
Shuwah
Maxfield Road
Shuwah Creek
Maxfield Creek
Maxfield Prairie
Apple Creek
Tassel Creek
Gunderson Creek
Flow
13.7 mi.
13.2 mi.
Whitcomb-Dimmel Road
FR 29
Forks
Olympic National Forest
To Bogachiel
East Fork Dickey River
Calawah River
La Push Road
Bogachiel River
8 mi.
Quillayute Road
Quillayute
Moriarty Road
Mina Smith Road
Dickey River
0 mi.
Kilmer Road
Mora Road
To La Push
Quillayute River
Bogachiel
101
110
110
101

© 2005 Wilderness Adventures Press, Inc.

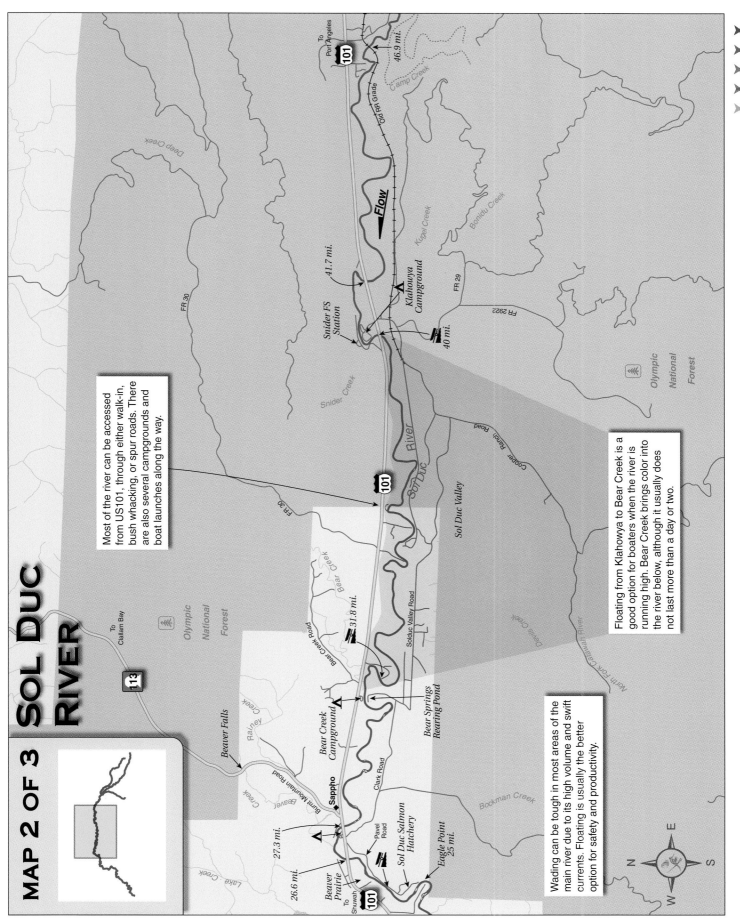

MAP 2 OF 3 SOL DUC RIVER

Most of the river can be accessed from US101, through either walk-in, bush whacking, or spur roads. There are also several campgrounds and boat launches along the way.

Floating from Klahowya to Bear Creek is a good option for boaters when the river is running high. Bear Creek brings color into the river below, although it usually does not last more than a day or two.

Wading can be tough in most areas of the main river due to its high volume and swift currents. Floating is usually the better option for safety and productivity.

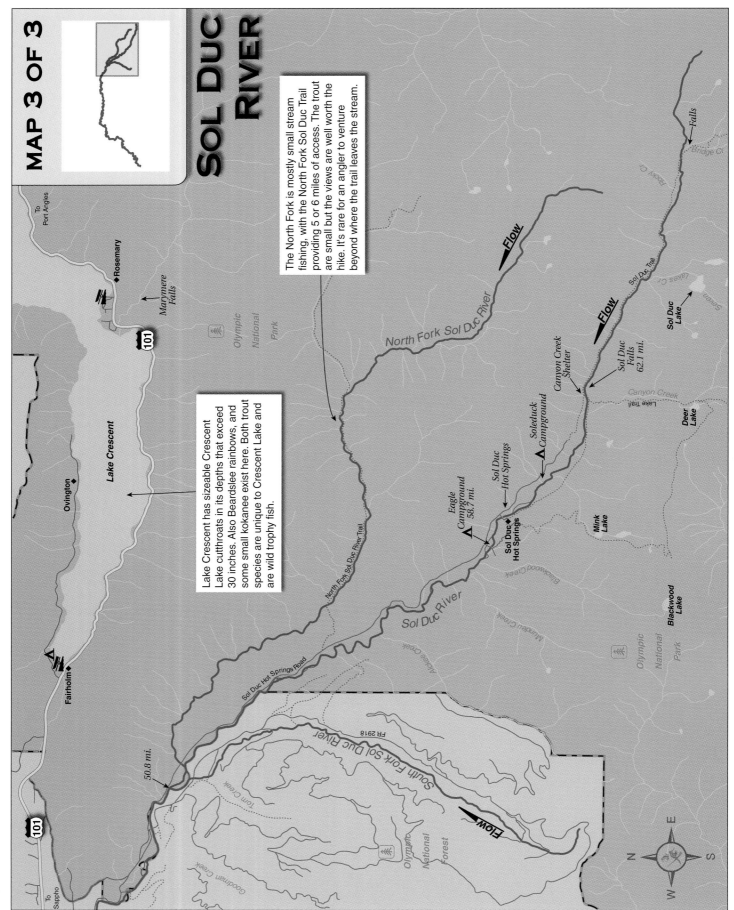

MAP 3 OF 3

SOL DUC RIVER

The North Fork is mostly small stream fishing, with the North Fork Sol Duc Trail providing 5 or 6 miles of access. The trout are small but the views are well worth the hike. It's rare for an angler to venture beyond where the trail leaves the stream.

Lake Crescent has sizeable Crescent Lake cutthroats in its depths that exceed 30 inches. Also Beardslee rainbows, and some small kokanee exist here. Both trout species are unique to Crescent Lake and are wild trophy fish.

To Port Angeles

Rosemary

Marymere Falls

101

Lake Crescent

Ovington

Fairholm

To Sappho

101

Olympic National Park

North Fork Sol Duc River

North Fork Sol Duc River Trail

Flow

Flow

Sol Duc River

Sol Duc Hot Springs Road

50.8 mi.

Tom Creek

Goodman Creek

Eagle Campground 58.7 mi.

Sol Duc Hot Springs

Sol Duc Hot Springs

Soleduck Campground

Canyon Creek Shelter

Sol Duc Falls 62.1 mi.

Canyon Creek

Lake Trail

Deer Lake

Sol Duc Lac Trail

Sol Duc Lake

Lakes Cr.

Falls

Bridge Cr.

Rocky Cr.

Mink Lake

Blackwood Lake

Blackwood Creek

Murdaue Creek

Aideaa Creek

Olympic National Park

South Fork Sol Duc River

FR 2918

Flow

Olympic National Forest

N E S W

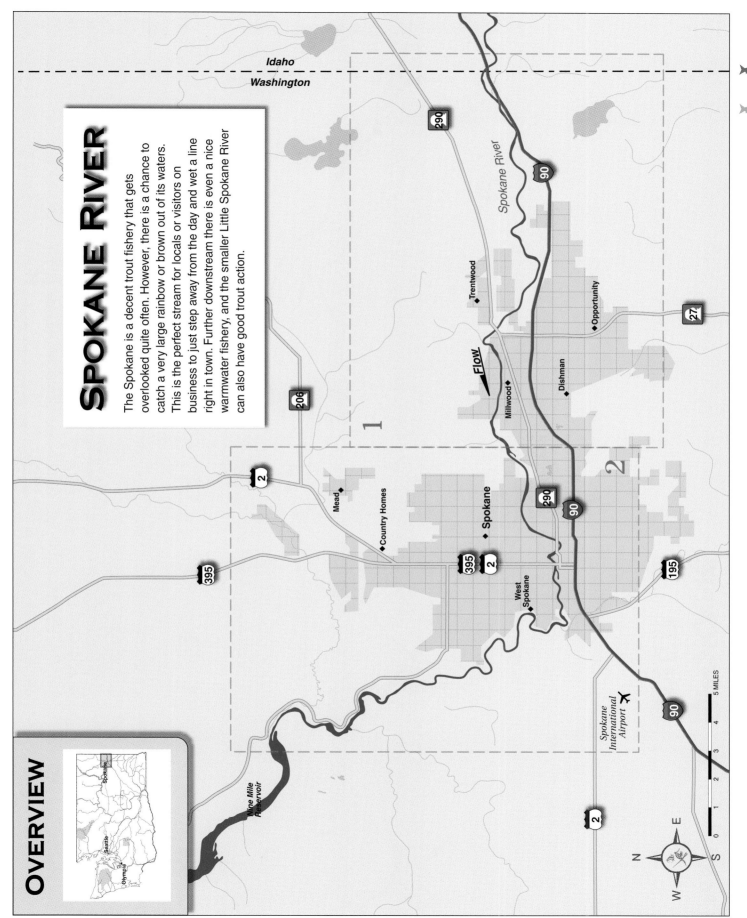

SPOKANE RIVER

The Spokane is a decent trout fishery that gets overlooked quite often. However, there is a chance to catch a very large rainbow or brown out of its waters. This is the perfect stream for locals or visitors on business to just step away from the day and wet a line right in town. Further downstream there is even a nice warmwater fishery, and the smaller Little Spokane River can also have good trout action.

OVERVIEW

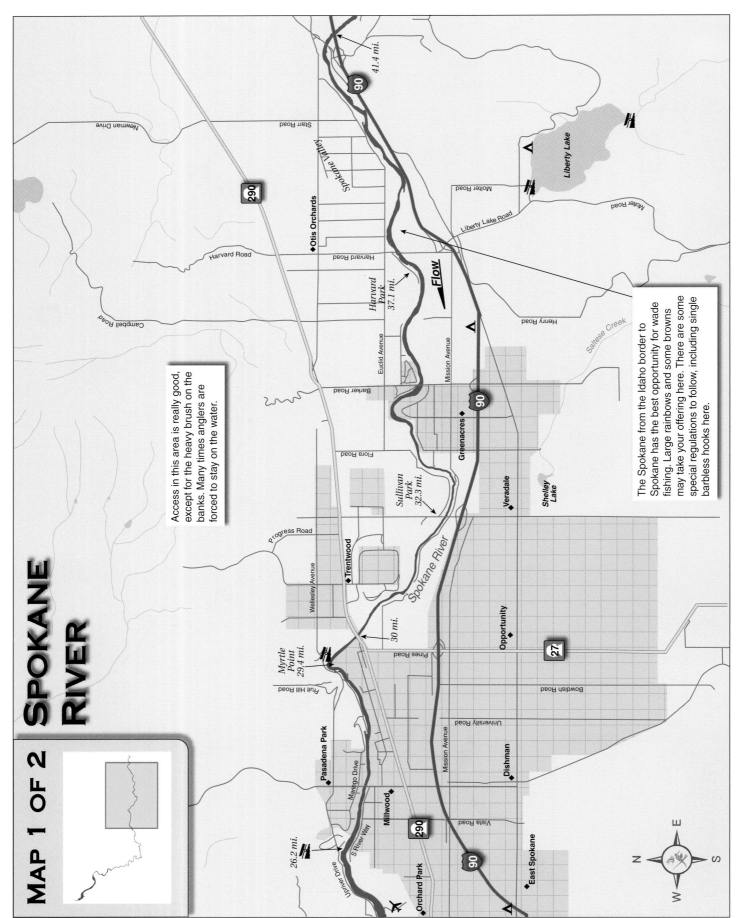

MAP 1 OF 2 SPOKANE RIVER

Access in this area is really good, except for the heavy brush on the banks. Many times anglers are forced to stay on the water.

The Spokane from the Idaho border to Spokane has the best opportunity for wade fishing. Large rainbows and some browns may take your offering here. There are some special regulations to follow, including single barbless hooks here.

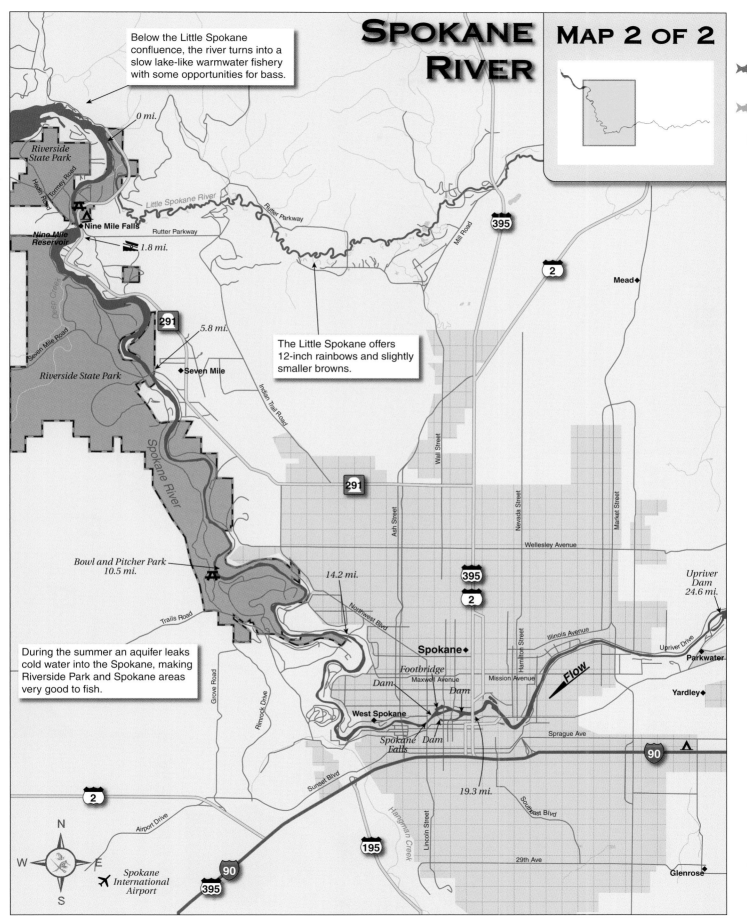

Below the Little Spokane confluence, the river turns into a slow lake-like warmwater fishery with some opportunities for bass.

0 mi.

Riverside State Park

Nine Mile Falls

Nine Mile Reservoir

1.8 mi.

Little Spokane River

Rutter Parkway

Rutter Parkway

Deep Creek

Seven Mile Road

291

5.8 mi.

Riverside State Park

Seven Mile

Indian Trail Road

Spokane River

Heath Road

Tormey Road

The Little Spokane offers 12-inch rainbows and slightly smaller browns.

395

2

Mead

Mill Road

Wall Street

Nevada Street

Market Street

291

Ash Street

Wellesley Avenue

Bowl and Pitcher Park
10.5 mi.

14.2 mi.

Northwest Blvd

395

2

Upriver Dam
24.6 mi.

Upriver Drive

Parkwater

Trails Road

Spokane

Footbridge

Maxwell Avenue

Mission Avenue

Hamilton Street

Illinois Avenue

Flow

Yardley

During the summer an aquifer leaks cold water into the Spokane, making Riverside Park and Spokane areas very good to fish.

Grove Road

Rimrock Drive

West Spokane

Dam

Dam

Spokane Falls

Dam

Sprague Ave

90

Southeast Blvd

19.3 mi.

Lincoln Street

Sunset Blvd

Hangman Creek

2

195

90

395

Airport Drive

Spokane International Airport

N
W   E
S

29th Ave

Glenrose

© 2005 Wilderness Adventures Press, Inc.

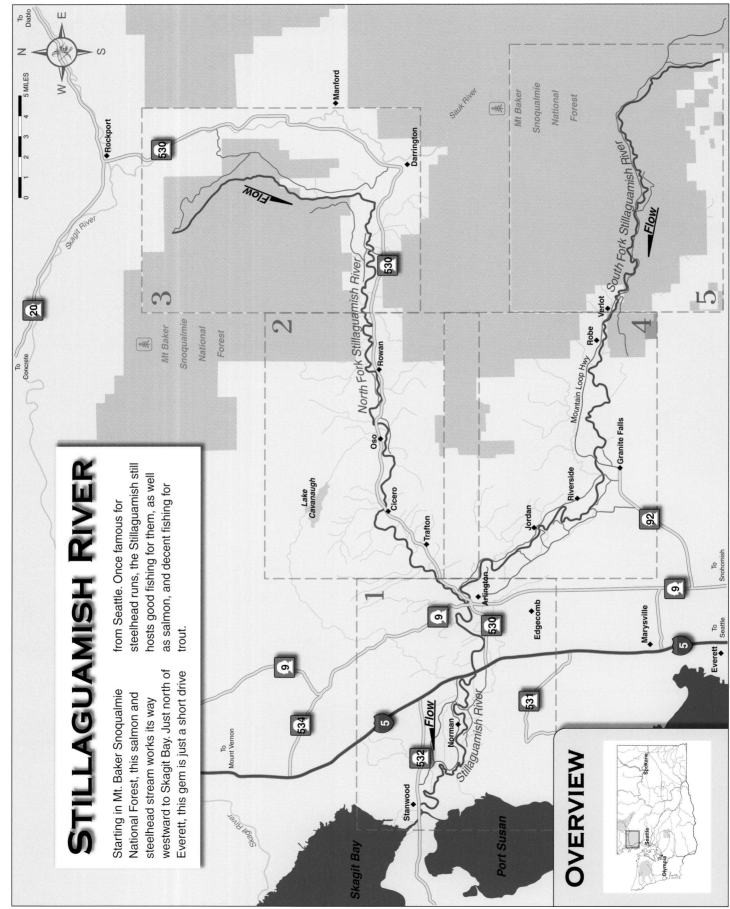

STILLAGUAMISH RIVER

Starting in Mt. Baker Snoqualmie National Forest, this salmon and steelhead stream works its way westward to Skagit Bay. Just north of Everett, this gem is just a short drive from Seattle. Once famous for steelhead runs, the Stillaguamish still hosts good fishing for them, as well as salmon, and decent fishing for trout.

OVERVIEW

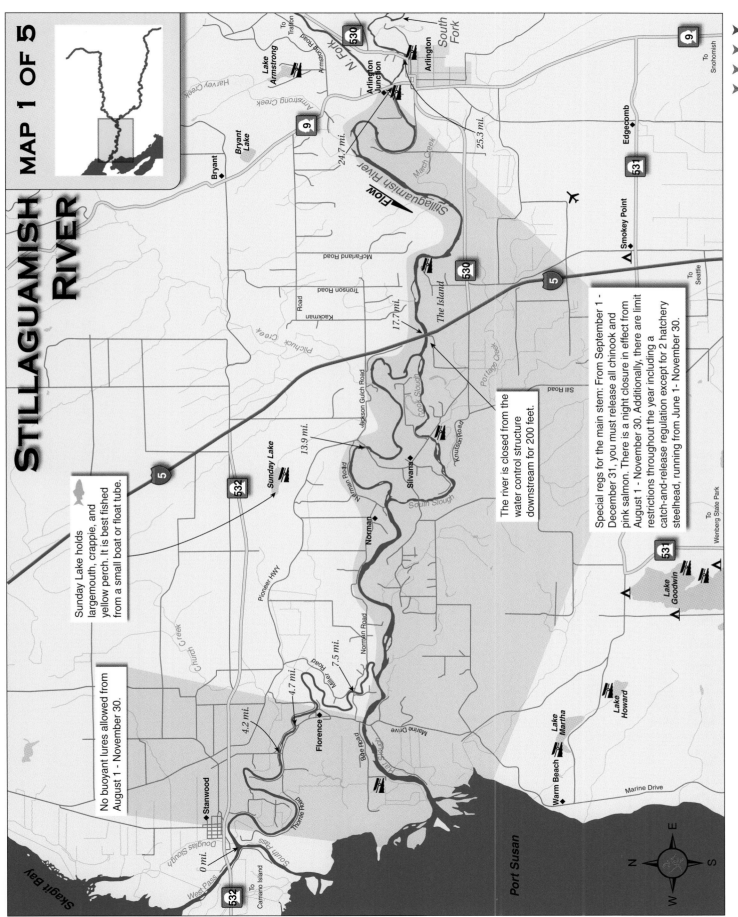

STILLAGUAMISH RIVER

MAP 1 OF 5

Sunday Lake holds largemouth, crappie, and yellow perch. It is best fished from a small boat or float tube.

No buoyant lures allowed from August 1 - November 30.

The river is closed from the water control structure downstream for 200 feet.

Special regs for the main stem: From September 1 - December 31, you must release all chinook and pink salmon. There is a night closure in effect from August 1 - November 30. Additionally, there are limit restrictions throughout the year including a catch-and-release regulation except for 2 hatchery steelhead, running from June 1- November 30.

© 2005 Wilderness Adventures Press, Inc.

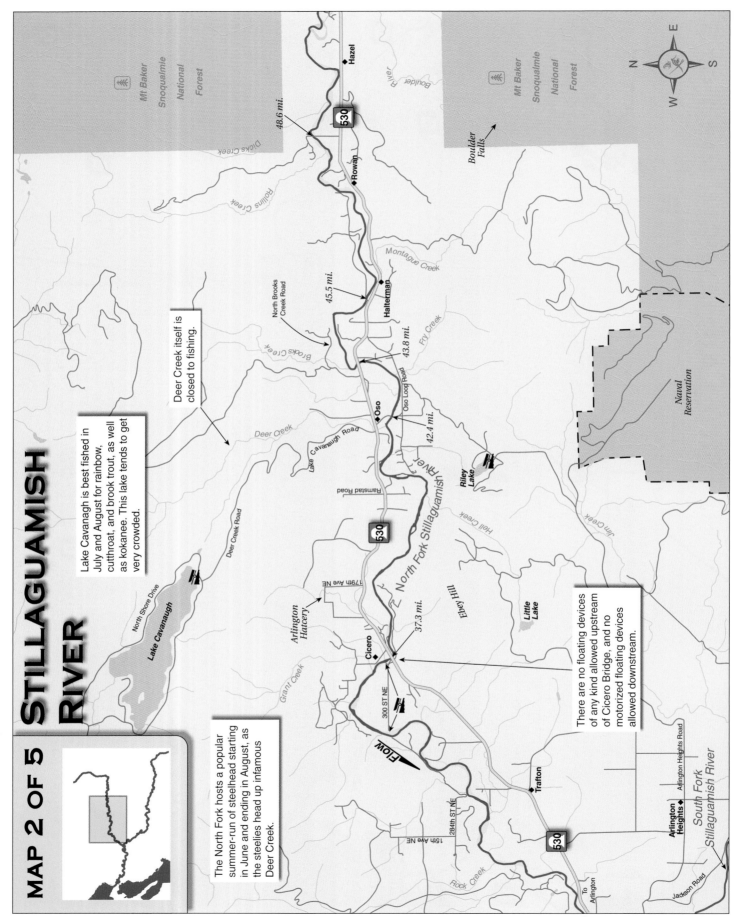

STILLAGUAMISH RIVER

MAP 2 OF 5

Lake Cavanagh is best fished in July and August for rainbow, cutthroat, and brook trout, as well as kokanee. This lake tends to get very crowded.

Deer Creek itself is closed to fishing.

The North Fork hosts a popular summer-run of steelhead starting in June and ending in August, as the steelies head up infamous Deer Creek.

There are no floating devices of any kind allowed upstream of Cicero Bridge, and no motorized floating devices allowed downstream.

Mt Baker Snoqualmie National Forest

Hazel

Rowan

48.6 mi.

Boulder Falls

Halterman

45.5 mi.

North Brooks Creek Road

Brooks Creek

43.8 mi.

Fly Creek

Montague Creek

Oso

Oso Loop Road

42.4 mi.

Naval Reservation

Deer Creek

Lake Cavanaugh Road

Ramstad Road

Riley Lake

Hell Creek

Jim Creek

North Fork Stillaguamish River

530

Ebey Hill

Little Lake

37.3 mi.

179th Ave NE

Arlington Hatcery

Cicero

Grant Creek

Deer Creek Road

North Shore Drive

Lake Cavanaugh

300 ST NE

Flow

Trafton

284th ST NE

15th Ave NE

Rock Creek

Arlington Heights

Arlington Heights Road

South Fork Stillaguamish River

Jackson Road

To Arlington

530

© 2005 Wilderness Adventures Press, Inc.

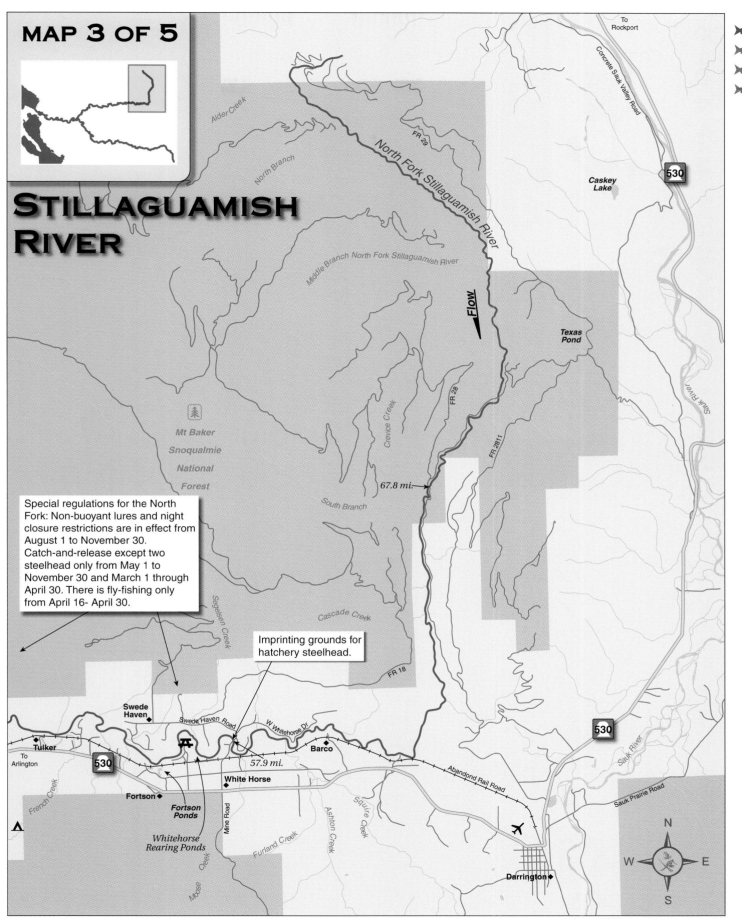

MAP **3** OF **5**

STILLAGUAMISH RIVER

To Rockport

Alder Creek

North Branch

North Fork Stillaguamish River

FR 29

Middle Branch North Fork Stillaguamish River

Caskey Lake

530

Texas Pond

Flow

Crevice Creek

FR 28

FR 2811

Mt Baker
Snoqualmie
National
Forest

67.8 mi.

South Branch

Special regulations for the North Fork: Non-buoyant lures and night closure restrictions are in effect from August 1 to November 30. Catch-and-release except two steelhead only from May 1 to November 30 and March 1 through April 30. There is fly-fishing only from April 16- April 30.

Cascade Creek

Segelsen Creek

FR 18

Imprinting grounds for hatchery steelhead.

Swede Haven

Swede Haven Road

W Whitehorse Dr

Tulker

To Arlington

530

Barco

57.9 mi.

White Horse

Fortson

Fortson Ponds

Mine Road

Abandond Rail Road

Sauk River

530

Sauk Prairie Road

French Creek

Whitehorse Rearing Ponds

Moose Creek

Furland Creek

Ashton Creek

Squire Creek

Darrington

Sauk River

N
W   E
S

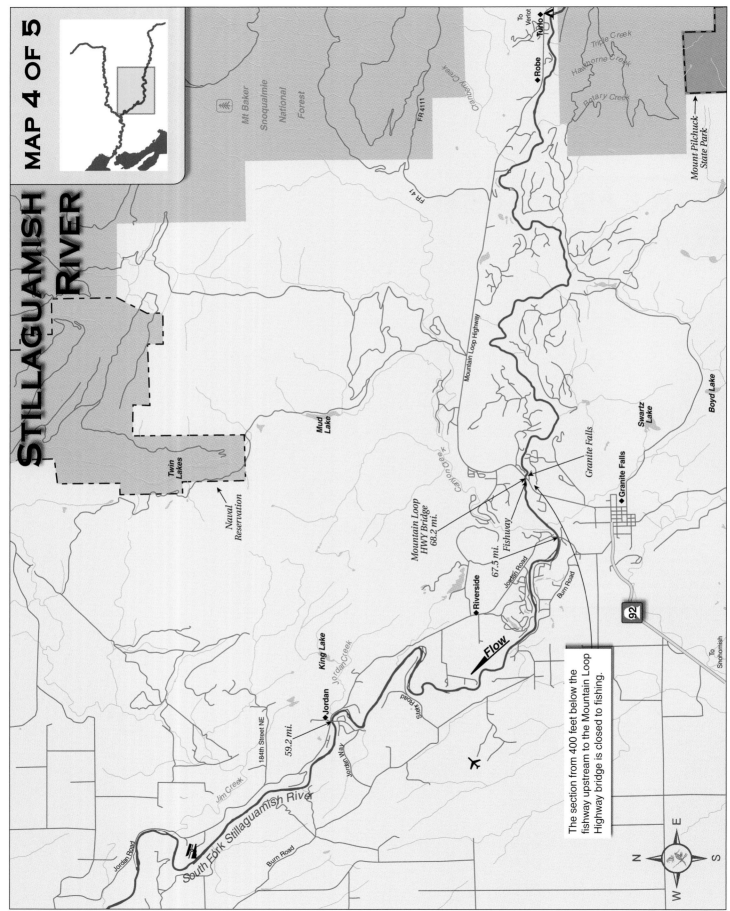

STILLAGUAMISH RIVER

MAP 4 OF 5

To Verlot
Tulio
Robe
Triple Creek
Hawthorne Creek
Botary Creek

Mt Baker Snoqualmie National Forest

Cranberry Creek

FR 4111

FR 41

Mountain Loop Highway

Mount Pilchuck State Park

Mud Lake

Granite Falls

Swartz Lake

Boyd Lake

Twin Lakes

Naval Reservation

Canyon Creek

Mountain Loop HWY Bridge 68.2 mi.

67.5 mi. Fishway

Riverside

Jordan Road

Granite Falls

Burn Road

King Lake

Jordan Creek

Flow

92

To Snohomish

Jordan

59.2 mi.

184th Street NE

Jordan Nav

Stark Road

Jim Creek

The section from 400 feet below the fishway upstream to the Mountain Loop Highway bridge is closed to fishing.

South Fork Stillaguamish River

Jordan Road

Burn Road

N E W S

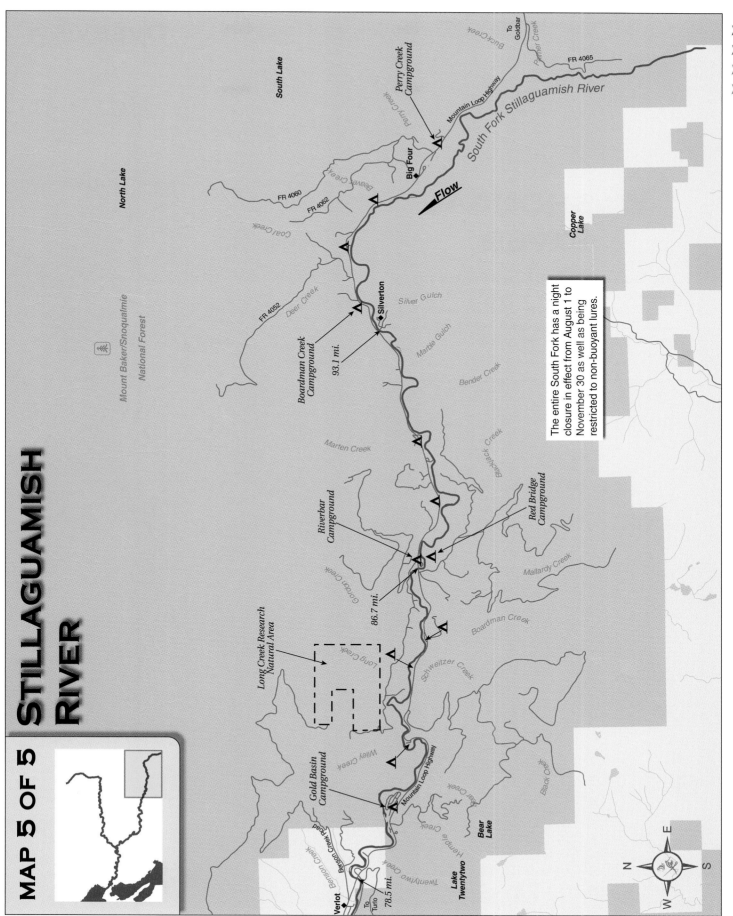

MAP 5 OF 5

STILLAGUAMISH RIVER

The entire South Fork has a night closure in effect from August 1 to November 30 as well as being restricted to non-buoyant lures.

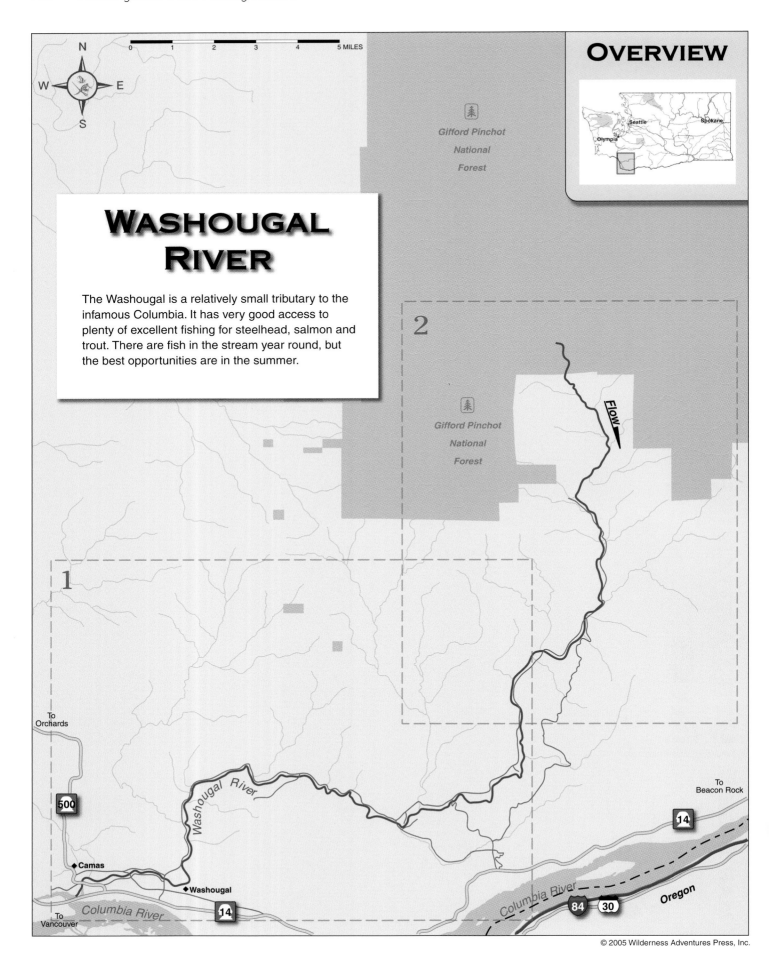

WASHOUGAL RIVER

The Washougal is a relatively small tributary to the infamous Columbia. It has very good access to plenty of excellent fishing for steelhead, salmon and trout. There are fish in the stream year round, but the best opportunities are in the summer.

OVERVIEW

0 1 2 3 4 5 MILES

N
W E
S

Gifford Pinchot National Forest

Seattle Spokane
Olympia

2

Gifford Pinchot National Forest

FLOW

1

To Orchards

To Beacon Rock

500

Washougal River

14

Camas

Washougal

14

To Vancouver

Columbia River

Columbia River

84 30

Oregon

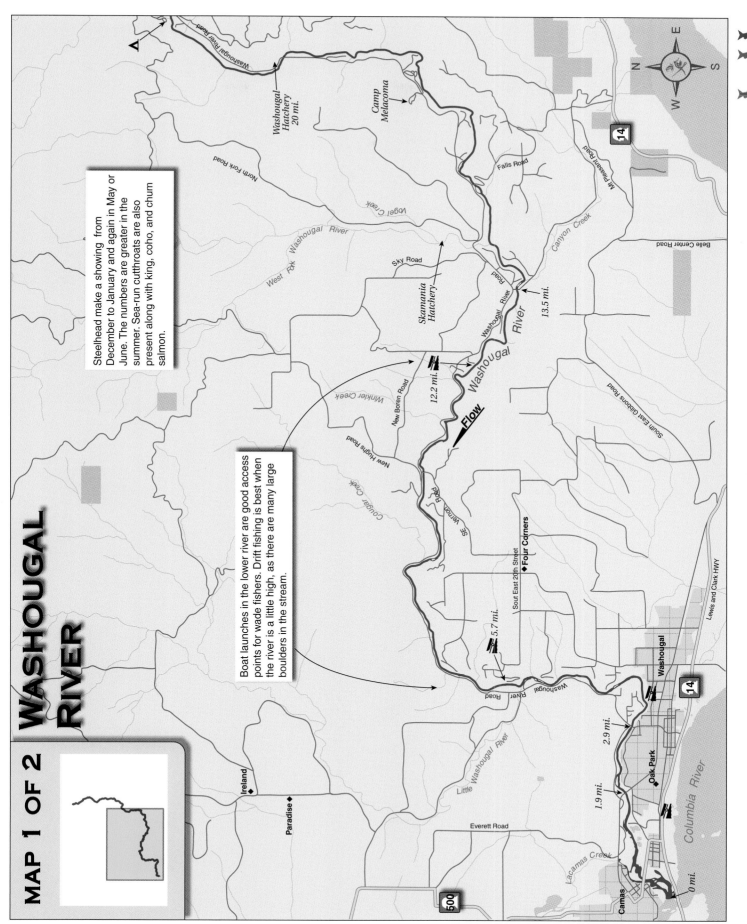

MAP 1 OF 2 WASHOUGAL RIVER

Steelhead make a showing from December to January and again in May or June. The numbers are greater in the summer. Sea-run cutthroats are also present along with king, coho, and chum salmon.

Boat launches in the lower river are good access points for wade fishers. Drift fishing is best when the river is a little high, as there are many large boulders in the stream.

Washougal River Road

Washougal Hatchery 20 mi.

Camp Melacoma

North Fork Road

Falls Road

Vogel Creek

West Fork Washougal River

Sky Road

Skamania Hatchery

Canyon Creek

Washougal River Road

13.5 mi.

Mt Pleasant Road

14

Belle Center Road

12.2 mi.

Winkler Creek

New Boren Road

New Hughs Road

Cougar Creek

Washougal River

Flow

South East Gibbons Road

SE Vernon Road

Sout East 20th Street

Four Corners

5.7 mi.

Washougal River Road

Ireland

Paradise

Everett Road

Little Washougal River

2.9 mi.

1.9 mi.

Oak Park

Washougal

14

Lewis and Clark HWY

Lacamas Creek

Camas

0 mi.

Columbia River

500

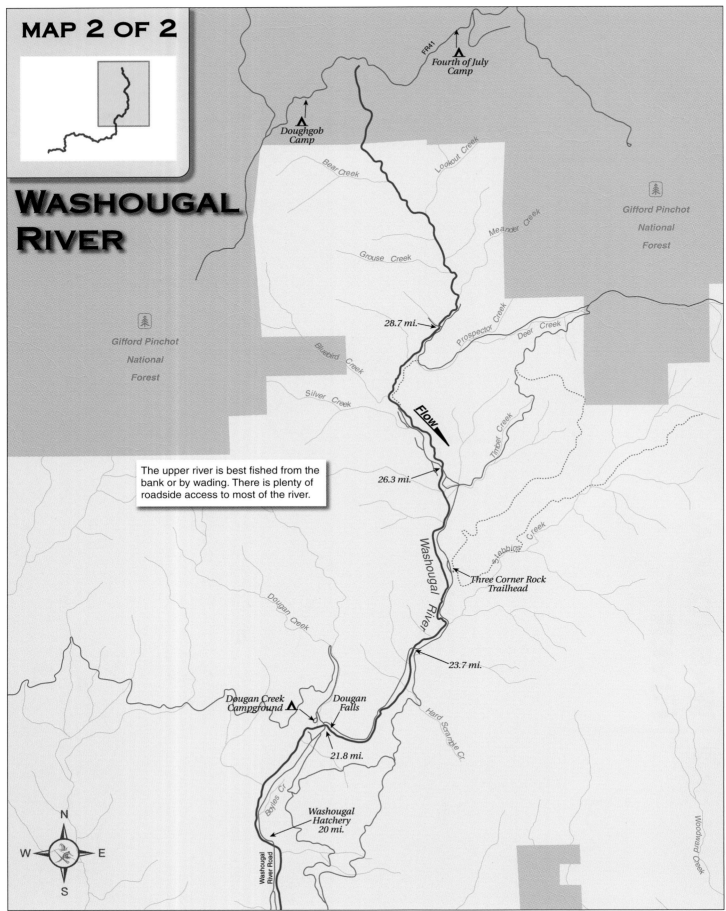

MAP 2 OF 2

WASHOUGAL RIVER

Fourth of July Camp

FR41

Doughgob Camp

Bear Creek

Lookout Creek

Meander Creek

Gifford Pinchot National Forest

Grouse Creek

Prospector Creek

Deer Creek

28.7 mi.

Gifford Pinchot National Forest

Bluebird Creek

Silver Creek

Flow

Timber Creek

The upper river is best fished from the bank or by wading. There is plenty of roadside access to most of the river.

26.3 mi.

Stebbins Creek

Three Corner Rock Trailhead

Washougal River

23.7 mi.

Dougan Creek

Hard Scramble Cr.

Dougan Creek Campground

Dougan Falls

21.8 mi.

Boyles Cr.

Washougal Hatchery 20 mi.

Woodward Creek

Washougal River Road

N
W   E
S

© 2005 Wilderness Adventures Press, Inc.

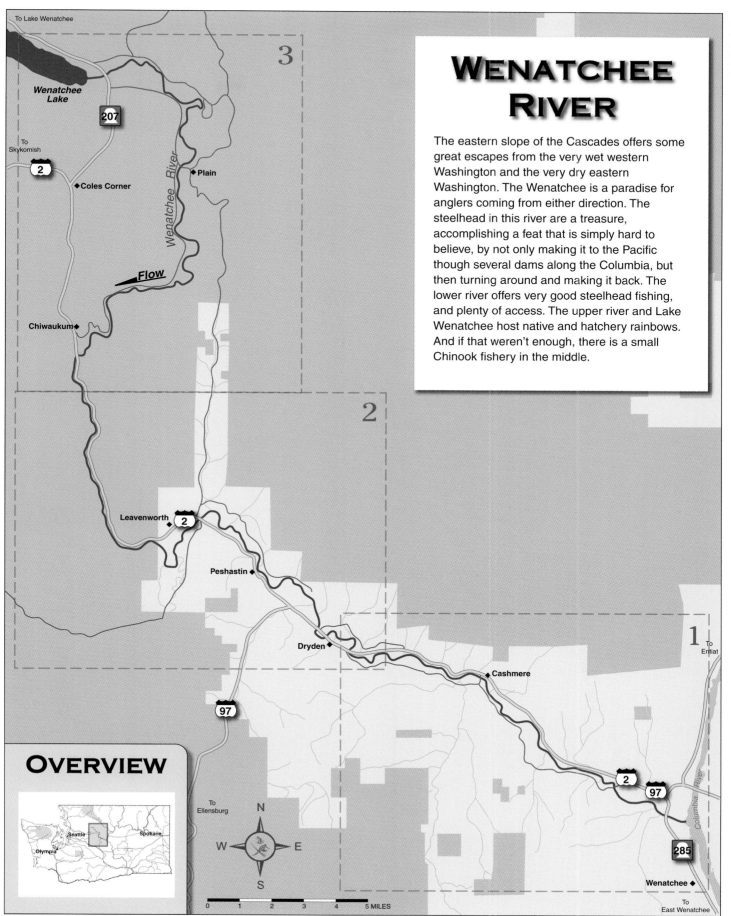

WENATCHEE RIVER

The eastern slope of the Cascades offers some great escapes from the very wet western Washington and the very dry eastern Washington. The Wenatchee is a paradise for anglers coming from either direction. The steelhead in this river are a treasure, accomplishing a feat that is simply hard to believe, by not only making it to the Pacific though several dams along the Columbia, but then turning around and making it back. The lower river offers very good steelhead fishing, and plenty of access. The upper river and Lake Wenatchee host native and hatchery rainbows. And if that weren't enough, there is a small Chinook fishery in the middle.

To Lake Wenatchee

Wenatchee Lake

207

To Skykomish

2

◆Coles Corner

◆Plain

Wenatchee River

Flow

Chiwaukum◆

3

2

Leavenworth ◆ 2

Peshastin ◆

Dryden ◆

1
To Entiat

Cashmere ◆

97

To Ellensburg

OVERVIEW

Seattle
Spokane
Olympia

N
W   E
S

0 1 2 3 4 5 MILES

2 97

Columbia River

285

Wenatchee ◆

To East Wenatchee

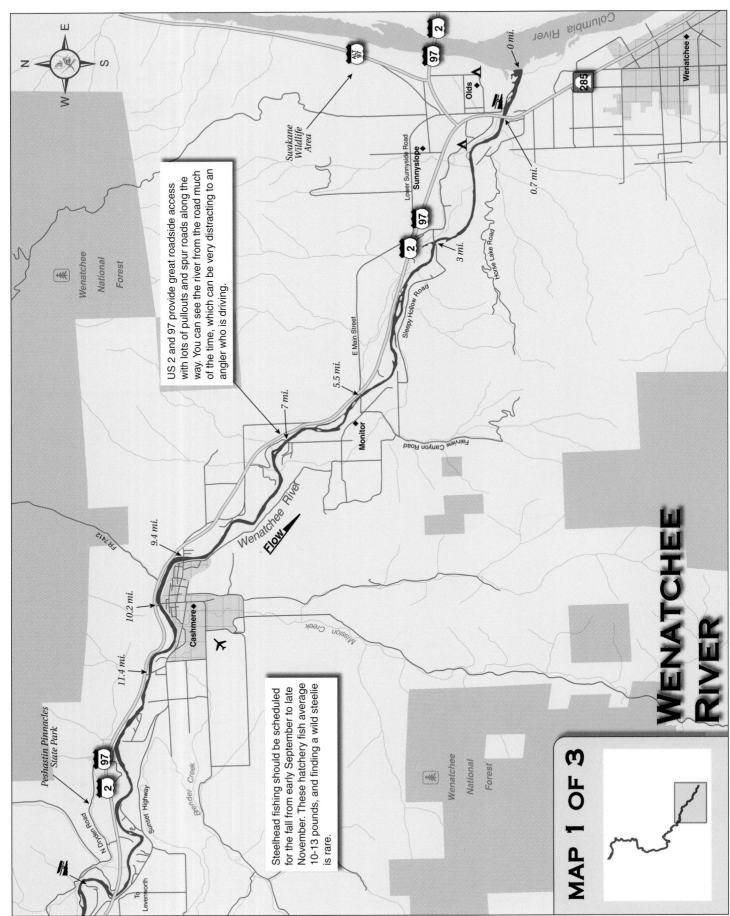

US 2 and 97 provide great roadside access with lots of pullouts and spur roads along the way. You can see the river from the road much of the time, which can be very distracting to an angler who is driving.

Steelhead fishing should be scheduled for the fall from early September to late November. These hatchery fish average 10-13 pounds, and finding a wild steelie is rare.

WENATCHEE RIVER

MAP 1 OF 3

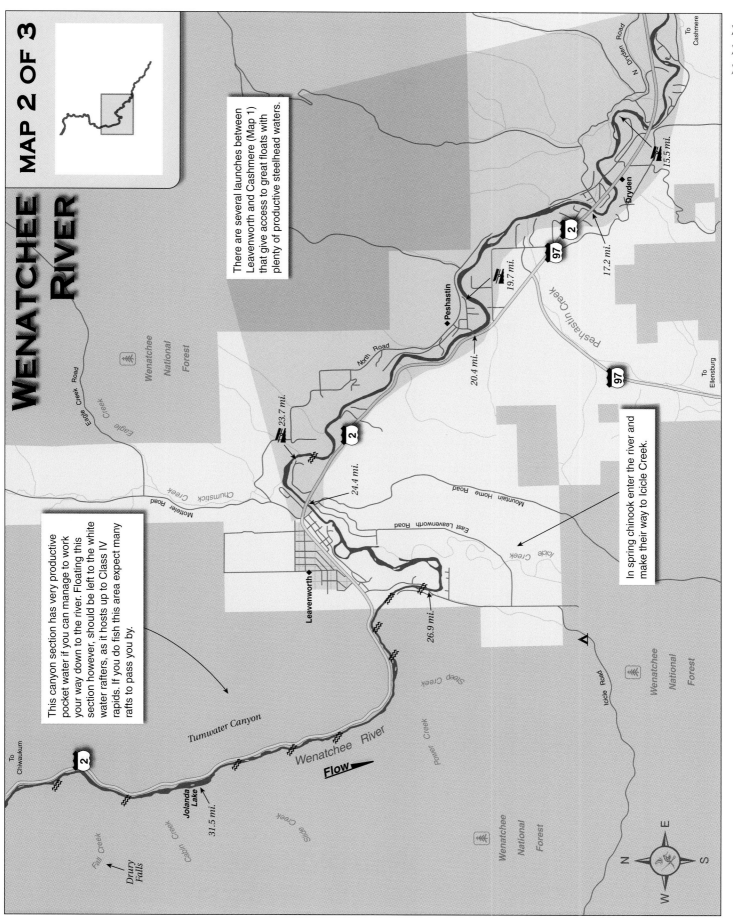

WENATCHEE RIVER

MAP 2 OF 3

There are several launches between Leavenworth and Cashmere (Map 1) that give access to great floats with plenty of productive steelhead waters.

This canyon section has very productive pocket water if you can manage to work your way down to the river. Floating this section however, should be left to the white water rafters, as it hosts up to Class IV rapids. If you do fish this area expect many rafts to pass you by.

In spring chinook enter the river and make their way to Icicle Creek.

Leavenworth

Peshastin

Dryden

Tumwater Canyon

Wenatchee River

Flow

Jolanda Lake

Drury Falls

15.5 mi.
17.2 mi.
19.7 mi.
20.4 mi.
23.7 mi.
24.4 mi.
26.9 mi.
31.5 mi.

Wenatchee National Forest

Eagle Creek Road
Eagle Creek
Chumstick Creek
Mottelar Road
North Road
East Leavenworth Road
Mountain Home Road
Icicle Creek
Peshastin Creek
Dryden Road
Icicle Road
Steep Creek
Power Creek
Slide Creek
Cabin Creek
Fall Creek

To Cashmere
To Ellensburg
To Chiwaukum

N E
W S

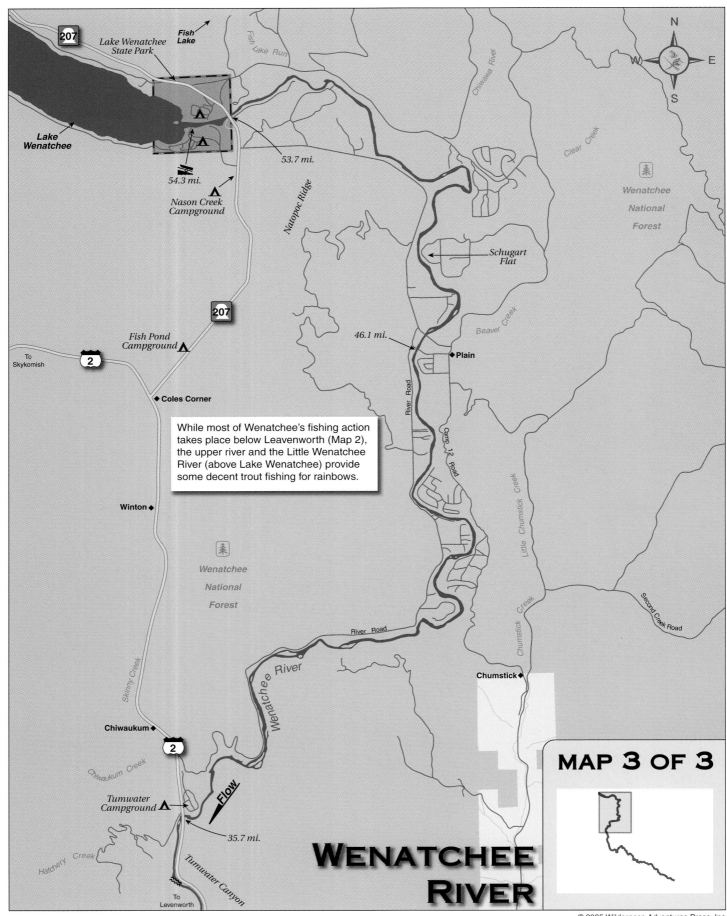

207

Fish Lake

Lake Wenatchee State Park

Fish Lake Run

Chiwawa River

Clear Creek

Wenatchee National Forest

Lake Wenatchee

53.7 mi.

54.3 mi.

Nason Creek Campground

Natopoc Ridge

Schugart Flat

Beaver Creek

207

Fish Pond Campground

46.1 mi.

◆ **Plain**

2

To Skykomish

◆ **Coles Corner**

River Road

Camp 12 Road

Little Chumstick Creek

While most of Wenatchee's fishing action takes place below Leavenworth (Map 2), the upper river and the Little Wenatchee River (above Lake Wenatchee) provide some decent trout fishing for rainbows.

Winton ◆

Wenatchee National Forest

Second Creek Road

Chumstick Creek

Skinny Creek

Wenatchee River

River Road

Chumstick ◆

MAP 3 OF 3

Chiwaukum ◆

2

Chiwaukum Creek

Tumwater Campground

Flow

35.7 mi.

Hatchery Creek

Tumwater Canyon

To Levenworth

WENATCHEE RIVER

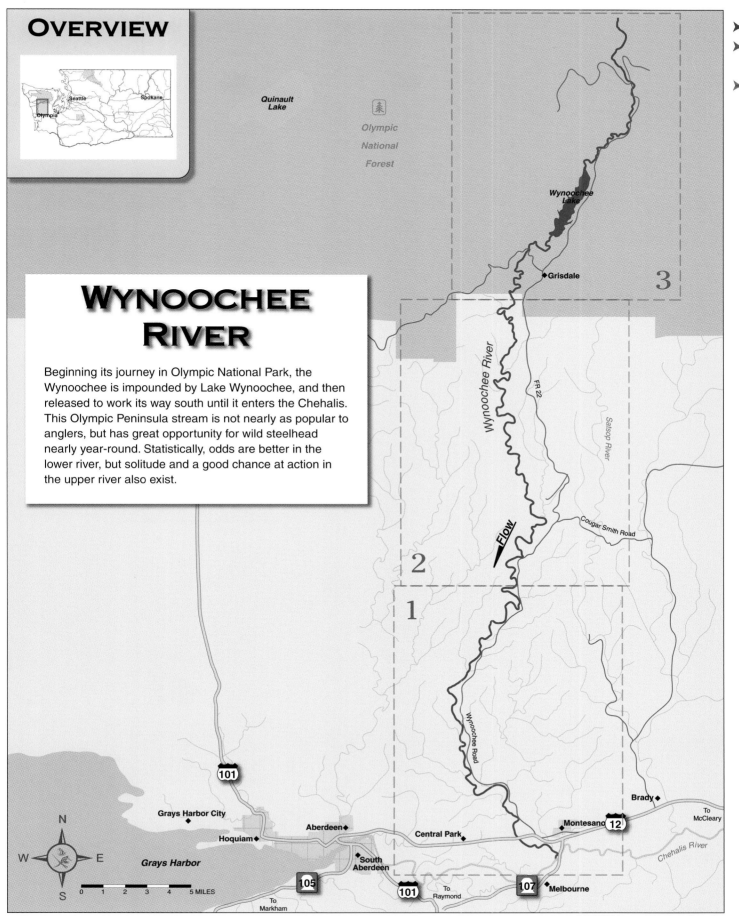

OVERVIEW

WYNOOCHEE RIVER

Beginning its journey in Olympic National Park, the Wynoochee is impounded by Lake Wynoochee, and then released to work its way south until it enters the Chehalis. This Olympic Peninsula stream is not nearly as popular to anglers, but has great opportunity for wild steelhead nearly year-round. Statistically, odds are better in the lower river, but solitude and a good chance at action in the upper river also exist.

Quinault
Lake

Olympic
National
Forest

Wynoochee
Lake

◆ Grisdale

3

Wynoochee River

FR 22

Satsop River

Cougar Smith Road

Flow

2

1

Wynoochee Road

Brady ◆

To
McCleary

N
W   E
S

Grays Harbor City ◆

Aberdeen ◆

Montesano ◆ 12

101

Hoquiam ◆

Central Park ◆

Grays Harbor

105

South
Aberdeen ◆

101

107 Melbourne ◆

0   1   2   3   4   5 MILES

To
Markham

To
Raymond

Chehalis River

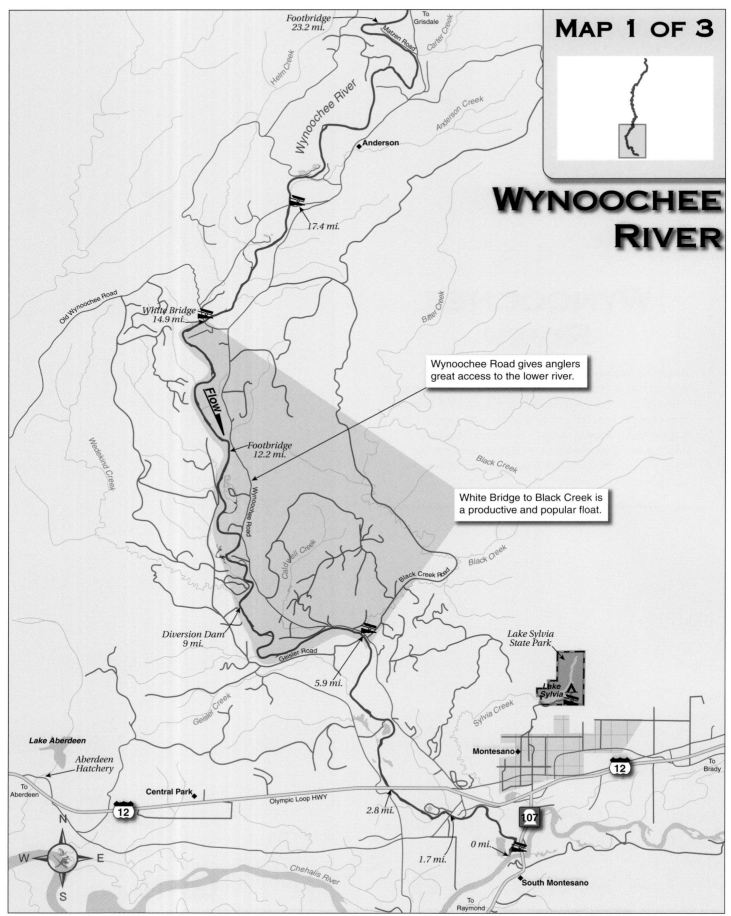

Footbridge
23.2 mi.

To Grisdale

Matzen Road

Carter Creek

Helm Creek

Wynoochee River

Anderson Creek

◆ Anderson

17.4 mi.

Old Wynoochee Road

White Bridge
14.9 mi.

Bitter Creek

MAP 1 OF 3

WYNOOCHEE
RIVER

Flow

Footbridge
12.2 mi.

Wynoochee Road gives anglers
great access to the lower river.

Black Creek

Wedekind Creek

White Bridge to Black Creek is
a productive and popular float.

Black Creek

Caldwell Creek

Black Creek Road

Diversion Dam
9 mi.

Lake Sylvia
State Park

Geisler Road

Lake
Sylvia

5.9 mi.

Geisler Creek

Sylvia Creek

Lake Aberdeen

*Aberdeen
Hatchery*

Montesano ◆

To
Brady

To
Aberdeen

Central Park ◆

Olympic Loop HWY

2.8 mi.

12

107

0 mi.

N

1.7 mi.

W   E

Chehalis River

S

◆ **South Montesano**

To
Raymond

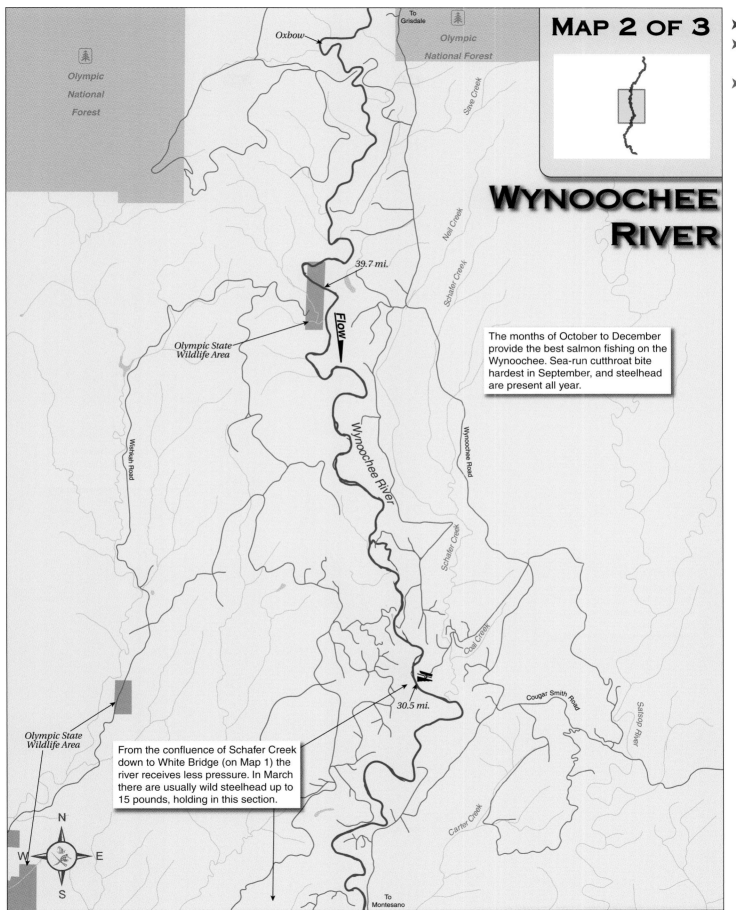

MAP 2 OF 3

WYNOOCHEE RIVER

Oxbow

To Grisdale

Olympic National Forest

Olympic National Forest

Save Creek

Neil Creek

Schafer Creek

39.7 mi.

Flow

Olympic State Wildlife Area

Wynoochee River

Wishkah Road

The months of October to December provide the best salmon fishing on the Wynoochee. Sea-run cutthroat bite hardest in September, and steelhead are present all year.

Wynoochee Road

Schafer Creek

Coal Creek

30.5 mi.

Cougar Smith Road

Satsop River

Olympic State Wildlife Area

From the confluence of Schafer Creek down to White Bridge (on Map 1) the river receives less pressure. In March there are usually wild steelhead up to 15 pounds, holding in this section.

Carter Creek

N
W E
S

To Montesano

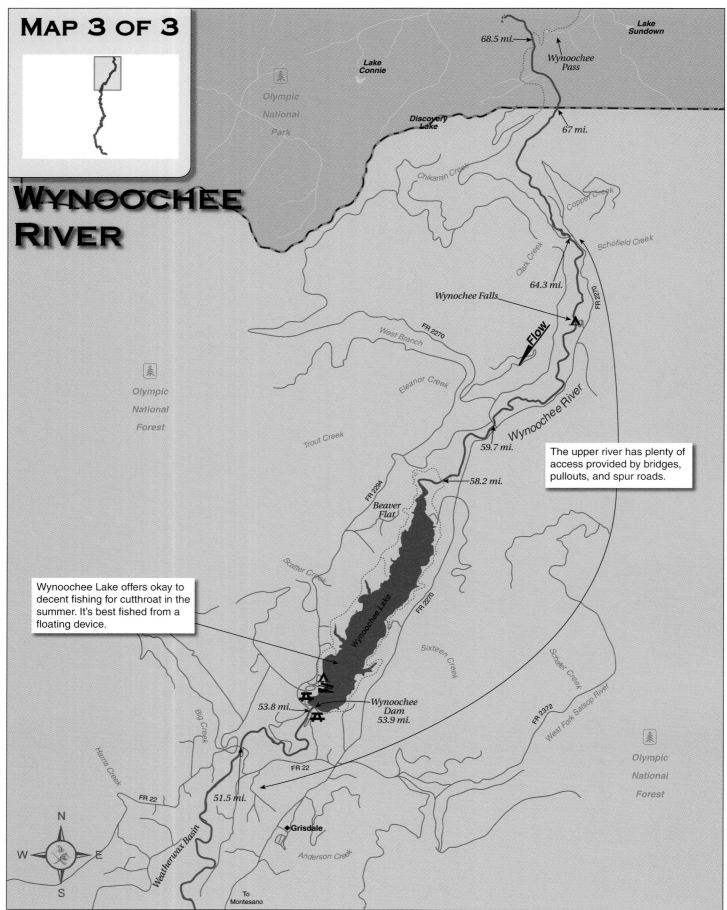

MAP 3 OF 3

WYNOOCHEE RIVER

Lake Sundown

68.5 mi.

Wynoochee Pass

Lake Connie

67 mi.

Olympic National Park

Discovery Lake

Chikamin Creek

Copper Creek

Schofield Creek

Clark Creek

64.3 mi.

FR 2270

Wynochee Falls

Flow

West Branch

FR 2270

Olympic National Forest

Eleanor Creek

Wynoochee River

Trout Creek

59.7 mi.

The upper river has plenty of access provided by bridges, pullouts, and spur roads.

58.2 mi.

FR 2294

Beaver Flat

Scatter Creek

Wynoochee Lake offers okay to decent fishing for cutthroat in the summer. It's best fished from a floating device.

Wynoochee Lake

FR 2270

Sixteen Creek

Schafer Creek

West Fork Satsop River

FR 2372

53.8 mi.

Wynoochee Dam 53.9 mi.

Big Creek

Olympic National Forest

Harris Creek

FR 22

FR 22

51.5 mi.

Weatherwax Basin

Grisdale

Anderson Creek

N
W E
S

To Montesano

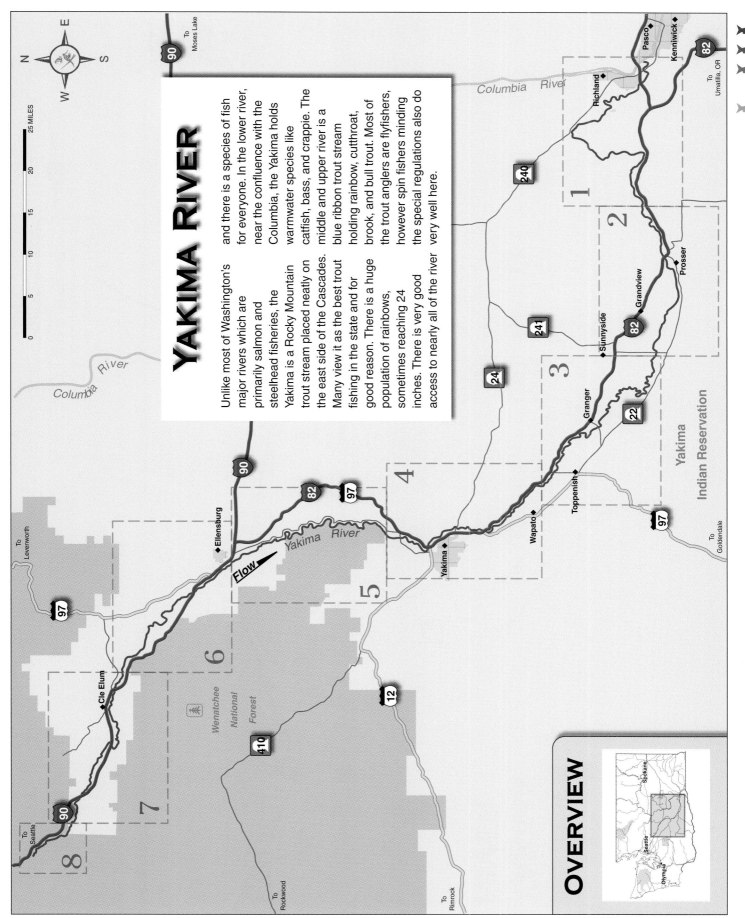

YAKIMA RIVER

Unlike most of Washington's major rivers which are primarily salmon and steelhead fisheries, the Yakima is a Rocky Mountain trout stream placed neatly on the east side of the Cascades. Many view it as the best trout fishing in the state and for good reason. There is a huge population of rainbows, sometimes reaching 24 inches. There is very good access to nearly all of the river

and there is a species of fish for everyone. In the lower river, near the confluence with the Columbia, the Yakima holds warmwater species like catfish, bass, and crappie. The middle and upper river is a blue ribbon trout stream holding rainbow, cutthroat, brook, and bull trout. Most of the trout anglers are flyfishers, however spin fishers minding the special regulations also do very well here.

OVERVIEW

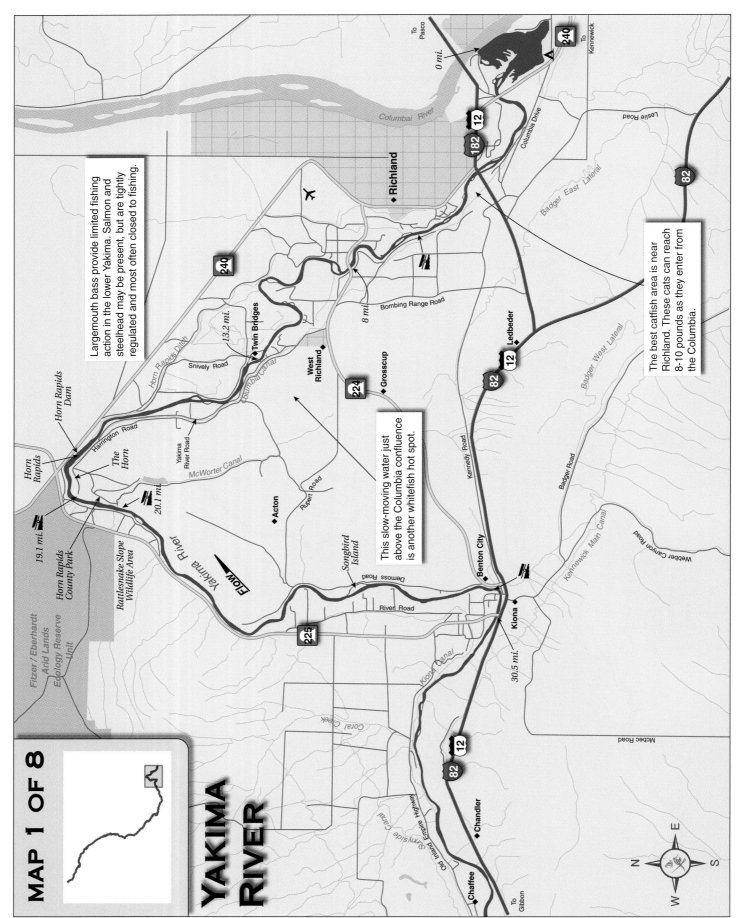

Largemouth bass provide limited fishing action in the lower Yakima. Salmon and steelhead may be present, but are tightly regulated and most often closed to fishing.

The best catfish area is near Richland. These cats can reach 8-10 pounds as they enter from the Columbia.

This slow-moving water just above the Columbia confluence is another whitefish hot spot.

MAP 1 OF 8

YAKIMA RIVER

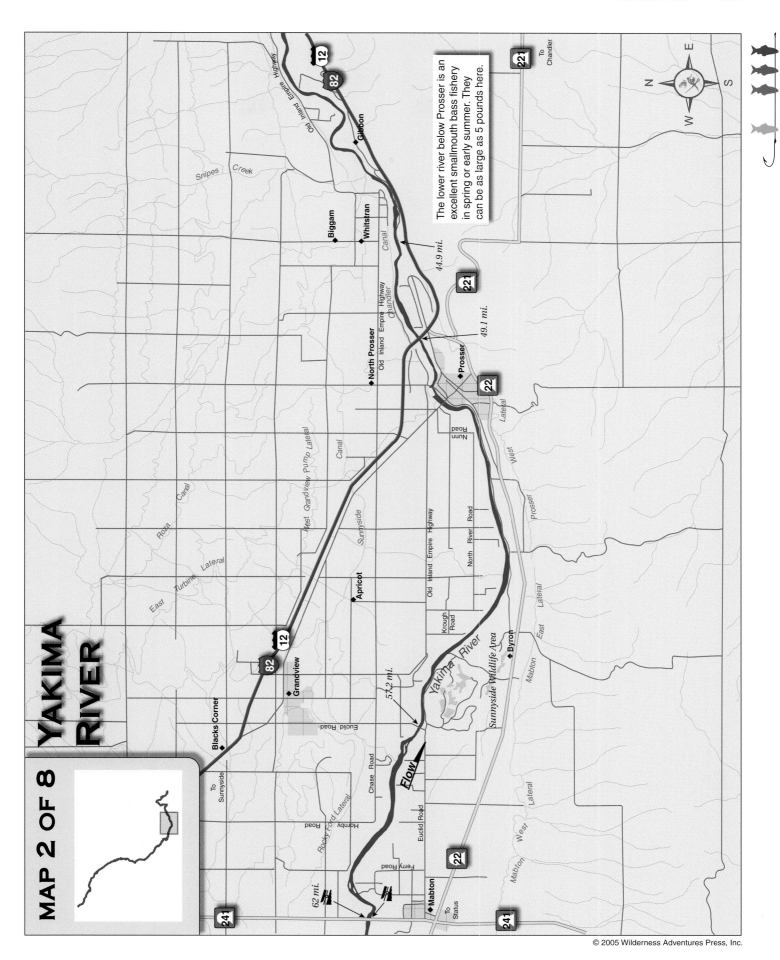

MAP 2 OF 8

YAKIMA RIVER

The lower river below Prosser is an excellent smallmouth bass fishery in spring or early summer. They can be as large as 5 pounds here.

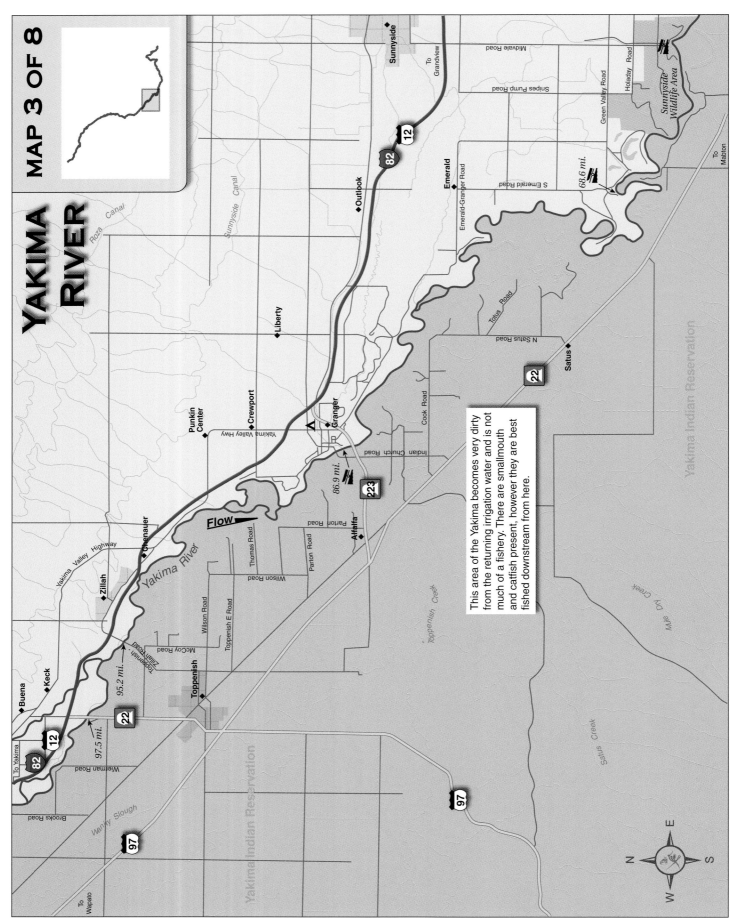

YAKIMA RIVER

MAP 3 OF 8

Roza Canal

Sunnyside Canal

Sunnyside

To Grandview

Midvale Road

Snipes Pump Road

Green Valley Road

Holaday Road

Sunnyside Wildlife Area

To Mabton

82

12

Outlook

Emerald

Emerald-Granger Road

S Emerald Road

68.6 mi.

Liberty

Totus Road

N Satus Road

Satus

22

Yakima Indian Reservation

Punkin Center

Crewport

Yakima Valley Hwy

Granger

Cook Road

Indian Church Road

86.9 mi.

223

Chenauer

Yakima Valley Highway

Zillah

Yakima River

Flow

Thomas Road

Parton Road

Parton Road

Wilson Road

Alfalfa

This area of the Yakima becomes very dirty from the returning irrigation water and is not much of a fishery. There are smallmouth and catfish present, however they are best fished downstream from here.

Toppenish Creek

Wilson Road

Toppenish E Road

McCoy Road

Zillah Road

Toppenish Road

95.2 mi.

Keck

Buena

82

12

To Yakima

97.5 mi.

Wierman Road

22

Toppenish

Yakima Indian Reservation

Brooks Road

Vanity Slough

97

97

Dry Creek

Satus Creek

To Wapato

N E S W

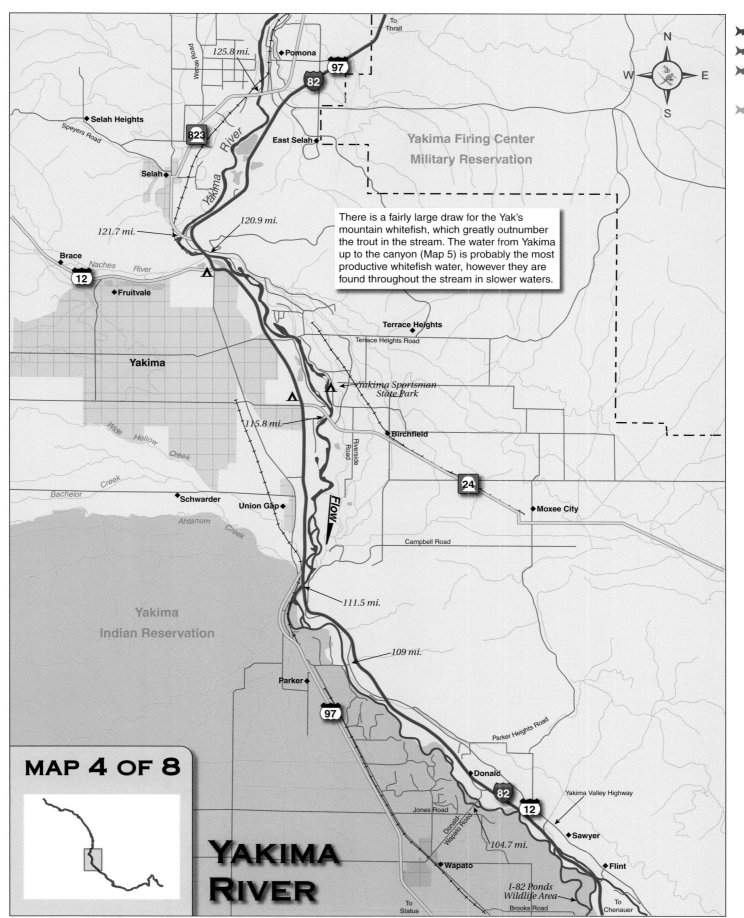

There is a fairly large draw for the Yak's mountain whitefish, which greatly outnumber the trout in the stream. The water from Yakima up to the canyon (Map 5) is probably the most productive whitefish water, however they are found throughout the stream in slower waters.

To Thrall

97

82

125.8 mi.

◆ Pomona

■ Selah Heights

Speyers Road

Wenas Road

823

Yakima River

East Selah ◆

Yakima Firing Center
Military Reservation

Selah ◆

121.7 mi.

120.9 mi.

Brace ◆

12

Naches River

◆ Fruitvale

Terrace Heights ◆

Terrace Heights Road

Yakima

Yakima Sportsman
State Park

115.8 mi.

◆ Birchfield

Riverside Road

Wide Hollow Creek

Bachelor Creek

24

◆ Schwarder

Union Gap ◆

Flow

◆ Moxee City

Ahtanum Creek

Campbell Road

111.5 mi.

Yakima
Indian Reservation

109 mi.

Parker ◆

97

Parker Heights Road

MAP 4 OF 8

◆ Donald

82

12

Yakima Valley Highway

Jones Road

Donald-Wapato Road

104.7 mi.

◆ Sawyer

**YAKIMA
RIVER**

◆ Wapato

◆ Flint

I-82 Ponds
Wildlife Area

To Status

Brooks Road

To Chenauer

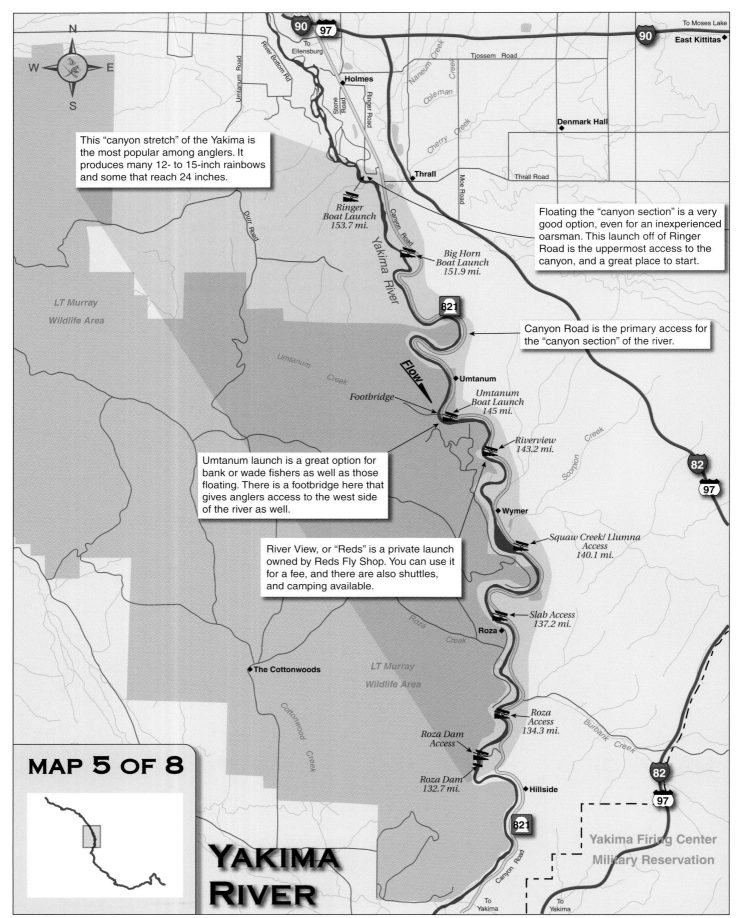

This "canyon stretch" of the Yakima is the most popular among anglers. It produces many 12- to 15-inch rainbows and some that reach 24 inches.

Floating the "canyon section" is a very good option, even for an inexperienced oarsman. This launch off of Ringer Road is the uppermost access to the canyon, and a great place to start.

Canyon Road is the primary access for the "canyon section" of the river.

Umtanum launch is a great option for bank or wade fishers as well as those floating. There is a footbridge here that gives anglers access to the west side of the river as well.

River View, or "Reds" is a private launch owned by Reds Fly Shop. You can use it for a fee, and there are also shuttles, and camping available.

Ringer Boat Launch 153.7 mi.

Big Horn Boat Launch 151.9 mi.

Flow

Footbridge

Umtanum Boat Launch 145 mi.

Riverview 143.2 mi.

Squaw Creek/ Llumna Access 140.1 mi.

Slab Access 137.2 mi.

Roza Access 134.3 mi.

Roza Dam Access

Roza Dam 132.7 mi.

To Moses Lake

East Kittitas

To Ellensburg

Holmes

Denmark Hall

Thrall

Umtanum

Wymer

Roza

The Cottonwoods

LT Murray Wildlife Area

LT Murray Wildlife Area

Hillside

Yakima Firing Center Military Reservation

To Yakima

To Yakima

MAP 5 OF 8

YAKIMA RIVER

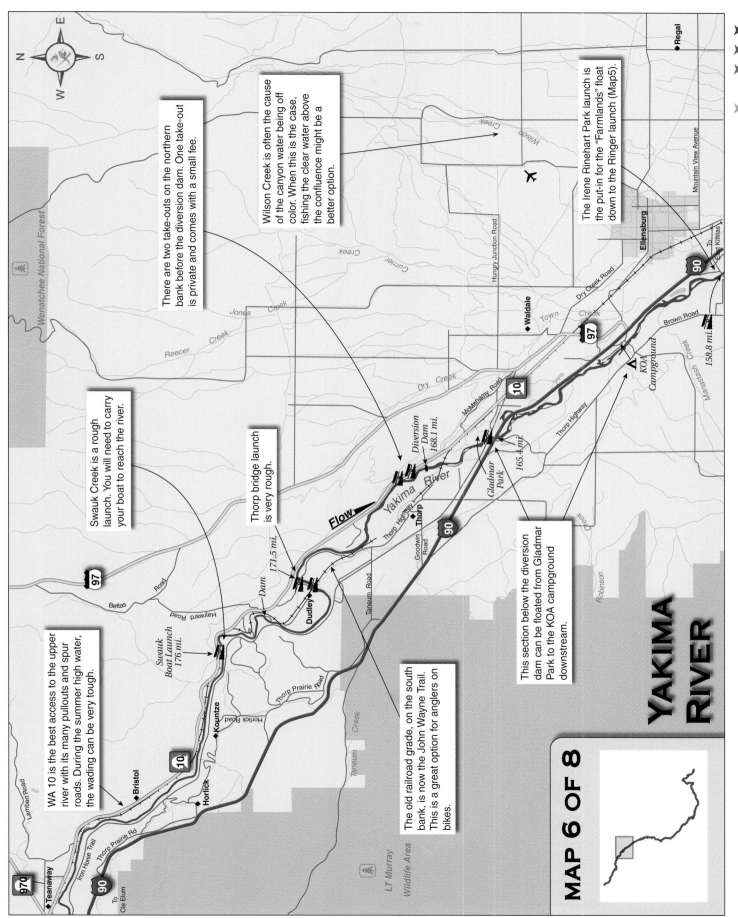

♦ Regal

There are two take-outs on the northern bank before the diversion dam. One take-out is private and comes with a small fee.

Wilson Creek is often the cause of the canyon water being off color. When this is the case, fishing the clear water above the confluence might be a better option.

The Irene Rinehart Park launch is the put-in for the "Farmlands" float down to the Ringer launch (Map5).

Swauk Creek is a rough launch. You will need to carry your boat to reach the river.

Thorp bridge launch is very rough.

This section below the diversion dam can be floated from Gladmar Park to the KOA campground downstream.

WA 10 is the best access to the upper river with its many pullouts and spur roads. During the summer high water, the wading can be very tough.

The old railroad grade, on the south bank, is now the John Wayne Trail. This is a great option for anglers on bikes.

Wilson Creek

Ellensburg

Mountain View Avenue

Hungry Junction Road

Currier Creek

Dry Creek Road

♦ Waldale

Town Creek

Dry Creek

McManamy Road

Thorp Highway

KOA Campground

Brown Road

158.8 mi.

Manastash Creek

Jones Creek

Reecer Creek

Diversion Dam 168.1 mi.

165.4 mi.

Gladmar Park

Goodwin Road

Thorp

Flow

Yakima River

Robinson

Wenatchee National Forest

Bettas

Road

Hayward Road

Dam

171.5 mi.

Dudley

Taneum Road

Swauk Boat Launch 176 mi.

Thorp Prairie Road

Horlick Road

♦ Kountze

Taneum Creek

LT Murray Wildlife Area

Lambert Road

Iron Horse Trail

Thorp Prairie Rd

♦ Horlick

♦ Bristol

♦ Teanaway

To Cle Elum

YAKIMA RIVER

MAP 6 OF 8

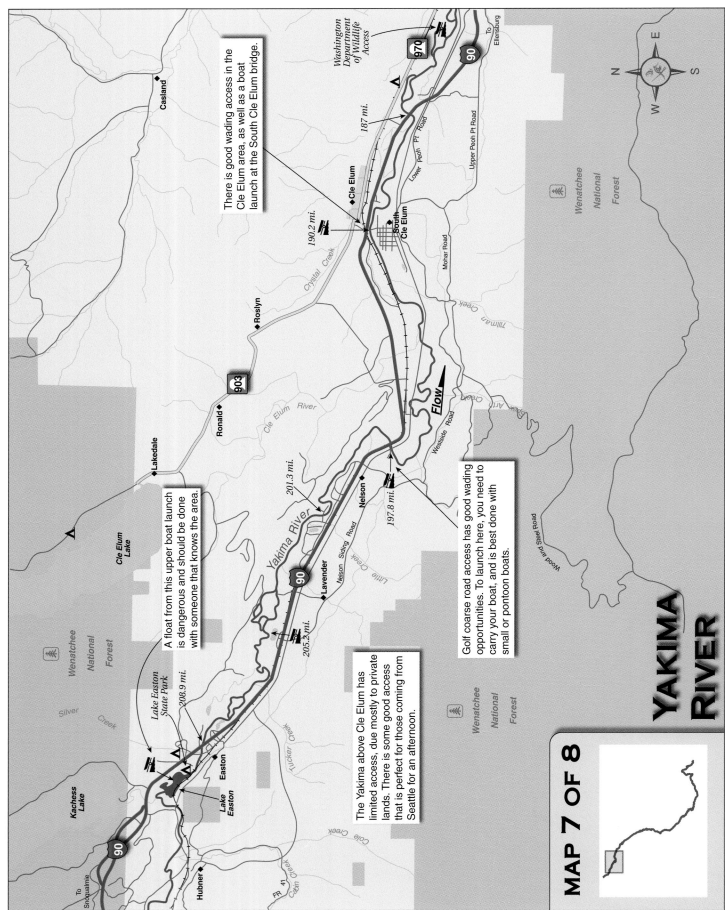

There is good wading access in the Cle Elum area, as well as a boat launch at the South Cle Elum bridge.

Washington Department of Wildlife Access

187 mi.

190.2 mi.

Golf coarse road access has good wading opportunities. To launch here, you need to carry your boat, and is best done with small or pontoon boats.

197.8 mi.

201.3 mi.

A float from this upper boat launch is dangerous and should be done with someone that knows the area.

205.2 mi.

208.9 mi.

The Yakima above Cle Elum has limited access, due mostly to private lands. There is some good access that is perfect for those coming from Seattle for an afternoon.

Yakima River

Cle Elum River

Crystal Creek

Tillman Creek

Little Creek

Nelson Siding Road

Westside Road

Wood and Steel Road

Mohar Road

Lower Peoh Pt. Road

Upper Peoh Pt Road

Wenatchee National Forest

Wenatchee National Forest

Wenatchee National Forest

Silver Creek

Tucker Creek

Cole Creek

Cabin Creek

Cle Elum Lake

Kachess Lake

Lake Easton

Lake Easton State Park

Casland

Roslyn

Ronald

Lakedale

Cle Elum

South Cle Elum

Nelson

Lavender

Easton

Hubner

Flow

To Ellensburg

To Snoqualmie

970

90

90

90

903

FR 41

Yakima River

MAP 7 OF 8

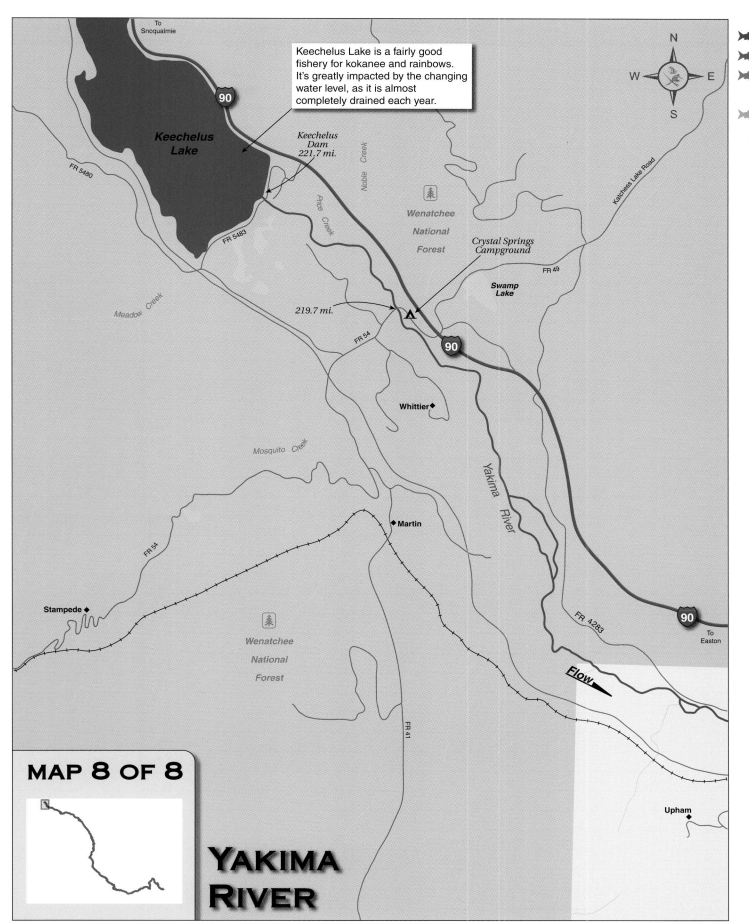

Keechelus Lake is a fairly good fishery for kokanee and rainbows. It's greatly impacted by the changing water level, as it is almost completely drained each year.

Keechelus Lake

Keechelus Dam 221.7 mi.

Noble Creek

Price Creek

Wenatchee National Forest

Crystal Springs Campground

Swamp Lake

FR 49

Katchess Lake Road

219.7 mi.

FR 54

90

Meadow Creek

Whittier ◆

Mosquito Creek

Yakima River

◆ Martin

FR 54

FR 4283

Stampede ◆

90

To Easton

Wenatchee National Forest

FR 41

Flow

MAP 8 OF 8

Upham ◆

YAKIMA RIVER

To Snoqualmie

90

FR 5480

FR 5483

WASHINGTON FLY SHOPS AND SPORTING GOOD STORES

Streamside Fly Shop	Po Box 295	Arlington	98223-0295	360-435-1043
Hook Line And Sinker	5200 172nd St Ne Ste 104	Arlington	98223-4703	360-435-5052
Auburn Sports And Marine	810 Auburn Way N	Auburn	98002-4198	253-833-1440
Northwest Angler	275 High School Rd Ne Ste C1	Bainbridge Island	98110-3665	206-842-0480
Orvis Seattle	911 Bellevue Way Ne	Bellevue	98004-4207	425-452-9138
Kaufmann's Streamborn	15015 Main St	Bellevue	98007-5229	800-442-4359
Yeager's Sporting Goods	3101 Northwest Ave	Bellingham	98225-1652	360-733-1080
H & H Anglers & Outfitters	814 Dupont St	Bellingham	98225-3103	360-733-2050
Guides Fly Shop	3960 Guide Meridian Ste C	Bellingham	98226-5548	360-527-0317
Windward Ways	1005 Lone Tree Ct	Bellingham	98229-3167	360-714-5172
Holiday Sports	680 Highway 20	Burlington	98233-3406	360-757-1221
Steelhead Anglers	Po Box 594	Carnation	98014-0594	425-922-5413
River Run Anglers	3946 Tolt Ave	Carnation	98014-7502	425-333-4446
Sunbird's Shopping Center	1757 N National Ave	Chehalis	98532-2314	360-748-3337
Yakima River Fly Shop	118 E 1st St	Cle Elum	98922-1111	509-674-2144
Blue Dun Fly Shop	960 Valley Mall Pkwy Ste A	E Wenatchee	98802-7655	509-884-4070
The Evening Hatch	2308 S Canyon Rd	Ellensburg	98926-9752	509-962-5959
Reds Flyshop	PO Box 186	Ellensburg	98926	509-929-1802
John's Sporting Goods	1913 Broadway	Everett	98201-2315	425-259-3056
Olympic Sporting Goods	Po Box 538	Forks	98331-0538	360-374-6330
Creekside Angling Co	1180 Nw Gilman Blvd	Issaquah	98027-5303	425-392-3800
Pritchard's Western Angler	2106 Kalama River Rd	Kalama	98625-9624	360-673-4690
Clearwater Fly Shop	417 W 1st Ave	Kennewick	99336-3926	509-582-1001
Gart Sports #550	908c N Colorado St	Kennewick	99336-7617	509-783-7801
Sportsmans Warehouse	6603 W Canal Dr	Kennewick	99336-7810	509-736-2200
Puget Sound Fly Company	25616 Pacific Hwy S	Kent	98032-5556	253-839-4119
Fly Fisher (Washington)	5622 Pacific Ave Se Ste 9	Lacey	98503-1271	360-491-0181
Avid Angler	17171 Bothell Way Ne	Lake Forest Park	98155-5534	206-362-4030
Greg's Custom Fishing Rods	12405 20th St Ne	Lake Stevens	98258-9270	425-335-1391
Silver Bow Fly Shop	1338 N Liberty Lake Rd	Liberty Lake	99019-8523	509-924-9998
Bob's Sporting Goods	1111 Hudson St	Longview	98632-3158	360-425-3870
Ace Hardware & Sport	1736 Front St	Lynden	98264-1261	360-354-2291
Ted's Sport Center	15526 Highway 99	Lynnwood	98087-2341	425-743-9505
The Fly Smith	1515 5th St	Marysville	98270-4700	360-658-9003
Mazama Store	48 Lost River Rd	Mazama	98833-9707	509-996-3674
Pacific Fly Fishers	1018 164th St Se Ste A22	Mill Creek	98012-1763	425-742-2402
Sky Valley Traders	18600 Highway 2	Monroe	98272-1430	360-794-8818
All About The Fly	212 E Main St	Monroe	98272-1508	360-863-1833
Skagit Anglers	315 Main St Ste G	Mount Vernon	98273-3889	360-336-3232
Oak Harbor Hardware	150 Se Pioneer Way	Oak Harbor	98277-5712	360-679-3533
Fishy Business	2415 Harrison Ave Nw	Olympia	98502-4544	360-352-0383
Waters West	140 W Front St	Port Angeles	98362-2607	360-417-0937
Swains General Store	602 E 1st St	Port Angeles	98362-3304	360-452-2357

Bay Street Outfitters	130 Harrison Ave	Port Orchard	98366-5227	360-874-7880
Port Townsend Angler	940 Water St	Port Townsend	98368-5747	360-379-3763
G.I. Joe's - Puyallup #5	120 31st Ave Se	Puyallup	98374-1203	253-445-8090
Sportee's	16725 Cleveland St	Redmond	98052-4415	425-882-1333
Shoff Tackle Supply	Po Box 2056	Renton	98056-0056	866-867-4004
Barrier Dam Campground	273 Fuller Rd	Salkum	98582-9700	206-985-2495
Creekside Angling Co	1308 4th Avenue	Seattle	98101	206-405-3474
Kaufmann's Streamborn Fl	1911 4th Ave	Seattle	98101-1106	206-448-0601
Patrick's Fly Shop	2237 Eastlake Ave E	Seattle	98102-3418	800-398-7693
Outdoor Emporium	420 Pontius Ave N	Seattle	98109-5422	206-624-6550
Linc's Tackle Shop	501 Rainier Ave S	Seattle	98144-2038	206-324-7600
Reel Adventures/Seattle	2545 Rainier Ave S	Seattle	98144-5328	206-722-0633
Chinook Sporting Goods, Inc.	Po Box 314	Selah	98942-0314	509-969-8486
Swiftwater Sports	17703 15th Ave Ne	Shoreline	98155-3803	206-547-3377
Kitsap Sports	10903 Nw Myhre Pl	Silverdale	98383-7661	360-698-4808
Sportsmans Warehouse	9577 Ridgetop Blvd	Silverdale	98383-8500	360-307-6900
Swedes Fly Shop	1611 N. Ash	Spokane	99202	509-323-0500
Blue Dun Fly Shop	135 S Sherman St	Spokane	99202-1460	509-838-3474
White's Outdoor	4002 E Ferry Ave	Spokane	99202-4646	509-535-1875
Gart Sports	9620 N Newport Hwy	Spokane	99218-1221	509-466-2100
Sportsmans Warehouse	14014 E. Indiana Ave	Spokane	99216	509-891-1900
Terry Tyed Flys	220 S Custer Rd	Spokane Valley	99212-0763	509-534-2939
R&R Fishing Supply	109 E Woodin Rd	Sunnyside	98944-9278	509-837-2332
Morning Hatch Fly Shoppe	3640 S Cedar St Ste L	Tacoma	98409-5700	253-472-1070
Angler's Gear	302 Robart Ln	Toppenish	98948-1036	509-865-4503
Ray's Tackle Shop	13225 Tukwila Intl Blvd	Tukwila	98168-3166	206-243-2361
Flysmith	8825 Quilceda Blvd	Tulalip	98271-8085	360-654-2974
Streamside Anglers (Wa)	4800 Capitol Blvd Se Ste B	Tumwater	98501-4464	360-709-3337
Flether's Flys	Po Box 722	Twisp	98856-0722	509-607-2117
Greased Line Fly Shoppe	5802 Ne 88th St	Vancouver	98665-0941	360-573-9383
Great Longview Corp.	8213 Nw 12th Ave	Vancouver	98665-6990	360-574-5766
North Country Outfitters	1212 Nw 76th Cir	Vancouver	98665-7250	
G.I. Joe's	13215 Se Mill Plain Blvd	Vancouver	98684-6991	360-253-2420
Steve's Archery & Fishing Shop	2815 E Isaacs Ave	Walla Walla	99362-2262	509-525-8772
Central Fly Fishing	1720 5th St Ste F	Wenatchee	98801-1700	509-630-0460
Swedes Fly Shop	17419 139th Ave Ne	Woodinville	98072-8519	425-487-3747
Anglers Workshop	Po Box 1910	Woodland	98674-1800	360-225-9445
The Sport Cove	101 Butterfield Rd	Yakima	98901-2008	509-453-4866
Grumpy's South 1st Surplus	2318 S 1st St	Yakima	98903-1687	509-452-0868
Hill's Discount Flies	8101 Poplar View Way	Yakima	98908-1170	800-337-4483
Gary's Fly Shoppe	5110 Tieton Dr Ste 200	Yakima	98908-3401	509-972-3880

NOTES

NOTES

NOTES